Bedtime

Bedtime Horror Stories For Homeowners

Paul Pugliese

Bedtime Horror Stories for Homeowners

Copyright © 2012 Paul Pugliese

All rights reserved.

ISBN:1482068044
ISBN-13:9781482068047

Bedtime Horror Stories for Homeowners

Bedtime Horror Stories for Homeowners

TABLE OF CONTENTS

- **Chapter 1 A Short History of Housing from the Cave-Man to the Present**
- In the Beginning 17-33
- **Chapter 2 Why did we Pick This House?**
- Location Is Everything 34-37
- How Do We Pick the House? 38-47
- Marketing the Development Home 48-53
- **Chapter 3 The Victorian Home**
- The Victorian House 54-70
- **Chapter 4 Handyman Specials**
- The Handyman Special 71-74
- Now Back to The Handyman Special 75-77
- Adventures of Paul and Janice, the Leaky Drain 78-87
- **Chapter 5 Size Matters**
- Duplex Homes 88-89
- Contemporary Houses & Mc Mansions 90-94

- **Chapter 6 Money Talks**
- Financing the Castle 95-104
- **Chapter 7 Who Gave the Home a Name?**
- Naming Homes 105-106
- Who Names These Places? 107
- **Chapter 8 Getting Through the Legal Stuff**
- Closings on Houses 108-110
- Mortgage Insurance 111-113
- **Chapter 9 Things You May Need to Own or Know to Survive Home Ownership**
- Things to Own With a House 114-116
- Home Ownership Terms 117-124
- Neighbors, Good, Bad or Otherwise 125-128
- The House We Almost Bought 129-130
- The Very First Day Your Home 131-132
- You Are Now a Homeowner 133

- **Chapter 10 Human Pests**
- Vandals, Burglars, Religious Fanatics, Salesmen,
- Visitors & Borders 134-145
- **Chapter 11 Modern Cave Dwellers and Old Homes**
- Underground Homes 146-148
- Historic Homes 149-150
- **Chapter 12 Getting Wet and Naked**
- Wedding Day 151-153
- Water Pressure 154
- The Main Water Line Fiasco 155-158
- **Chapter 13 You Balance the Check Book, I Will Rip Off the Roof**
- Skills 159-168
- **Chapter 14 You Parked Where?**
- Good and Bad Parking Spaces 169-170
- **Chapter 15 Do I Look like Bill Gates?**

  Homes I Could Never Afford 171-173

- **Chapter 16 The People Next Door, Your New Family**
- Noisy Neighbors 174-178
- Neighborhood Whack Jobs 179-180
- Clean House / Messy House 181-185
- Naked Warrior 186
- The Slab and The Gay Guy 187-204
- Jerky John and Dad 205-207
- **Chapter 17 Dog Tales**
- Dogs and Neighbors 208-218
- Dog Beds 219
- Dogs and Ceilings 220-223
- **Chapter 18 Seeing is Believing**
- Visual Pollution 224-225
- Religious Wars in the Hood on a 226-229
- Crooked Walls 230-236

Bedtime Horror Stories for Homeowners

- **Chapter 19 Good Plans Do Not Always Work**
- Scotts Stockade Fencing 237-238
- A/C Fiasco 239-243
- Stupid Shop Roof 244-245
- **Chapter 20 Sometimes I Get Lucky**
- Cheap Fancy Doors 246-248
- Locked Out 249
- **Chapter 21 Playing With Fire**
- Jackie's New Gas Stove 250-254
- Fire in the Tool Shed 255-256
- The Embarrassing Fire Alarm 257-259
- **Chapter 22 Water Stories**
- Stevens Hot Tub 260-261
- The Sump Pump Fiasco 262-267
- **Chapter 23 Dealing with Animals and Fools**
- Meese and Other Critters 268-272
- Moving Day 273-277
- No Home 278-279

- The Dead Phone Issue 280-290
- Busted By the Fuzz 291-293
- Concrete and the Blind Old Lady 294-296
- Bob and the Basement Apartment 297
- **Chapter 24 Back on the Block**
- The Home As an Art Project 298-304
- Christmas at Home 305-306
- Pay Attention 307-308
- About the Author 309

FOREWORD FOR
BEDTIME HORROR STORIES FOR HOMEOWNERS

If you are politically correct, are easily offended or think keeping up with the Joneses is important, you *may* not like this book. On the other hand if you think all those type people are losers, dig in and enjoy it.

I originally started this book over 20 years ago, and had someone retype it for publication. That did not work out, so it sat on a shelf for 17 years. On the upside, I now have a lot more silly stories to tell you. This book was originally intended to be one volume. Due to the number of crazy stories I have encountered; there will have to be more than one volume, or I will never get any of these published.

One of the things which will work for you with this book is the fact that it is not a chronological type book. All the stories are separate stories. If you decide to pick out a story in the middle of the book and read it, you can do this because they do not always hinge on previous information. Have fun.

INTRODUCTION

These stories are not messy, blood sucking, ax murdering type horror stories; I am talking about the other kind of horror stories; funny, stupid ones. This book is about houses and the people who live in them. It explores the relationship between the houses, and the people. It will give you a lot of laughs as you should be able to identify with many of these folks and their thinking. I am sure you will also recognize a lot of the physical problems with the homes.

If you are politically correct, you may hate this book. If you like the three stooges; just remember we are all stooges at one time. We do not all make it to television. If you want to read about people doing both clever and really stupid things with their homes, and some of the thinking behind these deeds, you will love this book.

I do give you some real decent advice on financing and some repair work, but you have to read the book to find this advice. It will not jump out at you.

I spent a lot of time working on homes as a carpenter plus the work in my own homes. At one time, I was even considered as a replacement for Bob Vela' when he left *This Old House*. If I tell you my ideas on repair work, most times they work out just fine. I cannot guarantee any ideas will work for you. If they do not work; don't hold me responsible. Just enjoy the story.

One more thing, I suggest you read this book before you go to bed. "Why?" You may ask, because this is a lot more fun than watching the news about some poor slob being shot at a deli and the idiot TV guy asking him: "Are you going to miss your brother?" Give me a break. If you are a bed wetter, go to the bathroom before you read.

Bedtime Horror Stories for Homeowners

There are certain things that are important to be a homeowner. You don't have to be a genius, but it does pay to exhibit some intelligence. At one time I taught in a vocational school and I had sort of a bulletin board that I used to give the guys a heads up on safety. These ideas would appear to be just nothing but common sense; but just for laughs I'm going to put some of them in this book.

When you own a house you may be doing some type of repair work. These ideas may keep you from getting in trouble or getting hurt. Picture this; you are going to tear out a wall. Try to think how these ideas will apply.

- Work neatly; you don't want to trip over tools, debris, children or pets.
- Use the right tool for the right job; you don't need a sledgehammer to drive a thumb tack.
- Don't do this job when you are tired, drunk, stoned or in a bad mood.
- Wear eye protection, hearing protection or a dust mask if you need it.
- Any tool that can cut wood; can also cut fingers. This includes utility knives.
- Don't have anyone around who will distract you. Some people just have that type personality.
- Don't throw tools. Even a pencil can do damage.
- If you're not sure what you going to do, sit down and think it out first.
- Don't mix water and electricity, this seems to be obvious no-brainer, but I have seen people use electric saws while standing in a puddle.

Bedtime Horror Stories for Homeowners

Bedtime Horror Stories for Homeowners

Bedtime Horror Stories for Homeowners

ACKNOWLEDGMENTS

I thank my Mom, Helen Souza for proof reading the rough copy of this book and letting me know where she found mistakes. She is the person who originally taught me to read.

And I thank my wife the lovely Janice for putting up with me monopolizing this computer so I could do the book. Then again, she keeps me busy and I do not bother her. She may not have to read this book, as she has lived through most of it. I thank all the people who have given me stories; we have had a lot of fun.

DEDICATION

Dedicated to my Dad, Jim Pugliese who could fix anything, I think.

Chapter 1 IN THE BEGINNING

IN THE BEGINNING

Seems I've heard that phrase before. Oh well, I guess we might as well start there anyway. We all know; or at least should know, that homes as we know them today did not just exist from day one. I mean, who would want some guy dressed in a hunk of animal skin and smelling worse than the previous owner of that skin hanging out in your house.

This guy probably had feet that were as tough as your average pair of work shoes and just as big and ugly. How would you like those on your coffee table? He could lean his club in the umbrella rack and enjoy some bottled water, a couple gallons of it. Of course if he brought his woman with him, she would have a charm of her own. You would now know where the term ANIMAL MAGNITISM came from. This is nothing new, it is just rediscovered.

No, this lovely couple had a slightly different approach to the home. It was simply a hole in the ground or a mountain otherwise known as THE CAVE. Now we have to look at his home from the occupant's viewpoint. It had no mortgage, no electric bills or power.

When it got dark they either cranked up the fire or chased each other around the interior and made noises like the other local critters. I understand these people were into interior decorating. This was called Cave Painting.

Art history books are full of this type work, but to the untrained eye the paintings all look pretty mundane and this is probably the reason for the similarity. But they did the best they could.

If they were in high school today, the political correctness people would be so proud of them. Their names would be on one of those lighted signs as "STUDENT OF THE MONTH" or some other stupid title. They were not just into a minimal art existence. They wanted to let the world know they knew the score.

Bedtime Horror Stories for Homeowners

Furnishings were sparse. Do you really think they were the Fred and Wilma we all know so well? Do you think they would carry huge rocks into a cave for a lounge chair? Would you? Think about that. They would usually go for the FURNISHED CAVE. One that pretty much came as is, a sort of handyman's special where what you saw was what you got. Besides that, sitting on these rocks probably would make their butts as tough as their feet. The smarter people in this time would go and find something a bit softer like a log; or a pile of brush, or a pile of skins like the one our original guy was wearing, and use those to pad the furniture.

Convertible furniture was anything that could be used more than one way. Imagine for a minute the usefulness of a big animal hide, even the dead animal would be proud of its versatility.

As for recreation; there was no TV, or I don't think so. With the low lighting; sex was probably way ahead of whatever was in second place. Be thankful though. Where would you and I be, if not for efforts of these people to amuse themselves?

Remember Dino, Fred's pet dinosaur, really, who the hell would keep a pet that had dumpster breath. Besides that, do you think any of these pets are easy to housebreak? Any scientist will tell you dinosaurs and people did not live together. This is the only part of this book that is fiction, the rest are real true stories, and some of the names have been changed so nobody sues my ugly ass.

The New York Times Sunday Edition would barely cover one day's droppings. Plus these animals were not exactly known for high intelligence or loyalty; and when they decided to lie down in the cave, there probably was not a lot of room left. And do you have any idea WHAT IT WOULD COST TO FEED ONE OF THESE GUYS?

So much for domestic pets, trying to domesticate the children was hard enough. These little dears were in a class of their own. They had no toys or hobbies as we know them today. They did not need Transformers to take something apart. They just tore apart anything that was handy. Didn't put it back together, just took it apart.

Bedtime Horror Stories for Homeowners

Dino was not a pet to them; he was FAIR GAME, dinner for two or more. The kids average toys were a pointed stick (You'll poke your eye out with that) a club and a rock. An average game would be something like throw the rocks at each other. Whoever was still standing at the end, was the winner.

One great advantage to the cave homes is that this type of game could be played inside, or outside and not worry about breaking a window or Mom's favorite dishes. Schooling was not very formal; it was usually a sort of on the job training type thing, learning by doing. This is why some cave paintings were better than others. Also why some kids grew up to be great hunters and some became critter dinner.

The home was a place to train the youngster how to hunt and cook. Both of these activities are sort of basic, due to the limiting comforts of home and the boring diet. Besides that, language had not really developed.

Remember Raquel Welsh in Six Million Years BC? How many big lines did she have? If it wasn't for the fact she was such a hottie, even the cavemen would have dozed off during the filming.

Kids didn't have to worry about keeping up with the local fashions. Lack of TV, radio and the Internet kept media information rather low so they never knew too much out their local area. Aside from that, they wore what they could kill. Closet space was never a problem.

For variety, they would most likely switch outfits with each other. This was the beginning of hand me downs and transvestites. The children were not really aware of all this subtle stuff; they just wanted something to keep them from freezing their asses off. Now that we have some idea about the families, let's say they are out to find a cave of their own. There are a number of ways to do this, but the one I'll investigate is the:

DAILY ROCK CLASSIFIED

Bedtime Horror Stories for Homeowners

ROCKSTONE REALTY: One of a kind, great view, stream on property. This cave features One Great Room, three smaller areas with connecting tunnels. Entrance faces south for possible use as a solar heating system. Large East/West openings at rear of cave provide excellent cross ventilation. Excellent wall art.

HARDHILL REALTY: Handyman's Special, loose debris and leaks are trying the patience of the present owner. Good starter cave for the man or woman with the right talents. Make offer.

OUT OF STATE

PTERODACTYL REAL ESTATE: Unique cave with one entrance at each end. Mainly used by single caveman for weekend retreat. Good neighborhood, much game and fruit trees in area. Will trade for either six heavy animal skins or one fair skinned woman with long hair.

ONWARD AND UPWARD...THE GRASS HUT

Now as close as I can determine, people soon must have either outnumbered caves or got sick of chasing large animals out of them. Maybe they got sick of the dampness and the resulting physical illnesses.

At some point, someone decided there must be a better way. In the warmer climates the grass hut was born. Probably some sun worshiper who needed some sort of shade at times or protection from the rain.
Of course these huts had a few minor drawbacks. Bugs love them; they must consider a grass shack almost like a condo or a resort area.
Also the structures are not too great in storms. Snow would be a real problem but worse of all: NO SMOKING ALLOWED.

AND IN THE NORTH:

Bedtime Horror Stories for Homeowners

I mean, let's be realistic, Okay? Who the hell would want to live in a circular building which feels like a meat locker and because of that; the dress of the day is, you guessed it, ANIMAL HIDES. Sound familiar? Where the hell is the progress? You tell me.

PROGRESS REPORT

In the European countries, there were big shots; Kings, the Pope, other religious leaders and some rich S.O.B.'s. They lived in castles. The rest of the peasants lived somewhere between grass shacks to stone houses with grass roofs. There is still reality. The big shots are not that much better off than the peasants because the castles aren't really that warm and cozy, the only big difference is the size.

AND ON THE WESTERN FRONT

Here we find the development of the LOG HOME, actually better described as the: LOG CABIN

Think about this, have you ever seen a big log cabin from the time of the pioneers? Simple reason for that fact is that trees only come up to certain sizes plus the people were building these with hand tools and horses.

Aside from that, there was not much concern about social status. Most of the pioneers were in the same boat so there was a decided lack of BIG SHOTS.

This led to people who worked together just to stay alive. There were certain advantages to these houses.
1. Lots of building materials, no middle man to inflate the price of the logs.
2. Simplicity of construction, sort of like a big Lincoln Log Set.
3. A little heavier but the same basic concept.
4. Usually plenty of free labor.

Of course there were a few problems.

1. If the person building the home did not consider the fact that wood shrinks when it dries, he had instant air conditioning if he did not let the wood dry some before he built with it.

2. There was a limit on styles, usually one.

3. The actual construction took a lot of hard work, not a job for wimps.

AND IN THE NORTHERN UNITED STATES

As people moved to colder climates, STONE houses became more the order. A lot of this construction was due to the nature of the terrain in New England. Even today there are plenty of old stone walls in those states. I mean there were about a zillion rocks there, and you had to do something with them. They made lousy food and clothing, so housing was the next logical step. These were unique in the fact they were similar to the old castles in their construction properties and similar to the log cabins in the availability of materials.

THEN THERE WERE THE POLITICIANS

Have you ever been to Washington D.C.? Have you ever noticed the great houses people like George Washington and Jefferson owned? Did you check out the property? I mean these guys did not become powerful by being stupid. You will notice, they did not live in slums or crowded areas; or someplace the government was going to take their home to build a highway. Oh no, these guys had their act together.

Aside from the status needed for their professional positions they wanted to be comfortable with the weather and knew how to handle workers and slaves and money.

These houses were designed to take advantage of the weather and the property and of new technical advances.

They were the forerunners of our present housing. There was one group I have to mention though who was a slight exception to the rule.

THE MANSION OWNERS

If you ever want to see a serious expenditure of money, go take a look at a real live mansion. There was one used in the movie *Annie*. This building does really exist in West Long Branch, New Jersey. I have been inside it. It is on the campus of Monmouth University. It is called Wilson Hall. If you go to find it, you can't miss it. If you miss it, and your eyes are that bad, your next eyeglass prescription is a dog. The building in no longer used by Daddy Warbucks or the original owners, it is now an office building, a large, ornate office building.

One more great location is the mansions in Newport, Rhode Island. Talk about money, these people must have had more money than God. I spoke to people whose ancestors helped build these places.

The *skilled help* were making maybe a dollar a day. Correct me if I am wrong; I probably will not change the book, but welcome the input. I am just quoting what one of the locals told me. Visit the Biltmore Mansion in North Carolina.

There are houses there which had price tags in the millions, back in the early 1900's. These are really something to see.

The bottom line here, at least for a guy like myself is? How many places can you sleep at one time? How often do I go to the can in one day? Beds and bathrooms are like a coffin, you only use one at a time.

Just for the hell of it, go visit them some time. The Historical Society runs tours all year.

SO WHO'S HOUSE DO WE VISIT NOW?

Bedtime Horror Stories for Homeowners

YOURS, MINE. Most everybody else's house that we mere mortals know. The guy who keeps the country going. The carpenters, the auto workers, the teachers, nurses, accountants, businessmen, sales people, artists, musicians, photographers, doctors. In short, the AVERAGE GUY if he or she truly exists.

From a realistic standpoint, we are more alike than we are different and believe it or not so are our homes. You build a dog house or a tool shed with the same things you use to build a condo or a split level or a cape cod. The big differences are the size, style and level of workmanship and this is not always dependent upon money or social status.

THE AVERAGE GUY

What can we consider the "average guy"? The guy who makes a steady living building cars, the lawyer who works for the local Legal Services office, the doctor who makes $150,000 a year? The housewife who helps her husband run a coffee shop. Get the picture?

The census people give us numbers such as the "Average Income of a certain type person is X number of bucks." "The Average Weight of a man or woman at age 40 is such and such" and on and on and on. This nonsense could go of forever and there would always be an exception to the rule.

The way I feel personally; is that if I can stay ahead of my bills, keep a roof over my head, food in my mouth, and clothes on my back with some money left over for hobbies or other non-essential stuff I'm doing fine.

One economist said that your expenses expand to meet your income, and if you think about this, he is probably right.

So let's not get too involved in this business. This is a lighthearted book and I do not want to depress anyone by having them compare themselves to someone else. Everyone is average for this book.

To keep the picture complete during the book I will use a man and woman, two kids and a dog for my "AVERAGE FAMILY." They have just gone out for the "AMERICAN DREAM." Their own home.

THE CHICKEN OR THE EGG THEORY
OR WHAT CAME FIRST? THE HOUSE OR THE MORTGAGE?

Some people get lucky and have a house given to them, as a wedding present; some get one left to them in a will. Some even win them in contests. Well these are not the people about whom I talk. The people I'm talking about are the ones who find a home they feel will fit their needs and decide to own it. This should be so simple. HA.

There was a time when if our breadwinner made a certain amount of money, had a steady income and found the house, a mortgage was not all that bad to deal with. For my purposes I will call my average family, Pete the father, Mary, the wife, Tom and Patty the kids. The dog is Champ.

Now back in the "old days" like 1950, the family picked out a house back for about $8000 (really, I wouldn't kid you). Pete was making seventy five bucks a week; that was decent money back then. Pete went to the local bank where he had an account for maybe the last 10 years, told them he wanted to buy a house and needed a mortgage. Told them he could put down a certain amount for a down payment and got his loan. Wham, Bam thank you Mam' here's the money, enjoy the house. Good luck and all that other good stuff.

Today things are different, even the banks are making jokes about the situation just to get you to deal with their institution instead of the one down the block. There is no such thing as simply going out and getting a mortgage anymore. There are all different types today.

There is the traditional 30 year fixed rate type where you know the interest rate, and it stays there for the entire loan. This is fairly safe as long as you make the payments. Well, duh, that is the whole point of the deal.

Then there are VARIABLE RATE MORTGAGES, BALLOON MORTGAGES, MORTGAGES THAT CHANGE WITH THE INTREST RATES, MORTGAGES THAT CHANGE WITH THE ECONOMY AND SOME THAT CHANGE WITH THE WEATHER. I started writing this book years ago and since then there is another type mortgage which has popped up....THE INTEREST ONLY MORTGAGE.

In that case, you only pay on the interest on the loan; with the idea that at some point either you unload the house and make money, or have to cough up the actual money for the principal. This seems like a good idea till it actually happens.

Some people have made a lot of money doing this; other people have lost their homes, their equity, their everything, because of greed and stupidity. These are the people who thought they were going to screw someone while the housing market was hot, and when it cooled off, they were left holding the bag. Sort of makes me feel good to see these smart asses take a hit.

There are so many variables in this area; a lot of us would need a lawyer to even know what the hell we are signing. Compound this with CLOSING FEES, FINDER FEES, POINTS, DISCOUNTS, CROOKED REAL ESTATE AGENTS, DIRTY DEALING SELLERS AND BUYERS and all that other good fun.

THE DEVELOPMENT HOME

Now this type home makes up a lot of housing in this country. Just the term development house brings a funny feeling to me. It sounds like a rehab center for drunks or dopers. Maybe that is why builders have stopped using that term.

No matter what term is in vogue today, this type home is the type where all the houses in an area follow three or four designs and the big differences are the decorations and the colors. These are the Cape Cods, the Bi-Levels, the Split Levels, the Mc Mansions and Condos.

If you look around areas in old towns, you will notice there are certain homes which look a lot like each other, and with some research, you will find they were built by the same carpenters. The big difference here is that there are usually just a few in any one location, maybe three or four at a time.

CAPE COD

With the case of Cape Cods, this style goes back to about 1950. I know people who purchased homes like this that far back and paid about $10,000 with a 4% interest rate. Most homes like this today in my area are more like $300,000-$400,000 depending on location and upgrades. The interest rates go up and down according to the economy. When I got my house the interest rate was 14 ½ % back in the early 1980's.

For those of you who do not know what a Cape Cod looks like, it is a small house about 35 feet square more or less, Most of them came with a stairway that led to a second floor/attic which could be made into bedrooms and many of them had full basements.

On the first floor, there is usually a Living room, a Kitchen/Dining room area, not really either one, but a combination of the two. There are usually two bedrooms, and a bath. These homes were built for people who came out of WW II and needed housing.

Most of these couples had one or two small children and this was a nice alternative to an apartment in the city. It also kept them from moving back in with Mom and Dad.

Some people went for the optional dining rooms on the back of the house; some had the builder finish the attic and the basement. Many people just moved in and worked on them on their own.

Many of these developments were built a few miles out of big cities. Within 20 miles of New York City, just in New Jersey I can think of at least 20 of these developments.

Nothing wrong with this type housing, it is basically very nice. It gave people a place of their own; it brought together a lot of people with similar interests and led to the general development of a lot of areas.

If you look around developments of this type you will find a lot of families who have brothers, cousins and parents all within the same neighborhood. The people liked what they found, and recommended it to their friends and family.

You did not have to be a millionaire to own a house like this; if you were working steady, and had a few bucks down, you were in business. Besides that, if you were a veteran; you were in the right place at the right time.

Back in the late 1940's almost everyone who looked for housing was a vet or married to one. It was a good time, there was the baby boom and the U.S. wanted to settle down and get back to normal. A lot of builders made a lot of money back then and the housing market was hot.

Builders back then, as today had a fast system for putting up a development. They would buy a piece of property (a.k.a. dirt) and talk some bank into some financing. A lot of the homes were pre-sold through offices and buyers were waiting at the door for the C.O. (Certificate of Occupancy)

The builder would either buy, rent, steal, borrow, or finance a couple of bulldozers and where there was originally thirty or forty wooded acres, there were now thirty or forty acres of land scraped down to the dirt with a few small trees left. The reasoning behind this is simple. If there are no trees in the way, construction will go easier and faster. This is true.

So this system became a widespread practice, some builders would leave the trees at the back of the lots, but a lot of them also went. After the house was built, the owner would receive a few small bushes for the front yard. Most people really did not care, it just meant less leaves to rake in the fall. I'm sure this was used as a selling point.

Now, if the builder wanted to build 100 Cape Cods, he would estimate approximately what was needed to build one, multiply this by 100 and he knew what it would cost to create this development. This worked with both materials and labor costs. This of course led to the development of the framing crew.

THE FRAMING CREW

This is a type of carpenter which has had a rebirth in this country several times. When the economy is going strong, and building is going strong, framing crews are rampant. There have always been carpenters who knew how to do framing, except in housing developments that is all these guys do. It is sort of like outdoor factory work.

First the builder would get crews of masons to put down the cinder block foundations and the basement floors. That is another outdoor factory job. I'm sick of hearing and typing about concrete. I am going to let your imagination do the work here. Just multiply by 100.

A framer is basically a carpenter who builds the skeleton of a frame house from rough lumber. Most of this lumber runs in dimensions that is in the multiples of the number two such as 2 X 4, 2 X 6....etc....up to usually 2 X 10's . If you get a chance sometime, measure a 2 X 4 and find out the true size...... (This is referred to as two by four).

I have another word for a framer and this applies strictly to the young relatively inexperienced men and women in this work.

NAIL BANGERS

This is the main occupation of these guys; the boss had one lead carpenter who does the brain work, and the layout. Maybe another skilled man who knows how to lay out rafters and read blueprints. Then there are the bunches of nail bangers. I personally know a lot of young men who work on crews like this. They admit the boss does not like them to be near a circular saw, or allow them to do any brain work. They are a boogiellugger with a hammer.

This is nothing to be ashamed of, you have to start off somewhere, and this beats having no trade at all.

A lot of these "Nail Bangers" actually become well trained and skilled carpenters; some become builders and still others are content to stick with this type work for a career. Let me give you a general picture of the average nail banger.

To start with, most of them are young. The age range is from about 18 to 30. Most of them are males, though with the way roles have evolved, there are more women in the field today.

 The person is usually physically strong, able to withstand various weather conditions, can balance on a narrow piece of wood, and be like an acrobat at times. They can usually read a ruler, live in jeans or shorts and wear either work shoes or sneakers to work. They usually carry the biggest hammer they can buy or handle.

The smaller 16 oz. type hammers most homeowners use are too small, these guys use hammers up to 28 oz. This is like a throwback to the stone ages with the clubs.

They may be asked to use hardhats, but most do not like to use them. The circular saw is one of their favorite tools, sometimes with the guards removed on commercial jobs. Dangerous as hell, but fast.

The down side of this type thinking is that if you take off a finger doing this, you are going to lose a lot of that time you thought you were making up. Got to use your brains once in a while. A lot of these guys have at least one short finger. A nail apron and hammer holder are pretty much standard stuff.

There are no size requirements for this work, the heights vary, but there are no real fatties; an occasional beer belly, but not fat. Some of their favorite words are "DUDE," "YASSHOLE," "BITCH," and "GODDAMN SHITTY LUMBER."

They relate well to sports personalities, loud music, beer and bonuses. They whistle at women and if their whistle is not too hot....it's usually "Hey Baby!" This is most effective while standing on the top of the roof framing while not wearing a shirt.

These people have created the skeletons of the frame houses in the U.S. And they must be doing something right; most of these houses stand for a long time.

I met a guy one time who worked as a framing carpenter; he told me they had done so many of these type homes that they could frame them without using a ruler. Think about that. He had done so many of these homes; he could frame them in his mind.

The similarities in the home start to disappear as time goes by. People wanting to have their own identity start to landscape the properties, paint the homes something else than the stock three or four colors, add garages, and patios. Some add dormers; others just leave the house alone so when everyone else makes their changes, their house still has its own identity.

Many of these homes were originally done with asbestos siding which is fun stuff in its own right. Most of them also were heated with hot air heating systems. Those are the kind of systems which operates with a burner making hot air, and a fan blowing that hot air through a duct system to vents to keep the house warm. It is one of the simplest heating systems to install, cannot leak water and has few moving parts. The biggest problem is that when the heat goes off, it is off. I mean when the fan stops blowing, that is the end of the heat. The walls, furnishings and people will have absorbed some of the heat while it is on, but that does not amount to much.

One advantage a few people have told me, is the fact that if you stand directly over the vent when the heat is blowing the warm air feels great. This is really helpful right after a shower.

Of course if you know that the young woman across the street takes a shower and dries herself this way at exactly 6:30 A.M. every day; and thinks just because she has the attic bedroom she does not have to close the shades, well that might make you get up in time. Get your mind out of the gutter and get your perverted butt off to work, you slob.

Now, development homes have come along a bit, not that far, but there have been some changes. The Cape Cod is sort of out of favor. It is the "keeping up with the Joneses" bit. As people realized they could have spent a few more bucks and purchased a bigger house the styles of houses got bigger. Enter the Bi-Level.

THE BI-LEVEL

The entrance to a Bi-level is usually up a set of steps from the sidewalk. There is usually about six or seven steps to a small concrete porch with wrought iron railings. The front door opens out to the porch. You get just about enough room to sneak by with groceries.

The front door I refer to is usually a storm door. In today's "Heat or Eat" economy, most people have these. Inside the door is a solid door which opens to the inside. The outside door can knock you down the steps, this one can knock you down the inside steps. This is the heart of the Bi-Level.

There is a platform from which there are two sets of steps, one up and one down, the upper one leads to a kitchen, a living room, a dining room and a couple of bedrooms, the bottom one leads to a garage which may have been made into a bedroom, a laundry room with a heating system, usually another bedroom and a family room/den.

This is so when the Super Bowl is on the TV and hubby does not want to miss any action, he can stand in the potty with the door open and watch the TV in the mirror. Nobody else is going to much care if he leaves the door open; they have all gone elsewhere for the day.

The builders will either use this den as a big activity room for the family with a fireplace for "atmosphere." I've got a few things to tell you about fireplaces later.

One problem with the family room is that it is built on a concrete slab and has a tendency to be cold and transmit dampness, good for the arthritis.

If this room faces south, you may get lucky and be able to use it for some passive solar heating by using big sliding doors to collect sunlight and heat the slab during the day and then closing heavy drapes at night to trap the heat in the room.

The only problem here is you have to get to the builder before the floor is poured, so he puts foam insulation under it. Otherwise the heat will just go halfway into the room, and the rest of the heat goes into the dirt.

This home is just what it implies; it is built on more than one level. It's great if you want to stay in shape by running up and down steps. Also very good if you are a Jewish American Princess, the kitchen is a good excuse for eating out a lot. I have been inside a lot of bi-levels and thought about buying one years' ago.

I am yet to find one that has a kitchen which does not look like a closet with appliances and a sink. All the necessary stuff is there, it is just that it is small. The kitchen might be 8 by 8 feet with cabinets on the walls, a refrigerator in one corner and a stove in the other corner. Sort of like the kitchen in an RV, but smaller.

If it were used just to prepare food that would be Okay, except there is usually a table in the room with at least two chairs. This will help with the lack of counter space, better to eat in the dining room.

Most of the dining rooms are connected to the living room, so they are not that big either, but they are bigger than the kitchen. This is always a fun house with small children and light colored carpets. Maybe a sheet of plastic on the entire dining room floor would help.

The trick to this house is the living room. It is an optical illusion. It is the only large room on the upper floor. The living room being connected to the dining room makes you feel that the dining room is larger. Usually the side of the living room has an open railing by the steps which take up a big part of the center of the house. With the open area of the steps and the living room, the top floor looks a lot more open than it really is.

Chapter 2   WHY DID WE PICK THIS HOUSE?

LOCATION IS EVERYTHING

Simple Economics....If you buy a great looking house in a lousy location, you are in trouble. Better to buy an ugly home in a good location and fix it up.

LET'S TALK ABOUT LOCATIONS

From a realistic standpoint, there are certain obvious things you would avoid in location. You may want to avoid items such as FLOOD AREAS, LANDSIDE AREAS, AN INTERNATIONAL AIRPORT, OR AN AREA WHERE DRUG DEALING AND PROSTITUTION ARE THE MAIN BUSINESSES.

If you see things like this and still take the place, either you want part of the action, or have made a big mistake. Or maybe you are a nut. Sometimes there are no obvious signs of the problems. But you must hunt them down and take appropriate action. The action here is to sell the home to someone who has not read this book. Or burn it down and sell it to the insurance company.

When there are FOR SALE signs all over the area. This tells you something. Watch neighborhoods like that, ask questions. Sometimes it is just a good market and a lot of people want to make a change, sometimes it is something more subtle. Get your lazy ass out of the car and talk to the neighbors. It will pay off in the long run. Some more subtle signs are as follows:

"BAD" LOCATIONS

- The only road into the area is paved with dirt.
- This road is full of tracks from 4 wheel drive vehicles.
- All the neighbors drive four wheel drive vehicles. Not the sissy type SUV that you see on the road today. NO, I mean the type car or truck which has four VERY LARGE TIRES and you need a ladder to enter the door. They may be disguised with fancy paint jobs, but so was the Trojan Horse.
- The tires are always full of mud.
- When you drive under a railroad overpass to enter the neighborhood, there is a sign which reads.... SOUND HORN. You will notice the many colors of paint on the sides of the overpass.
- On this overpass you will notice water marks.
- Everyone in the area has a boat, not a cabin cruiser type, more like a rowboat or a rubber raft.
- There are no two story homes here. The weight would cause them to sink into the ground.
- The lawn is always wet.
- On the map to locate the area, there are funny marks and a light blue color.
- The local post office people have never heard of the street. If they have, you will hear them laughing as you leave the office.
- The area smells of one of the following; cheap perfume, medicine, rubber, gasoline, chemicals, sewage, or any of the above in combination.

MORE "BAD" LOCATION SIGNS:

- It is June 15th and there is no vegetation in the area.
- It has not rained for a month and the ground is soggy.
- There is nothing but brand new, *BIG* cars on the block. These are usually painted lavender.
- There are NO big cars in the area or new ones either.
- The drinking water in the house tastes lousy.
- It looks like an area where you may starve to death trying to make a living.
- There is upholstered furniture on people's front porches.
- There are no kids or pets in the area. The welcoming committee is a water rat.
- There are wrought iron grilles in front of windows and doors. these are not for looks, they are for security.
- You look for the sky and cannot see it.
- It is July, a weekend, nice weather and there is nobody in their yards.
- The only sound you can hear is that of heavy machinery.
- The hedges in the back yard are 30 feet high.
- The house smells like urine.
- There is an even coat of dust on the entire neighborhood.
- You pass a large number of boarded up homes and stores.
- You breathe deeply, you smell a landfill. Holy Crap!

HOW TO SPOT A "GOOD" LOCATION:

- The price of property will probably be about twice what you expected.
- All the property in the area looks well kept.
- People wave at you when you drive past.
- The color of the garbage cans compliment the color of the house.
- There is no major road construction.
- There are sidewalks and curbs.
- You can look up and see the sky.
- Your car is the worst one in the neighborhood.
- The local dogs do not fraternize with your dog.
- The house you are looking at does not have a FOR SALE sign in front.
- The garbage men wear ties and fetch the trash from the side of the homes.
- A number of cars in the area are of Italian origin and the names of them end in an "I".
- There are no bus stops in the area.
- The mailboxes and fire hydrants are all freshly painted.
- You don't recognize anyone in the area.
- Your dog is the only one who humps anyone.

SO MUCH FOR LOCATIONS, GO LOOK YOURSELVES!

HOW DO WE PICK OUT THE HOUSE?
More like, WHO PICKS OUT THE HOUSE?

Before you get involved with the home or the mortgage, or any of the paperwork involved, someone has to pick out the home. This *may* seem like a fun job, and sometimes it really is a fun job. At other times it can be frustrating, tiring, or annoying. Sort of like trying to find a new boyfriend or a new dog.

You may find yourself out driving around at night in the snow and the rain in zero type weather with a notebook, and your favorite pencil and a flashlight, writing down addresses and phone numbers of real estate agents.

If you work nights and the other person works days, this can be twice as much fun, or even more than that, when you take other half to check out the best house you have seen all day.

I will go into more detail about what you would look for, but before I do that, I must disclose a FACT that all real estate people know the day they are born......

THE WOMAN PICKS OUT THE HOUSE

No matter what the man says about the leaky plumbing, old drafty windows, water in the basement or anything else, she will say "That's not too big a problem, you can fix it!"

And keeping this in mind, if SHE likes it; YOU WILL BUY IT.

Believe me, I own my second home, have put deposits on several others either for possible occupation or rental properties and looked at in the past 35 years maybe 1000 homes.

Not that I have searched every nook and cranny of each one, some I checked out as I went by in the car and decided the neighborhood was the pits, or the firehouse next door may be too loud or some other problem.

But the thing is, I did a lot of looking and the women in my life did plenty of it with me. I hope you are getting the picture. If she walks in and sees a big living room and dining room, you're on your way. If the kitchen is huge, you bought it. Even if the man is the cook, and you only have visitors twice a year, this is how she thinks.

Do you think for two seconds, that spot in the basement is where your power tools are going? Fat chance. More likely, an exercise bike with full length mirrors. Do you think you're going to put solar collectors on the roof? The birds are lucky they don't clash with the color of the shingles.

See that nice sunny porch where you could spend the afternoon and watch the young lady next door sunbathing while you are drinking a beer? You'll never sit still long enough to drink a 16 oz. bottle. Better to get used to pony size. By the time you get a chance to sit down, that young hottie will be married with three kids, and driving a big ugly SUV full of toys and groceries.

That big garage in the back yard? Give it up pal. Do you think all that glorious sunlight coming in the window is going to last? The sun may keep shining, but you will never know it with the "Window Treatments".

I know one guy who considered permanently closing up the windows inside and out, complete with insulation, put up a full size photo of the previous view and let his wife knock herself out with all the drapes, and sheers and curtains she desires.

And think of the privacy. Most guys will walk around the house in their birthday suit. I don't' know why, but they do this, and could care less about who looks in the window. ("Maybe the woman across the street will get off on my bod!"). Maybe not! A woman on the other hand will close the curtains to change her socks. Even if she has fat legs and lives two blocks from the nearest neighbor. (That pervert probably has a telescope. Forget the fact that he is 86 years old, and almost blind anyway).

Back to the garage, do you think for one second, your custom van will ever see the inside of it? Maybe from across the street and through the "Winter Clothes."

MALE AND FEMALE CHECK LISTS

There are things a man looks for in a house and things that women look for. If you don't believe me, wait till you go looking. There are some common areas and this is how these people will decide on the home.

MALE HOUSE CHECKLIST:	FEMALE CHECKLIST:
Does the roof leak?	What color is the roof?
Is the basement full of water?	Where do I put my washer/dryer?
Is the kitchen full of old, useless appliances?	The sink is a horrible color, so is the floor, and the walls. Who picked out this shit anyway?
The house has drafty windows.	I could put up some great drapes in here.
The place has three bedrooms. (Man Cave?)	I'll make a closet out of the third bedroom. Good place for "Winter clothing".

Bedtime Horror Stories for Homeowners

MALE:	FEMALE:
We're only a block from the lumberyard.	I can see the mall from here.
Nice two car garage, good place for a workshop.	More "Winter Storage"
The dog will love the big yard.	That lousy mutt better not crap in my flowerbeds.
The insulation in this place is garbage.	Look at the room in this attic none of that fuzzy stuff up here either. More storage.
That school on the corner will create tons of garbage on my front lawn. Maybe a Doberman is in order. The other dog will get along with it.	How convenient for the kids.

HOW TO TRANSLATE REAL ESTATE ADS

    To start with, these ads are written in a text size that runs about this big. (House for sale).

    There is a reason for this. It costs money to run ads and the more ink a newspaper can put on the page, the more cost efficient it is to print the paper. (Who cares if the readers go blind? This will create income for the people who advertise eyeglasses in the paper). For the benefit of the people who buy this book, I am printing these ads at a larger size so you don't go blind and blame it on me. I am sooooo considerate.

Bedtime Horror Stories for Homeowners

RENT BEFORE YOU CLOSE

Beautiful spacious three bedroom brick front U-Shaped Ranch. Grand Master bedroom, stone fireplace full basement. Two car garage. Must be seen to appreciate. $192,800.

Translation: You will have to use the rent for the first 5 years for a down payment.

Try working out *that* deal, good luck.

PROFESSIONAL LOCATION

This 4-bedroom ranch home. Features fireplace, partial basement. Situated on 75 x 150 foot property.

Translation: This place is situated on a four-lane highway, and the basement is just about big enough for the heating system and the hot water heater. The fourth bedroom was probably the receptionist office for a chiropractor.

FOR SALE BY OWNER

BR, 1½ bath, LR, DR, GAR, FPLCE, GOOD STARTER HOME $89,000

Translation: To start with this guy is too cheap to go to an agent, so he is going at it with a sign on the lawn (Hand painted with a big black Sharpie marker) and he has abbreviated every word he can locate so he only has to make one sign. He will probably also try to sell you the furniture, the dog, and a kid.

EXECUTIVE RANCH
EXCLUSIVE, GORGEOUS LOCATION, CONTEMPORY

With 5 bedrooms, 2 ½ Baths. Huge family room, with fireplace adjoining Country kitchen. Formal dining room, sunken living room. All this on over 2 acres of rustic wooded property.

Toms River, A steal at $298,000

Bedtime Horror Stories for Homeowners

Translation: The important word here is EXECUTIVE. You get an automatic mental promotion from whatever you are doing at the present time. This is supposed to make you want to spend money like an executive.

MOTHER/ DAUGHTER HOME

Gas heated ranch on 75 x 100-foot lot. Featuring 2 Kitchens, 2 baths, 2 separate entrances, and a full basement. Great investment. $165,000

Translation: Have you ever heard the old thing about two women in the same kitchen? Wait till you try to work out a deal with two women. They probably do not get along with each other, (2 entrances). You can make a safe bet that they will not get along with you either. On the other hand, they may want to unload the house so they can get away from each other. Mom is ready for a senior citizen dwelling anyway.

MIRACLE HOME

I have no idea who came up with this sign for selling a home; I can only guess that the person selling the place has a Saint Joseph statue buried in the front yard to help get rid of the house.

MOTHER DAUGHER HOME, 200 FEET FROM THE OCEAN

2 Story, 3 bedroom, 2 full bath home. Only 3 houses away from the Oceanfront. It features 2 kitchens, enclosed porch, walk to boardwalk. Seaside Heights. $ 220,000

Translation: You and Mom will never talk to each other again after you get involved in this deal. Besides did you check to see where the high water line is on the house from last year's hurricane season? If you are not sure where this line is, look for a white line somewhere on the outside of the home. Also if you give Mom the bottom floor, is she going to get nosy when she hears your bed squeaking on the second floor? Think about this.

FIVE BEDROOMS, ONE MINUTE FROM THE BEACH

Vacation or second home for the busy executive or family man. This home has been in the area for the past 100 years, and is "A Landmark" in town. Sunny location, close to shopping.

Translation: You can make a bet this place was rented to college kids for most of that 100 years. Sure, the neighbors know where it is, the police do. The sunny location is due to the fact that the last renters accidentally burned down the home next in line to the beach and since most of these "slum lords" don't really care about anything except making money, none of the houses were properly insured. If you look around, you will find a place where someone had a kerosene heater hooked into the chimney, as this place was never intended for year round use. Of course there is shopping, you are around the corner from the liquor store, a pizza joint and an all-night 7-11.

THE REAL ESTATE AGENT

In theory, here is someone who must have a lot of knowledge in various areas. He or she should know something about the structure of houses, the zoning laws, plumbing, electricity and heating systems.

They do not have to know everything about all these subjects, but enough to at least to be able to carry on an intelligent conversation about these things.

Now for the reality viewpoint. I personally know some real estate agents who could not tell a hot water heater from a refrigerator.

It would stand to reason they would know something about finances and debt management. After all, they are going to try to sell a $200,000 house to someone who is making $14,000 a year. Hello? Do the math dummy. You would have to put all your income for the next 15 years into the house just to pay the principal of the home. This will leave you nothing for other small items such as food or clothing. This is also assuming Uncle Sam lets you keep every dime you make. I don't think so.

This real estate person must also know something about mortgages, interest rates, the V.A., F.H.A., Fannie Mae and Mae West. They should also know something about G.I. Mortgages, financing, taxes, long term investments and all the other nonsense involved in buying a home.

It helps if this person knows something about people and how to deal with them. You do not need someone who is a bigot, an anti-Semite, an extreme right or left wing thinker. We are not interested in their personal views on religion or sex. All we want to do is work with them to get a house.

He or she must know how people think. What motivates the buyer or the seller?

What motivates someone to accept or reject an offer? What turns them on about a house?

What gets the buyer excited? In some ways it is sort of like being a pimp. You have to know your clientele, what they want, how much they are willing to pay, and how to give it to them.

When a realtor states "WE HAVE BEEN SERVICING THIS AREA FOR 50 YEARS." Be careful, this may be like a bull servicing the local cows.

In all fairness, I must say that the agents I've worked with in my dealings were really great people. Most of them. Except for a few of them. One doofus tried to sell me a place that was in the middle of a flood zone.

I felt they not only looked out for the buyer, but for the sellers also and gave us all a deal with which we could live. I have also run into a few winners who tried to sell me homes which should have been named TITANIC or POSIDON. Another one tried to sell me half a house which was part of a duplex. No Kidding, these places actually exist.

Now visualize this, you decide to paint your side of the house. Say something like Mauve, and the idiot in the other half decides to go with Orange. Needless to say, that deal will never go through.

Had another live one tried to sell me a place, which was zoned for summer use only. Hello? Where do I live the rest of the year? A homeless shelter? That had something to do with some kind of recreational zoning or something like that.

One of the most memorable houses though was the house, which hung over the property line of the city by two feet. The poor slob living there had never received a proper title and didn't know it. If you do not stay awake, you are dead meat. For more details, see the chapters on duplex homes and the house we almost got.

VICTORIAN, CONTEMPORY, UNDERGROUND

OK, so now that we know who will make the big and not so big decisions about the house, we now have to find one with the right style for you. This should be so easy!

Aside from the color and the wallpaper and the area, now you have to deal with what STYLE house. You think you have seen styles in shoes, hats, coats or automobiles? Ha! Well you have not seen anything yet. There are big homes, small homes, fancy homes, plain homes, the variety is incredible.

Victorian, unbelievable, ranch houses, modern, contemporary types with about a million crazy angles and seven floor levels. Geodesic domes are another strange type.

The one person I know who lives in one of these loves it, yet there are some people who would say it looks like a beehive with windows. Underground homes have come into their own rights. Again, some of us would feel like a gopher. (Back to the caves?)

The things that do separate houses are the size, the price, and the appearance. A house is a reflection of its owner. The location is also very important. Think about this.

What is a better deal? A great house in a crummy neighborhood or a crummy house in a great neighborhood? No Brainer. You know what I mean. There are a few flood areas left in the world.

You can take the "Handyman Special" which is many times structurally solid, but needs some cosmetic work and turn it into a beauty. But in an area where you have to pack a gun to work on the place; no matter how nice you fix it up... YOU STILL OWN GARBAGE!!

Do this work in a good location and after a while, instead of people laughing at you for putting bucks into the place, they will be saying things like "I didn't know you knew how to do this kind of work" Or "I am so glad my daughter married a carpenter instead of that accountant she was so hot for." A lot of people will also think you are crazy for putting the time and money into it, but after all, it is your time and money. It's either this, or bad women and cheap booze.

Q. What do men, women and houses have in common?
A. You will never find one that is 100% perfect.

MARKETING THE DEVELOPMENT HOME

Now anyone who has studied any books on sales technique will tell you that you buy the sizzle, not the steak; housing is no different. Many people do not know all that much about the physical construction of a home, they have to rely on recommendations, appearances and luck.

The sellers are professionals. These people know how to word the ads, lay out the furniture, (check out a model home sometime, and take a close look at the physical size of the furniture) and most of all know how to name the developments. At one time, when this concept started the developer would name the area after himself, Levittown for example. Now this is a whole science in itself.

At last, I have figured out where all the English majors from college went if they could not get a position on the staff of a magazine. These have to be the people who make up the names. I would say if the person were a Literature major, even better. The names I will use are all fictitious just to keep from being sued, but you will get the idea.

DEVELOPMENT NAMES

WHISPERING PINES: Really, if a tree started talking to you, would you answer?

MEWS AT DEER MEADOWS: Five bucks says you don't know what a mew is either. Wait till you check it out.

SETTLERS PERCH: Who were the settlers? A bunch of birds?

OAKEN ACRES: Most people would not even know how big an acre of land is, and if there were any oak trees here, the developer chopped them down to make room to build the homes.

MORE EQUALLY DUMB NAMES

OCEAN VIEW LANDINGS: Usually this is the kind of name for an area which is about 10 miles from any body of water, and 20 miles from any sea water.

BRIARWOOD GARDENS: Have you ever been caught in briars? I bet you would not want your house caught in them either?

SHADY ELMS: About the only thing shady here might be the builders' reputation. Again there are only "token" trees here.

WOODED ACRES: They were wooded, and then the crew came in to work. Now we are back to the barren land. If we all live to about 115, we may be rewarded for our patience.

TALL OAKS: The only tall tree left here is at the entrance to the sales office. They had to impress you with something.

BENSONS CORNERS: At least this guy had the guts to identify himself with his work.

Seems builders favor names with nature themes. Water and any kind of wood or tree used somewhere go over big. More realistically, they could be called names like:

DUMPS ON THE SWAMPS, HIGHWAY CROSSING LOTS

LOWLIFE ACRES, FLOODHAVEN, WINDYTOWN. Get it?

Bedtime Horror Stories for Homeowners

Another ploy used is the descriptions used for the homes. One of my favorite is: PATIO HOMES

PATIO HOMES. Think about that for a minute. OK, your minute is up. What we have here, is a home constructed on a concrete slab. Now why are they not called slab homes? People think of slabs in a negative light....Slab brings up images of death...as in a slab in the local police morgue. The very word SLAB is not even pretty to look at; it fits in with SLAG, SLOP, and STAB. All sorts of negative ideas.

But on the other hand, a patio has a whole different image. I am inclined to think of summer, barbecues, and sunshine. Even as I type, I think of a young lady with a short dress, nice legs and a bit of lace where the legs meet the dress. You thought of it too? Nice going pervert. A patio is a fun place. It's hot dogs, music and a good time.

In a technical sense it is also a slab. See how this system works? Ask anyone who owns a home built on a slab how their feet feel after a day at home. The concrete does not give at all and by the end of the day, you feel like a day at U.S. Marine Basic Training. Yer Left. Yer Left.

Another term used is DECORATOR INSPIRED: Who was the decorator? Anybody we all know? Most likely; some poor guy who works at the local furniture store, has a large building full of furnishings and has to sell as much as possible. He may have some really good ideas, and a smart builder will at least will use these. He would not give the guy any credit, just use the ideas.

COLOR COORDINATED: This means all the walls are WHITE or OFF/WHITE. People in the industry call this kind of paint COMMERCIAL WHITE. This looks fine until some kid gets his dirty hands on it and you try to wash it, of course anything will go with white. Bring out the mustard carpet.

UPGRADE: This is a term used by builders to let you know the house can be built either with cheap stuff or a grade better. The local building codes say what type lumber and sheetrock etc. must be used but the upgrade bit is for items such as stainless steel sinks instead of painted cast iron, a better grade of carpet instead of the stock Astroturf stuff. One wall painted a light brown instead off-white.

When upgraded faucets are used in the bath, you can actually turn them on and off without using a pair of vise grip pliers, the cheap ones will cost more over the long run with the extra hot water being wasted because you can't shut the damn thing off.

CONTEMPORARY HOMES

Now this term has always made me wonder exactly what it implies. If a home is contemporary, I would assume this would mean a home which is newly constructed. On the other hand, take a look at these type homes. They are all considered state of the art as to the appliances and conveniences or at least that is how it should be. Take a closer look; they have the same basic items as any other new home.

There is usually nothing really radical about the construction. I would expect complete climate control, super high energy efficiency, automatic sliding doors (think Star Trek), and windows. Also a security system, no maintenance type exteriors and interiors, an intercom. A vacuum system built into the walls, the whole nine yards.

If you want to see these types of construction, take a trip to EPCOT in Florida to get a taste of it; don't go to your local builder. A fine example of a home like this was in the movie *Parental Guidance* with Billy Crystal and Bette Midler. There is a "smart house" featured in this 2013 film which would fit the bill.

Bedtime Horror Stories for Homeowners

The problem here, is that most builders take a basic home, change the roofs from the traditional gable roofs (this is the type roof shape which one usually associates with the shape of a house) and makes smaller sections of roofs what is known as a shed roof.

This is a roof which is half a gable roof and usually connects a short wall with a taller wall. These are placed at strange angles in relation to each other and many times have skylights installed. Not that there is anything wrong with this idea.

But here is some food for thought. A large amount of heat in the home just rises to the ceiling in this type home. If you do buy a home such as this, make sure there is a good old ceiling fan or two. They are back in style anyway and these can be used to keep your old lady from cranking up the heat every time the place gets a bit cool.

Another thought is that if there are skylights, you may consider small ones to keep some light in the house without overheating; and even with these, vented skylights may be the answer. Just remember, if a skylight is 20 feet from the floor, unless you are really, really, tall, it is going to be hard to open by hand. This means you will have to go for power operated skylights which open and close with a small motor which is a smaller version of the type motor used on a hospital bed. The mechanism is about the same except it is twenty feet higher and operates from a wall switch.

One more small detail to consider is the cost of these babies. I priced one back in the early 80's in a commercial roofing supply. The skylight was about two feet square and also about $600.00.

That price was just for the skylight with the motor, no labor costs or framing or electrical work. Of course if you are spending six hundred thousand for a small home for the summer, what are a few more bucks?

Now this type house will have rooms with names like THE GREAT ROOM and the MUDROOM. First let me explain what is really going on here. Many of these homes were fine with the original style house, but then the builder got spaced out on something either natural or synthetic and decided to turn the place into a contemporary.

This may have been inspired by almost anything. He could have had sex in the woods with his woman and decided to adopt this wide open feeling in his house.

He might have graduated college with a degree in fine art, and could not make a decent living in that field. Worked his way through school as a carpenter's helper because he liked to work with his hands, and somehow became a builder. Now he has to do something with all that stuff he learned about design, positive and negative spaces and all that other good stuff. Now is his chance to prove his teachers were actually wrong about him being a hippie druggist.

Chapter 3 THE VICTORIAN HOME

Caution: This part of the book moves slowly, just the way a Victorian House was built. It has a lot of details. If you start nodding off, go elsewhere and come back.

Chances are I will probably not go into a tremendous amount of detail about every kind of house, but a Victorian home is something worth telling you about. Besides that you may never get inside one unless you visit a bed and breakfast or a high-end brothel. I know someone who really lives in one of these houses.

For those of your who are not sure what a Victorian home is I can only describe it as one of the homes built about 100 years ago with big money and a taste for the large and ornate. Not quite a mansion, this is the type home in which old horror and murder movies were filmed. Just think of it without the spider webs. This one is three stories high with a big wrap-around porch.

On our visit to the home. We first encounter the property with the high steel fence around the yard. This is not the el cheapo wire fence you find in most places; the chain link crap. NOPE, this is the real thing. This fence has steel bars maybe ¾ inch square with a pointed end on top set vertically into a horizontal pair of pieces sort of like a steel picket fence. There are two gates. All painted flat black. This fence could hold tigers.

We open the gate, a double gate to be accurate; and walk up the entrance walk. This is surrounded by large trees and leads us to the WRAP AROUND PORCH.

This porch is a piece of work in itself. There are five steps leading to the porch. The original porch floor is yellow pine as was the original construction of those days, but after a few paint jobs the painted color is gray. The porch is built to go around the ends of the house besides just being in the front of the house.

There is a railing which goes from the edge of the steps all the way around to the side of the house. There is a similar one on the other side of the porch. This is truly a house painter's nightmare.

This is the kind of a porch where I could sit all summer in shorts and drinking beer with my feet on the railing, looking smug, getting fat and drunk and pretty soon I would be out of work and losing the place for lack of mortgage payments. If you took the wood on the floor of this porch and straightened it out it would look like the deck of an aircraft carrier. Find me an F-16.

Anyway, this material used on this porch with all the loads of fancy trim and woodwork. I can only think the painters must have used a lot of fancy brushes on a job like this, and probably did a lot of drinking.

This ceiling and most of the ceilings in this house are high, anywhere from ten to fourteen feet high. I guess heat was cheap back then.

The porch goes to the ENTRANCE DOORS (known elsewhere as the front door). The entrance door is a masterpiece in its own way. To start with, it is about ten feet tall with TWO DOORS.....excuuuuusssee me. These doors are joined in the center, which opens to the outside.

There are double doors like this on development homes today, they look good, but the hardware is flimsy. My 90 year old mother could kick those open. Now on this house, you could drive a small truck through the doors. Above the doors is a transom. A transom is sort of like a window which could be opened for ventilation (this is before air conditioning).

The doors and the transom have beveled leaded glass. This style is coming back again; the prices are like ransom money. Today, this is either an optional item or an after-market item to replace the cheap stock door on the development house.

Think about the weight of this door on the Victorian. This door is about 10 feet tall, about 3 inches thick, real wood, with beveled glass with a flat layer of glass in front and back for easy cleaning. The door only takes about six really big people to hang it.

This transom has the address done in stained leaded glass above the door. If the owner was a hunter, he may have a window done with ducks, or bullet holes if he has a sense of humor.

The doors on the other hand were probably done in glass for a couple of reasons. It let in light and a view. This is before those little fish eye viewers that go in doors today where you look through to make sure it is company ringing the bell and not some religious nut.

There are huge doors on this entire house. Tell you what; you don't ever want to get your fingers caught in any of these doors. It will take 6 weeks for the finger to stop looking like a baseball bat, and even then it will hurt to pick your nose.

THE HALLWAY

This hallway is pretty big. You could hold a skating party in it. As we enter the entrance doors, we notice there is another set of doors inside the first set. This was the Victorian answer to storm doors. The distance between the two pair of doors is about two feet. This creates airspace, and a place to leave your boots and umbrella. This was probably done for insulation purposes and to add to the grand design of the home.

The wood used between the doors in this case look like mahogany or walnut. (The price of walnut like this today for those of you who are interested; is about $6 a linear foot for 1 inch thick by 5 inches wide) You do the math, expensive trick today. Not counting labor costs to install it.

Of course all the doors have fancy doorknobs and hinges. The hinges here are about 8 inches tall, thick and engraved. Recent price on these would be maybe $100 a pair. Chump change. I guess if you are going big time, well… go big time.

The pins, which hold these hinges together, could be used for weapons, and the brass doorknobs could be used to drive spikes. Real brass, solid, not like we have today. I mean this is all heavy duty expensive goodies, and you are still at the front door. Excuse me, the entrance door. Of course this was not only done to make a big strong house, but also to impress all the peasants who might visit. Sort of like keeping up to the Jones; but on steroids. You know the people we are trying to impress. Guys like your poor brother in law who is trying to make it as a poet, he is living on bread and water and who makes an occasional visit at the holidays. This kind of door also scares the hell out of door to door salesmen. They take one look at the place and think. "What the hell could the owner of this place need?" ..."Gold toothpicks?"

This is also good to elevate your own status if for example you married a man who owns this type home and he made all his money selling vacuum cleaners or by being the local trash disposal mogul. The guy may be worth a fortune or picked up the place as the winner of a bet on Super bowl X. Regardless of how he acquired the place, maybe it is his one claim to good taste and culture. Maybe he still spends Sunday afternoons sitting around in his underwear with a beer and watching NASCAR.

He then falls asleep and refuses to get dressed when you sister comes to visit. "She's seen it all before, or maybe it is time she did." Make you wonder about those two, especially considering the sister is a nun.

THE STATUS THING

Of course if the intellectual snot nose in the family is still renting a one-bedroom apartment and comes to visit, this house will give the owner a definite status advantage. Regardless of what Mr. Snotnose PhD. says, HE IS NOT BLIND. So take it for what it is worth. It is all nonsense anyway, so you might as well have some fun with the game anyway. Back to the house.

The hallway here is about the same size as a small singles apartment. Of course the ceiling, like all the ceilings in the place is pretty high, so that does increase the size both physically and visually. This particular hallway is about 40 feet long, 10 feet wide and 14 feet high. On the left hand side starting half way down is the stairway leading upstairs. This particular one is "only" a straight stairway with a railing. The stairway is about 5 feet wide.

Even the width of the hallway does not diminish the feeling that one is going to heaven when walking up those long stairs. Regardless of the size of the stairway, it is in proportion to the rest of the hallway.

Look at the flooring here and the trim work. The floor is about two million small pieces of wood, parquet flooring as it is known. Except that this looks like it was installed one piece at a time. All the trim work as in the rest of the house is massive and everywhere. There is no such thing as a bare corner in a house like this. Even the ceilings have a huge piece of fancy woodwork to cover where the ceiling meets the wall. I can only surmise this was done for the style of the house as the exposed areas of the home do not show any sloppy work that would have to be hidden with trim, at least not with trim that size. This hallway has four doorways, two singles two doubles. The doorway as we face the hall on the left-hand side leads to THE LIBRARY.

Now please try to follow me around the floor plan of this place so you can appreciate the size and layout of the home so back to:

THE LIBRARY

Seeing as many of us do our reading in bed or on the crapper, this is a bit much. The original owner of this house used this room as a library and the man who owns it now wants to use it for the same purpose.

With any kind of luck he may get to do this in his lifetime; but for the time being, the room has another purpose. It is presently being used for his wife's warehouse.

To start with, I'll tell you the room is about 30 feet long, 18 feet wide with the high ceiling a fireplace and tall windows. The double doors lead in from the hallway with another pair at the back of the room.

Now here is where this guy screwed up. He did not set the room up completely before he met his wife. In this situation, the girl collects everything. She got one look at this room and fell in love with it.

Talk about winter storage, we are only on the very tip of the iceberg. When he met her, the room was in the almost painted stage. So why put books in an unpainted room (just needed a fast coat to cover the old stuff) besides….

"I have a few things I would like to store in here temporarily." RIGHT! So far this has been going on for about 25 years. Sort of like temporarily taking a dog till a suitable owner is found. You got the picture. The dog will have a good funeral and burial at your expense.

This lady, (mind you, she is a nice woman, who would do most anything for you) has an unusual habit. This habit was fueled by the fact that she lived home till she got married in her thirties, worked till she got married, had lots of credit cards and knew how to use them. She is one of these people who not only has matching dresses and gloves, but also probably has matching underwear under those clothes. I can't tell you that for a fact. Just guessing.

Not being strapped by a husband or kids she had the luck to be able to buy whatever she needed or wanted in multiples. Instead of going to K Mart and buying one blouse, she would go to Macy's and pick up a blouse but in every color available with all the accessories, shoes, skirts, jewelry, gloves, etc. A commissioned sales ladies' wet dream.

This same habit would prevail when she would buy small items such as ball point pens, paper clips, or rubber bands. She could probably supply a small business for two or three years. Fortunately, she never got into pets or assault weapons.

Aside from her ability to collect things, she is very methodical.

Everything and I don't kid you; is cross-indexed, she must have a memory like a mainframe IBM. She tells me she remembers being born. I think I actually believe her.

At one time I needed a small American flag for something and asked her if she had one. Big as life, she had one, in perfect condition. In the original box and EXACTLY in the location it was assigned. The U.S. government could learn a few things from this lady. I can lose things such as a car, and it takes me a week or so to remember where I put it. I am not even on drugs.

At last record, the most recent visit to this place impressed me with the order and quantity of the warehouse. These are in this one room. Enough clothes to cover the population of Rhode Island; paper clips that if placed end to end would reach the moon, enough rubber bands to make a catapult that would throw an army tank.

Also 12 cans of spray paint, 11 racks of shoes, 10 pair of socks in every color, 9 business suits, 8 boxes of purses, 7 hat boxes, 6 sets of shelves, 5 rows of coat hangers, 4 clothes hanging racks, 3 small tables, 2 boxes of casual clothes, and 1 exercise bike. If you can put this list to music you are better than I am.

And this was only the crap I could see at a fast glance.
I get tired just thinking of the work involved keeping all this stuff in order. Remember that this is only one room; we aren't even to the rest of the storage areas. When she moved out, her mother's house devcloped an echo.

Now through the back doors of the library to: THE OFFICE

The man of the house was smart enough to set up this room, and has probably used it as a tax loophole for years. Here is where he has some of the books that were originally intended for the library, has a desk, a couple of small lamps and a computer.

Toward the rear of the room with a large stuffed desk chair. The desk is about 30" x 60". This is pretty much the size of a commercial metal desk in an office building.

The only difference here is that it is in a home and fits easily in the room. There are also a few bookcases, enough books in them to supply a small high school, and a little room left over for new additions. The floor is carpeted with a better rug than most people have in the living room and there is original art work on the walls. No K-Mart stuff. The great thing about this room is the location.

Ron can hide here for weeks and Gloria his wife would not even have a clue. He could have a girlfriend living here and the place is so big, nobody would notice.

Ron the owner, likes to read, and this room is perfect for that purpose. The only place more quiet than this has six feet of dirt on top of it, and even though it is a good size room it has a cozy feeling to it. This is the kind of room that makes interior decorators drool.

I hear he kept this room secret from Gloria for 6 months till he really checked her out to make sure she wouldn't get his books off the shelves and replace them with her lifetime collection of Better Homes and Gardens, Redbook and Cosmopolitan. The third collection I don't understand. She does not even like sexy clothes. Now through the back doors to:

THE UTILITY ROOM

Here is a room, which probably had been used for storage when the house was built, but with the advent of the washer and dryer and other items such as freezers, it has become a more useful room.

To start with it is a fairly large room, maybe 16 feet square, with a window, electricity, and a cold water line. It is located where most guests don't even realize there would be a room. This is great for ducking out on a boring party, especially being right next to the office. There is a washer, dryer, a refrigerator, a freezer and a half-mile of clothesline in this room.

I understand they tried to add a hot water line at one time, but the floor is 18 inches of solid stone. On the upside, at least you don't shrink clothes with cold water.

As for drilling through this floor, you don't do it with the average ¼" drill that you get in Sears or Home Depot. This kind of job is more for the commercial jack hammer crowd and the compressor the size of a car. There is nothing that exciting about this room unless you are into dirty clothes or getting to the beer before it makes it to the bar.

THE BAR

Now how many people do you know with a bar in their home? I don't mean the cheap stuff you get in IKEA that you put together with a screw driver. I mean a real life type bar, complete with a sink, lighting, two million glasses and enough booze to float the Titanic.

They have every type glass that is shown on the Southern Comfort recipe book. If you ask for an Old Fashioned glass for a scotch on the rocks, you get just that, not an old jelly glass with a picture of a cartoon character painted on it.

When these people entertain, they go with the class of the house. Their bar has more variety than my local restaurant and all good stuff. None of that rotgut stuff in expensive bottles. The bar is located physically behind the end of the hallway one of the doors we saw when we entered the home. It is built just for its purpose. A drunk would love to die in a place like this.

THE KITCHEN

There is a doorway, which leads out of the bar into the kitchen. I understand this was not the original kitchen for the house but part of a later addition. Regardless. This is another large room, the only clues to its age are the fact the ceiling is only about 8 feet high and the cabinets are finished in plastic laminate.

Houses this old were built way before Formica became a household word. At least it is done well and the average person cannot tell it is not wood.

The room itself is as big as a two-car garage. Maybe 50 feet of cabinet space just running around the top half of the room. Add another 50 feet on the floor level. As one realtor told me about a kitchen. "You could cook for 50 people here." I don't even know 50 people. Actually I do, but I wouldn't cook for them all at the same time.

This room has a stove, a microwave, an oven, a large refrigerator with an ice cube maker. Remember the stone floors and the jack hammer? How about spending 7 hours to run a small water line for the ice maker? That had to be fun. There is also a table for two, some counter space and a floor big enough to roller skate on while waiting for dinner to cook. It is not really as fancy as the rest of the house, but it is nice enough. There is also a rear door, which opens to a porch. On the porch is one of these motorized awnings for those of us too lazy to use a hand operated one. The only thing I don't like about this kitchen is there is not much natural light, so it is a bit dark. You can't have everything. The alternative is to chop down some large trees. And the trees were here first so they stay. Good.

Out of the kitchen, through the bar into the:

GREEN ROOM

In contrast to the kitchen, this room has a sunny disposition. It is not painted green. It is called the green room because of all the green plants in it. It is bright and sunny and looks out over the yard. With the plants here; if they ever want to do *"Tarzan in New Jersey"*, this is the location. This is a really great room. It is about 30 feet square, with the plants, enough furniture to do a small apartment, a sound system, a nice view. Everything my first house had, without my dizzy ex-wife.

When the owners have a party, a few people; maybe 20, can retire to this room and have their own party, and go on for a few days. Nobody will notice. The only problem with this room is someone got carried away with insulating the room and insulated the floor thus eliminating some of the benefit of the heating system in the basement which would help keep the room warm. Aside from that, it could be rented to a small family

ONE MORE ROOM

Yes, but with all these rooms on this floor what are we missing?

You know, a BATHROOM. Actually you can't take a bath in this one unless you can fit in either the sink or the toilet, but it is here for the really important stuff. This room is sort of stuffed into the end of the hall. Remember the hall? And it is long, and narrow, and of course a high room. It has white tile, which sort of looks like smooth white bricks. It is pretty much only a functional room with nothing of a really impressive nature, except for the tile if you are impressed with that type thing. Now don't leave. This floor contains two more rooms which run off the hall. Must be nice to be rich, I wouldn't know.

THE FORMAL DINING ROOM

This room has double doors on one end, two single doors, and mirrors on one wall, chair rails, a complete dining room set and still has enough room to ride your Harley around the table. There is also a chandelier over the table, more of the long narrow windows, and some more of the flooring that was found in the hall. The furniture is all antique or good reproductions, there is a house portrait hanging on one wall. A big tree was taken out of the painting so the home would show up better. Artistic license or something like that. Works better than a Jackson Pollock in this room.

The furnishings go with the house and there is more of the same type trim and HUGE SLIDING DOORS. The person who hung these doors must have been built like The Incredible Hulk and eaten automobile tires and Wheaties for breakfast. These are one set of the double doors I told you about.

They must be at least 10 feet tall and four feet wide ....each. They also about 3 inches thick with trim. Can't forget the trim. They are fitted into the walls. These are called pocket doors. Keep that in mind the next time you see them somewhere and you want to impress someone. Like anybody really cares.

These are fitted into the walls and when they are closed they meet in the middle. So now you also know what pocket doors are, big deal! That and $5 will get you a Starbucks coffee. These doors are also known as panel doors mainly due to their construction of several small pieces of wood, which are joined and interlocked to create this door. The trim is a different color than the side pieces and the panels are also different.

The workmanship on these doors is incredible and again there is a lot of fancy hardware. The hardware is solid brass to be exact. Even the pulls are solid brass.

A pull is a handle built into the edge of a door that stays flat till needed to move the door. It took me five minutes to figure out how to open these pulls; which is strange, seeing how I am usually pretty good at this type stuff. Also when you pull out these doors, you do not want to be in the way.

When they squeak, make sure you oil them. Not only do they probably need the oil, but if they ever decided to stop doing what they are supposed to do, you would have to go get the guy with the big muscles to help you get them back in order. Now would you believe we have hit the last room on this floor? Thank God.

THE FORMAL PARLOR

This room is very formal. How formal do you ask? If you plan to sneeze or make some other body noise, you have to make a formal written request on bond stationary two weeks in advance. There is a couch in this room which has more good leather on it than an average herd of buffalo, and weighs about the same as the leader of the herd.

As could be expected, this room has the high ceiling, the trim, the fancy doors and a fireplace. Now, no matter how energy inefficient a fireplace has been proven to be, this was the original heating system in many older homes and people still use them when in the room.

Now this fireplace usually creates a cozy atmosphere in the room and does keep it a bit warmer. Though in a house of this age; the walls are usually not insulated, so the heat goes through them and the tall windows. I heard it cost them $6000 to heat this house one year. For that price I would have burned it to the ground. Don't want to ruin the historical value with something stupid like insulation and vinyl siding and new windows.

I do have a fast story about the fireplace for you. The room is meant to be a formal type place, but the owners like to have people over for the holidays and all that good stuff. One Christmas when I visited them they had gotten screwed on a live tree.

You may not know this, but the live trees which are not sold are sometimes frozen till the next year, so by time this happens, you have a stick with needles.

Between the fact that the tree was dry to start with and the fireplace created a lot of hot air, the tree started to look like something out of a cartoon. This is the only time I have seen a tree drop needles as it was being decorated. This tree was bigger than the ones at a Boy Scout camp so when it fell apart, it really fell apart. You could sing Christmas carols in time to the sound of the needles hitting the wood floor. Every time a foot hit the floor, more needles came with it. I think the tree went in on the 23rd of December and was out on the 26th.

The trees after that were usually better.

That was probably the most lighthearted thought this room has entertained in a long time. This room has the two sets of double doors, and looks out on the porch. I am surprised it does not have those velvet ropes at each of the doorways that are used in theaters. They're also another 10,000 small pieces of wood in the floor. See what I mean about detail? It can get a little out of control.

THE SECOND FLOOR

I'll bet you thought I would never get off the first floor of this house. Don't feel bad, remember I'm sitting here typing all this down and I type a lot slower than I think, talk or read. I thought I'd never get off it either.

Anyway, on the second floor this is where the master of the house must have a great time with the mistress of the house. There are, let's see three, no four bedrooms, a dressing room, another bathroom or two and a great view from all the treetop height windows.

A sex maniac would love this place, if they wanted to try a different room each night or a different position, it would take years to use all the bedrooms up. Maybe 50 or 60 years. Of course; I am being crude and rude, but you were getting too relaxed with the tour.

"ON YOUR FEET", as they say in the Army. If you take a New York City apartment with a $1000 a month rent, you can visualize the size of each of these bedrooms. You want to know something strange though? The closet space here is the pits. Simple reason, when this house was built, people usually had two sets of clothes. Work clothes and Sunday clothes, so who needed a lot of closet space?

There is a dressing room next to the master bedroom; I guess that had to do with old time modesty standards. This way the woman could spend all day getting dressed and leave the old man sitting on the porch with his beer. In the bedrooms though, were these huge wooden cabinets called wardrobes or something like that.

They would hold a lot of stuff, clothes, books, and guns, whatever. These cabinets are big and heavy. About the same size and weight as a small car.

They also had to be ornate to match the style of the house, so that was sort of interesting. These homes also did not always have indoor plumbing so showers and baths were less common, hence not a big need for an underwear drawer. It was just a whole different lifestyle.

The bedrooms in the front of the house have fireplaces located directly over the ones downstairs, more or less. The back bedrooms did not have these. "So let the kids freeze a bit. It will either kill them, or make them stronger."

Of course when central heat was installed, things changed a bit. There are thick walls between the rooms and the old place was done in what is known as balloon framing, which if I remember, I may explain in detail later. This type construction makes renovation work a lot of fun. Even running a phone line can be a major project.

Toward the rear of the house is a small bedroom, most likely a room for a guest. It also has its own bathroom. See how easy it is to get lost in a house like this? Instead of going on and on, just remember. High ceilings. Lots of trim. Big windows, you have the idea. I have to take you up one more floor. Good house if you have a heart condition.

We are going to: THE SERVANTS QUARTERS

If you were a servant back in those days, you had to carry flight insurance in case you fell out a bedroom window. This floor feels like a high rise apartment building with fancy trim. If you look at this house from the street and see all those high windows. Just remember there are rooms behind them. There is more trim, the windows are not just for looks. This part of the house is the equivalent of a small three-bedroom apartment. The servants are no longer there.

It is *so* hard getting help these days. But the rooms have been put to good use. You guessed it. *More storage.* Now you can understand why Gloria's father was helping her move out of his house.

There is a section where the help used to sleep, this is full of boxes, and long pipes used to hang a ton of clothes. Gloria also stores stuff up here for her yearly yard sale. She has people give her stuff and she sells it. Either that or it goes in the trash. I have no idea if the donors get any $$ out of the deal. I don't care either. The best part of this floor is the view. It has 5 rooms and all the windows are high, plus you don't build a house like this overlooking a train yard.

As a kicker, there is also a set of servant's stairs that run from the top of the house to the first floor. More of that status crap.

SO MUCH FOR THE FLOORS OF THIS HOUSE

Get a load of the basement:

To start with, Gloria is not a basement person. Too bad. She is missing out on a few thousand cubic feet of storage space. This place has a full basement which is bigger than an average ranch house, and has high ceilings. I think Ron keeps one snow shovel down there.

THE GROUNDS

The property surrounding this home is not as large as one might expect, but it is still twice the size of a regular building lot. Twice one way, twice the other way. That makes it four times as big. Do the math...c'mon...use the gray stuff...Thanks. Most of the land is only grass and trees but instead of a garage, there is a CARRIAGE HOUSE, as the building is called. This was originally intended for old time horse drawn carriages, horses, feed, etc. Now it was used as a two-car garage, the place is so big the cars sort of disappear in there.

I live in a decent size house, and this car barn is larger than my house and at least three times the size of the first house I had. It makes most garages look like dog houses. The only problem here is that it has never been taken care of, so it is sort of like parking the car in a tent. It does need work, but it does the job.

O.K. Everyone out of the carriage house, down the driveway, close the gate. Don't pinch your fingers in the gate. This carriage house got demolished after Ron and Gloria helped lead a group of locals against some people who wanted to put office space in the building next door. After the office space got approved, the new owners came after Ron and made a big deal out the fact that the car barn was beat up. For what it cost him to knock it down I could have renovated it and still have a two car garage. Not my business, not my problem. Move it; we are now going to visit an old house in need of repair. You know the term:

THE HANDYMAN'S SPECIAL

Chapter 4   HANDYMAN SPECIALS

Buying a handyman special is sort of like buying a Saturday Night Special. It may work out fine, or it may blow up in your face. This is where it pays to have some technical knowledge. If you do not have this knowledge, try to bring along someone with you who does.

You want someone who has a clue about carpentry, plumbing, electric, roofs, floors and pretty much everything else that can be right or wrong with a home. These houses do not have to be ready to go on the Historic List; they can be much newer, but poorly maintained. Think about it; if you lived somewhere and never painted or fixed anything there, at some point the home would turn into a mess.

There are reasons these homes become handyman specials. One is just plain old laziness; some people do nothing to help themselves or the family. Sometimes the home has been used for rental property.

Some renters do not take care of the place and since it is not theirs, this is not their problem. There are cases where there is a divorce, these can be real messy. One party or the other will destroy the place just to torment the other person.

There is also ignorance, such as not actually knowing they are living like slobs but think this is normal. Or the other kind of ignorance, someone who cannot fix anything. I know people like this. Another problem is some homeowner who has no extra money to repair anything. Or someone who thinks they know what they are doing, and make the problems worse than they started.

There are some homeowners who also just do not give a damn, as long as the house does not fall down on them, they are happy. I know someone like this. The funny thing is this guy supposedly makes a living doing repair work. Better not have his address on his business cards.

If you decide to look at homes like this just use your brains. There are laws today which tell the sellers they are supposed to tell buyers about problems with the house. I do not know how well these laws are enforced. I guess it all depends on the town, and who calls the shots there.

I mean; if you walk on the front porch and the wood floor is rotted in ten places and you have to walk on it like a circus performer, you can figure it will need work. If you see ceilings where they curve toward you with a dip the size of a football in the center; there might be a water leak somewhere on top of that ceiling.

If the wallpaper is peeling or looks like it was put up the year Eisenhower was elected, you can figure on changing it when the time is right. Same thing goes for horrible paint jobs. If all the paint looks old and dull, it is time to repaint.

People with dogs will occasionally have some damage. Some of this is solved with stain killer and some paint. Some repairs will take a more aggressive approach. I have two big dogs and one of my window sills is pretty well beat up. They put their paws on it and bark at other dogs. I know one of these days I will have to smooth this out and repaint it. I will also work out something that keeps it from happening again. I know you animal haters would just get rid of the critters. That is not going to happen anytime soon.

You do not need dogs to destroy a home; kids will do it just as well. At least my dogs do not put handprints all the way up the walls. They also do not put up crayon art on the walls.

Some of the reasons folks buy handyman specials are interesting. Some are money issues, or it could be a creative urge thing. The buyers may want to buy a home like this in order to express their own ideas of what they consider good design.

Sometimes this works. That is one reason I got my home. One other reason was the money issue. We were not broke, but did not want to spend the rest of our lives paying off the place.

Another reason is that one person or both of them for whatever reason just fell in love with the place. This is much like picking out a mate. You know the deal. Some really hot woman is married to a fat idiot who thinks farting is an art form. She says she really loves the guy. Don't worry about it, not your problem. Stay out of closed rooms and elevators with him.

Some people just like the location, the school system or the look of the neighborhood. Maybe they have friends who live nearby. Let's see how good a friend they are when you ask them to help you do a concrete sidewalk when it is 100 degrees.

Some family's kids help make the decision. The horny teenage kid wants to live near the girl who makes him wake up in the middle of the night with a sticky pair of shorts. "Yeah Pop, this house is great, look at the yard for the dog. I love to cut grass."

Sometimes the decision is because of the dog and the fenced in yard that is big enough for him to run and pee. Not all decisions are based on cold facts or logic. If you doubt that, look at yourself and others and some of the choices that have been made. Some people will find some old home that reminds them of a previous home; maybe where they grew up or wished they grew up. Some people just want a challenge. The old, "Watch and see what I can do with this dump." Guys are usually the ones who show up strong on this reason. How many wives know the guy cannot hang a picture but go along with a handyman special because he convinced her he has some skills she does not know about.

There are some people who just love the look of old beat up homes, they have a personality, as someone told me once. So does my old car, but I am the only person who rides in it. My dogs will ride in it also, but they would ride in anything with wheels.

One thing I like about the old handyman specials; I mean the ones which are about 100 years old. When these were built and they were done with real two by fours, which was the real size of the lumber. They were put up to last.

My home is about 100 years old and for the most part it is still pretty solid. These are also the places which end up on some reality show where a crew comes in and totals the place to make a new home for some "deserving" family. These people usually have some kid with a handicap, or some other ugly situation which prevents them from getting their life in order. Makes you appreciate the problems you do not have.

Artsy types love places like this, they can either add to the place or subtract from it and call it artistic license. Sounds good. But as I mentioned elsewhere, watch the location. I met someone years ago who did a great job on a home, but the neighborhood was sort of a problem, I am not sure they even live there anymore.

Some people actually look at this as either fun or an educational experience. That can be scary. Or they think they can do anything, when in reality, they are a danger to themselves and others. If you fall into any or all of these categories, you may end up with one of these homes. Just try to have fun and not shoot yourself.

NOW BACK TO THE HANDYMAN SPECIALS

That was the original subject of this area of the book.
The house has possibilities if it has most of the following items:
- Decent size rooms or a chance to knock down walls and make some decent sized rooms.
- A yard.
- A basement that a normal size person can stand in. This all depends on your idea of normal. Many old homes have a tendency to have low basements. I saw one which was advertised as having a full size basement. If you were taller than a large dog, you were scraping the floor joists above your head, full basement my ass.
- All the outside of the house is covered with at least sheathing.
- It has heat.
- Some of the windows are still intact.
- The owner of the place is sick of working on it. This can be a good bargaining point.
- The neighbors' dog is quiet, and neighbors are quiet.
- Only *some* of the pipes leak.
- The water marks on the basement walls are only 12 inches from the floor.
- You can find the place without a hunting dog.
- The rooms are large, but painted ugly colors.
- The basement doors are still on the building. These may fall off upon closer inspection.

SO WHY THE HELL NOT?????

I mean you passed the local Adult Education Handyman class. You own some tools, you remembered to flush the toilet and try the oil heating system on/off switch. Goddamn, you are a slick article. We can fix this dump up in two or three weeks. RIGHT?

Bedtime Horror Stories for Homeowners

There are several things you will find out about handyman specials. I can only think of a few thousand at this point. First you will notice, EVERYTHING LEAKS.

This includes but is not limited to the faucets, drains, sinks and roof. Of course if the basement does not leak, give it time. No matter what type siding is on the house. Your wife will hate it.

These houses are usually painted in some outrageous color. Pink and black have proved to be big colors. The electrical service may be a bit undersized. There will be no more than one outlet in any room except for the parlor. There are usually no closets worth using, and these all have at least 4 clothing bars in each one. The insulation is old newspapers.

The kitchen may be done in contact paper and the kids' room done in last month's New York Times Classified Section. (They did not read it, just that there is a lot of paper for the price of the paper). The rest of the paper went to housebreak the puppy.

The floors may squeak. The radiators may sound like a concrete mixer when the heat goes on. You can get great ventilation next to all the windows, even though they are closed. The owner has all the original manuals for every appliance in the house....even stuff he no longer owns. The yard looks like a war zone. The garage door only opens six inches. When you flush the toilet, the sink stops running. When you drain the sink, and tub fills. The outside water faucet (if there is one) is broken. There are no outside electrical outlets. The owner will throw in the washer, dryer, refrigerator and the cat. There will be flock wallpaper somewhere. The bathroom runs off the kitchen. It is hard to find the house since one of the address numbers is missing.

REACTIONS TO A HANDYMAN SPECIAL

Mother in Law....Vomits.
Father in Law.....Laughs.
Wife...Hates the colors.
Your dog...Will pee on the living room floor.

Bedtime Horror Stories for Homeowners

You think you have found a jewel in the rough and at times your wife will agree. But not in front of her parents. She feels stupid enough showing them the house in the first place.

Your friends will say things like "Wow, with your talents you could really do something with this place" or "It this $55,000 looks like?"

The realtor will say something like "The previous owner loved this place" or "The place only rattles when the LATE train comes through." Or, "It only needs a little cosmetic work and some TLC." (Tender Loving Care)

The mortgage company will hand you a short list of items they would like to see corrected before you take title, or they give you the mortgage. This list is usually about three pages long. If you show a really sincere interest in doing all this work, they will usually let a lot of stuff slide. Remember, they are making money on this deal.

>The V.A. will suggest you re-enlist and sign up for Peru.
>
>The F.H.A. will charge you extra interest for being adventurous.
>
>The local guy at the lumber yard will give you a dozen short "How to do it" booklets and a credit agreement form.
>
>Your mother will praise you for your sense of value.
>
>Your father will cry.

SO, GO FOR IT!!!!!

Instead of me telling you a lot of general situations regarding handyman specials, I'd like to relate to you instead some real live stories starting with: Adventures of Paul and Janice, the leaky drain.

ADVENTURES OF PAUL AND JANICE, THE LEAKY DRAIN

This is a series of true stories relating to a handyman special, my wife's and mine. We have had a lot of fun with it and feel you might also. I will later go into some stories about other people who have done some wild things in the same vein.

Remember, I told you in a house such as this everything leaks? Our place was a prime example of that system. Let me start with the BATHROOM DRAIN.

This drain is connected to a sink in my bathroom and also to the kitchen sink. It works fine now, but when we moved in there was a small leak. Now let me tell you I don't care how old or new a house is when a leak develops; they all have one thing in common. YOU CAN'T GET AT THE S.O.B. They always manage to happen in a place where you cannot visually locate them and after you take out some major framing under a floor to see the sucker; you still have a rough time physically getting at it.

This leak was directly located over a floor joist which supported the wall and the floor between my kitchen and the bathroom. It started out as a simple drip...drip....drip...and when I went to look for it, I couldn't even see it. I felt the water, but the source was not there. Well, after crawling into the crawl space which was shared by a large boulder, a skeleton of a bird, and old coal shovel and a couple of beer bottles I saw the problem. Now this is sort of like seeing the moon. You know it is there, but you can't get at it

Fortunately I have a pretty good idea of how to repair a lot of problems, so this type thing does not look too bad. My wife, (The Lovely Janice) on the other hand has gotten all her knowledge from magazines and friends who were good at guesswork. She knows a lot more at this time, but in the beginning she needed some education.

When the leak was discovered, it was only a small hole about one eighth inch in diameter. Some people would just let it leak. After all it is only in a drain line over a basement wall.

I am one of those nuts who just have to repair the damn thing. It even annoys me to visit someone and see a leaky faucet in his or her bathroom.

People make me leave my tools at the door when I visit. They sometimes make me dress formal or come nude so I can't smuggle in any tools. This makes them think their homes will still be in one piece when I leave.

So my first line of attack is to see how much pipe is really in bad shape. This was easy; I just poked at the hole with an old screwdriver for a few seconds. NOW I HAVE A RESPECTABLE SIZE HOLE. This one was maybe two inches one way and an inch the other way, a manly leak. The hole replaces what used to be some of the threads inside the steel pipe.

Now I have to change something, or my basement will look and smell like a toxic waste dump. I took this on myself about 10 o'clock at night. Maybe because when it is late at night, drips are easier to hear. Maybe, I just like to get myself in messes after all the supply houses are closed.

This only inconvenienced me for about two days, till I got a chance to really repair the mess. I mean emptying a pail under the pipe every few hours under a drain is not all that bad, especially if I let Janice do it.

Anyway, we did not get to the pipe till Saturday. My father decided it would be nice of him to come up and help me do the job, or more like I would help him do the job. Dad never had all that much faith in my abilities to do mechanical work.... DAD ARRIVES.

When my father was alive he was a carpenter contractor, which meant he could build or repair almost anything except the pyramids; he had the tools and the knowledge to do the job.

So when he arrives; it is like having a plumbing supply truck show up, complete with a ton of tools. There are wrenches small enough to fix a supply line to a toilet right up to a huge pipe wrench, which could possibly be used to remove a fireplug.

Also a torch, solder, flux, brushes, a million parts, solvent and glue for plastic pipe, matches, rags, pieces of pipe and a thermos of coffee. Hell, you would think we wouldn't give the old guy coffee.

Meanwhile, when I brought the house with Janice, he had given me two or three truckloads of repair stuff to help me along. He had also owned a house like this and knew what I was up against. I imagine at night he had hoped I would forget his phone number. Or maybe he went to sleep laughing at the house and me. No, really he was a great guy; he had a sense of humor.

He arrives early, about 7:30 A.M. which is not all that early for anyone in my family. We grew up kicking the rooster in the ass to get the day started, Dad was not all that familiar with Janice, but felt she must get up early. She was a nurse and usually by now she is sticking a needle in some poor slobs arm. The weather is nice that day. It was the middle of October, and not cold yet so we could open the doors to the yard and not drag junk through the house.

FIRST THINGS FIRST

Before we even look at the problem, we have to have a cup of coffee. We are all coffee drinkers and who the hell starts the day without a fix. We all had breakfast, so this was just more coffee to get us going. So with a short break, we have our coffee and discuss the problem. A discussion is *always in order* regardless of the situation in case one of us misses an important detail.

We do a lot of small talk, for two minutes and get on to the pipe situation. Dad always would tell me about of couple of old Jewish carpenters he knew in his younger days. They discussed everything about twenty times before one nail was driven. They would put the problem on the table and talk it out till it was isolated as only a technical problem. Believe me this system actually works.

Well, both he and I developed this habit. So we did the discussion bit for a while. There were angles to be analyzed, pipe sizes to be discussed, what type pipe is used, how it is connected. ALL THIS BEFORE HE GOES DOWN THE BASEMENT WHERE THE ACTION IS. Detroit should put this much thought into one of their cars.

NOW DOWN TO THE BASEMENT

Remember that we moved in here about a week ago, we had the stuff from an apartment, which was no problem. But we also had my goodies from a furniture repair shop. Do you really want to know where all that stuff is located? You got it.

Not wanting to look like a total bozo, I have at least cleared the area near the repair job, and hooked up a couple of spotlights. Of course being an old house, I have them hooked up with about 200 feet of extension cords. These cords got in the way at every opportunity.

The back door is open, the area is clear; Dad looks for the leak. I am kind enough to show him. "It's here, where else do you think it would be?" He is used to this, sort of the story of his life.

If you want to work on a problem like this, you have to be able to get at it. So first, we tear out a short chunk of a beam, which supports what used to be an outside wall of the house. Now, you do not just cut out a hunk of wood like this without some preparation. This work we did with a couple of short pieces of 2"x 8" lumber located on the cinder block wall below the beam. Then we wedged and nailed in place two heavy support pieces between the 2x8 lumber and the beam. This created a strong vertical support for the section, which would be removed to work on the pipe.

This type work is the reason that a job takes twice as long as expected. (One of Murphy's Laws I think). Of course if the prep work is not done, there will be a lot of repair and cleanup work, which is your reward for laziness.

So now, we took a reciprocating type electric saw and remove about 10 inches of the beam, just enough of it to get to the pipe. Without going into all the ugly details, I can only say that with a torch, wrenches, some magic words (cuss words) and luck, we took out not only the bad part of the pipe, but a couple of other sections to boot.

If you ever wonder why a pipe does not drain properly, take one of these guys apart. Where there was a 2 inch pipe, the insides of the pipe were so coated with old soap, grease, gook and whatever other nasty stuff goes down a kitchen drain that the pipe no longer was two inches inside. It was more like the size of a soda straw. Maybe.

The bad pieces of pipe we replaced with plastic pipe, which is great stuff to work with. Actually this stuff would make a good Christmas present for any kid with mechanical abilities. With twenty feet of pipe, some solvent, sandpaper, glue and firecrackers, the kid could probably make a small ICBM and take over the neighborhood.

Naturally; with all the parts and pieces we owned collectively, we were short a few small pieces of plastic pipe. This amount of pipe was worth maybe $5, but the trick was to buy the stuff.

The local plumbing supply places, which deal with the professional plumbers, know all the locals and will not talk to you if they do not know you. With their attitude, you would think they were selling women instead of pipe.

I know the reasoning behind this attitude, but I still think it is B.S. The commercial places only want to deal with the regular plumbers so they can keep their "secrets" to themselves.

These guys act as if they are brain surgeons and their license is a gift of the gods to help us mere mortals, or take us to the cleaners whenever possible. Call a plumber for a small job sometime. You would think you were calling the Pope to bless your car. If the Pope could not make it due to something important such as Christmas Mass, he might at least send you a card or a priest from the local church.

The plumber would not even answer your phone call, and if by some mistake he did answer it and show up, he would give you his "brain surgery rate". You would also have to wait till the south end of Hell freezes over before the job gets done. The commercial plumbing place in my area upholds this attitude so we didn't spend much time there looking for parts. Instead, we ended up in the local hardware store. Now here is an experience for the virgin hardware store shopper.

Being new to the area, I asked around for a local store and was directed to this place. The attitude here was different than the plumbing supply. For one thing, it was friendly. It also was a bit slow paced. This is fine if you have nothing to do and all day to do it; but sucks if your basement is filling up with water at the rate of 100 gallons a minute. Let me tell you about this place.

THE LOCAL HARDWARE STORE

This business was owned by a guy named Herb. One of the nicest guys you ever met; and also one of the most knowledgeable. I hear he had a college degree in English Literature. He was also like an encyclopedia of repair work, a regular Renaissance Man.

Herb was about 70 at the time, looked good for his age, and was in better shape than some people I know who are half his age. He was tall, thin and wore rimless glasses. His whole attitude is that of the Golden Rule in low profile.

He would rather spend a half hour telling you a good way to save a few bucks on a project that spend 5 minutes selling you a bunch of extra parts. A store like Home Depot or Sears would lose money if he worked there.

Going into Herb's store was like a trip back in time, sort of like a Twilight Zone experience. Like going into another time period. The place was clean, well-organized and in good condition, and also carried parts from the past 50 years. These are the kind of parts you find in an old house like mine.

See, when he started this business; there were certain parts that were popular in homes at that time. He still carried much of this stuff, with original prices on many items. Just like the stuff today that someday will be an antique.

Now a younger person would usually not have a clue as to what some of this stuff is, but he would sell you a 50-cent item instead of having you put $5000 into a new bathroom. He was just that kind of guy. Plus, if you are polite, he will tell you how to install the thing.

The store itself was a long high room with the cast iron radiators installed about 7 or 8 feet off the floor along the walls. I can only figure this is so they did not get in the way of shelf space. Then again the old ceiling fans would push the heat down. Smart old guy. It looks strange, but works fine. There are about a half-mile of shelves on the walls, down the center of the floor and the back and front of the building. Everything from mouse traps to hammers and welding stuff.

Herb sold everything from window glass to doorbells to bug sprayers. Another amazing thing is that he knew exactly where everything is located. Then I guess if I had spent 30 or 40 years there, I might know it also, duh. He also dealt with new items just on the market. His prices were decent, and his patrons are varied.

If you planned to visit Herb, don't plan to rush out. I have gone there for one small item and came home the next day. On an average trip when I arrive, there are two or three people ahead of me, but this is no big deal. If I stuck around and listened, I would pick up about the same amount of information as is in this month's Popular Mechanics magazine.

Herb will be telling one guy how to install a hot water heater complete with how he installed one in his sister's house in 1946. He will then find some ancient part for a 1910 electrical system. This will be in the original box with the original price.

This will all be done with discussions about someone's kids, the dog, the fire downtown last night, the price of oil and some really corny jokes. The kind of jokes you tell kids when you are not sure what they will understand.

So now it is my turn. Remember we were working down the basement with the leaky drain pipe? Well, right away, my old man likes this guy because of the low key atmosphere of the place and Herbs personality; maybe the place reminded him of his youth.

I only knew Herb slightly at this point, but still I introduce my Dad to him. Well, big as life he has exactly what we need. He even has the pieces in a scrap box reserved for small pieces of pipe. He also has whatever other small parts we need to finish the job. We had spent maybe 5 minutes in the plumbing supply store, and an hour and a half in Herb's.

Janice went to the neighbor's house to go to the bathroom, as she was not sure what was taken apart under the floor. Smart woman.

Of course since we have been out for like 2 hours, it is time for another cup of coffee. Since the drains from the sinks are open, we clean the pot outside with the faucet in the yard and fill the pot there. Water is water. We do another discussion of the problem, finish the coffee, and take another cup along for good measure and head for the basement.

Now today; being Saturday, this is a special day at my house. Picture this if you can. Dad and I are in a rotten little crawl space, our heads about six inches from the floor joists, with a folding ruler, a hacksaw and some black plastic pipe. The lighting is not too bad, but I wouldn't read racing forms with it either. We are about to get our measurements right to cut and fit the pipe. (This stuff is great, but there are technical problems to work out, so it is a little tricky). Just as we get the little brass extension from the rule into the inside of the plastic elbow, there is a great roar over our heads. Sort of like a jet plane.

Bedtime Horror Stories for Homeowners

"WHAT THE HELL IS THAT NOISE?" Dad yells, trying not to cry from the lump on his head from when he hit it on the beam. I should have known better. It is the vacuum cleaner directly over our heads on the wooden floor.

Janice would not know a broom if she tripped over one; she uses a vacuum cleaner for everything. I'm surprised she does not use it to pick up grass clippings in the yard. She also has a system, which is unique. I call it, the one square inch system. Here is how it works.

You know the pipe on the end of a vacuum cleaner? The piece of chrome stuff about an inch in diameter? Janice will sit on the floor and do the whole house like this with the end of this pipe. One square inch at a time.

Says she finds this to be relaxing. About as relaxing as a root canal. Mind you, she only does this once a week, but she is so thorough with this system, that dirt is afraid to come into my house. I once had a flea jump off the dog at the door and ask permission to come into the house. I politely told him to get lost!

We all know the sound of a vacuum cleaner comes close to that of a jet fighter, which is fine at a few hundred yards, but right over my head. Give me a break.

Since this is my house, and my woman, I elect to ask Janice to do something else not so noisy, like walk the dog or go visit her sister. The one who lives two hours away. The dog has disappeared and the sister is not home, so she decides to find something quiet to do for the time being. To this day, I don't really know how she spent the time, but neither of us has ever brought it up again.

After about two hours work which included some time chasing parts and Janice, we have the drain straightened out. Thank God. And the best part is, it actually works. Dad sticks around for lunch, watches me make up one of my weird vegetarian sandwiches and opts for something else he can recognize. After lunch he took off for home.

Since the original job with the bathroom sink drain I have also replaced the one in the tub and the kitchen drain under the sink. These were not nearly as much fun, even if I did have to work in the crawl space for the tub drain. That one was a piece of cake seeing as I had already been well acquainted with the crawl space.

Bedtime Horror Stories for Homeowners

Chapter 5   SIZE MATTERS

DUPLEX HOMES

I am not sure when this type home came along. I am not sure if they were intended to be Mother / Daughter places or what. Either way I had the luck to look at two of these in my life. One was in some town in North Jersey. I think it was in Randolph; find it on a map, it is still a small town. The funny thing about this place is that I would have been buying the whole place. Two kitchens, two living rooms, double bedrooms, baths, everything. There was a not so funny thing, and this just amazed me. The property was zoned to only be occupied during summer months. That meant that if I did buy it, for nine months of the year I would have to live elsewhere. That deal went nowhere. Probably still trying to sell it if the deal is still the same.

The other one I looked at was in Ocean Grove, NJ. This is a small town near Asbury Park, Deal and Neptune. I think they share the Neptune police department. This is a cute little town, lots of Victorian type homes. One problem in this town at least in my opinion, is that a lot of the homes are about four feet apart. If there is a fire, the entire block could go up. I decided to take a look at this duplex home here. I took my parents with me. Janice was working that day.

So, when we got there, Dad wants to make conversation with the agent just to be civil. At one time, there was a situation in this town. The town was run by a religious group and there was a rule in place that nobody was allowed to drive a car in town on Sunday. This must have been a lot of fun for people who lived there. Dad made some comment referring to this rule.

The agent must have been in favor of it staying that way.

"AND WE WANTED TO KEEP IT THAT WAY!" Dad was smart enough to keep his mouth shut on that deal. This rule has since changed. Now we get to the home.

The agent is telling me how I am never going to find a free standing house in my price range in this market. She gets us to the duplex. Cute home, two entrance doors, windows, steps and so on. She opens the door; we go in to take a look at the place. It is old, but we knew that already.

Dad scores another big hit; says to me "What are you buying here, half a house?" I thought the agent was going to have a stroke right there.

He says to me "What happens if you want to paint your half of the house orange and the guy next door wants to do his half in purple?" That pretty much made this deal go to pieces. The back yard here was also a joke. I have had vans where the inside of a work van was as big as this yard. The yard also had an oil tank. So much for this duplex.

CONTEMPORARY HOMES AND MC MANSIONS

This term has always made me wonder exactly what it implies. If a home is contemporary I would assume this would mean a home which is newly constructed. On the other hand, take a look at these type homes. They are all considered to be state of the art as to the appliances and conveniences, or at least that is how it should be. Take a closer look they usually have the same basic items as any other new home. There is usually nothing really radical about the construction.

I would expect climate control to be super high energy efficiency, like being able to heat the place with a toaster. I would be looking for automatic doors and windows, sort of like a Lexus automobile. Also a security system, no maintenance type exteriors and interiors, an intercom, a built in vacuum system, radiant heating and solar panels.

If you want to see this type construction take a trip to EPCOT in Florida to get a taste of it, don't go to your local builder. The problem here is that most builders take a basic home, change the roofs from the traditional gable roof (this is the shape roof kids' use when drawing a house) and make smaller sections of roofs known as shed roofs.

A shed roof is half a gable roof and usually connects a short wall with a taller wall. These are placed at strange angles in relation to each other and may have skylights installed. Not that there is anything wrong with this idea, but here is some food for thought. A large amount of the heat in a home just rises to the ceiling in this type home. You do pay for this heat you know.

If you do buy a home such as this, try to make sure there is a ceiling fan or two. They are back in style anyway and these can be used to keep the old lady from cranking up the heat every time the place gets a little cool.

Another thought is that if there are skylights; you may want to consider small ones. These get some light in the house without overheating the rooms. Even with those, vented skylights may be the answer. Of course, get them with energy efficient glazing.

Just remember though that if the skylight is 20 feet from the floor and you want to be able to open it, there either has to be a hand operated system or a power operated system.

I have three skylights and a vent window which are about 10 feet up which I open and close by hand with a long pole which has an end made just for this. The power operated ones will cost you a lot more money. These open and close with a small motor which is set up with a gearbox and operates from a wall switch on the wall. These are really pretty neat. They are also pretty expensive.

I priced one of these years ago, talking like 1986 and at that time in a commercial roofing supply place they were using this with a two foot by two foot square skylight and they were going for about $600. That price was for the skylight and the motor. No wiring, no installation, no labor costs. Of course if you are spending a half million on a summer home, what is a few hundred more.

These type homes will have rooms with names like THE GREAT ROOM and the MUDROOM.

First let me explain what is really going on here. Many of these homes were fine with the original style home, but then the builder got spaced out on something either natural or synthetic and decided to turn the house into a contemporary. This may have been inspired by almost anything. Maybe the builder could have had sex in the woods with his woman and decided to adapt the wide open feeling in his house.

He might have graduated college with an art degree and could not get a "real" job in his field, worked his way through school as a carpenters' helper and because he liked to work with his hands he somehow became a builder. Now he has decided to do something with all that design stuff he picked up in college. He has to show off what he knows about positive and negative space and all that other good stuff he learned in design classes. Now is his chance to put some practical use to all that stuff.

Let me tell you about a couple of these rooms:

GREAT-ROOM

Whatever the motivation, the great room was created. This usually is a large room that takes up a lot of space in the center of the home and actually is a sort of combination living room, dining room, and den all in one. It is also as large as a small apartment. This room may also even contain a conversation pit. This translates to a hole in the floor which has been upholstered.

Maybe there will be a hot tub or a small swimming pool. The pit or the hot tub will serve the same purpose. It gives you a place to hang out and talk, smoke dope. No, if you have that kind of money you are probably doing cocaine instead.

You can warm up a new date here with the climate, the small trees over the hot tub and a good line of crap. It is also a good place to have sex if you are careful not to drown in the process.

MUD-ROOM

Now the mudroom I mentioned is not to help you get your feet clean after your encounter in the great room. Actually it is intended to keep the mess out of the house in bad weather. This is a small room, usually with a closet and some sort of storage area to hold wet boots and mittens. Some old houses have these, but they are known as the back porch. See, as the status connected with money and the houses change, the names go with it. Macaroni is now Pasta.

Most contemporary homes I have seen all seem to have all the rooms run off the great room. This is really convenient when you have to make it to the crapper after loosening your insides in the hot tub. Oh, you say you just saved the trip to the can by warming up the hot tub? What is the big deal, the water is hot anyway.

All this open space allows air circulation much easier, so if the smell of supper does not impress you; you can save the trip out to the kitchen and pig out at The Olive Garden later.

There are also some drawbacks to this open scheme. If your kid is into some slightly loud rock group like Metallica and you are into Johnny Mathis; when he cranks the stereo in his room to "rock concert" volume, you and Mr. Mathis may go take a ride in the car. Or you may just throw the kids stereo out of the window.

This open space is usually great for family fights, you and the other half can scream at each other over a variety of distances instead of being confined to a little dinky bedroom. It is also advantageous to those of us who throw dishes in a fight. You can turn those dishes into ceramic Frisbees.

The Mc Mansions are a type home that has evolved since about 1990, give or take a few years. I think what got these going was the loose credit that flowed through the United States much like loose stools in a goose.

People were buying these oversize homes which were only a larger version of whatever they owned before. There are more bedrooms, dens, family rooms, great rooms, more bathrooms. Two, three or four car garages.

I guess the builder figures if you can pay for this oversize house, you must have enough cars to fill a used car lot, some families do. There is nothing extraordinary about most of these homes. Even though there are a lot of rooms; that means nothing.

I know someone who had one of these. They could put their dining room inside mine and ride a bicycle around it. That was the size difference of these two rooms. An outside feature of many of these Mc Mansions is what looks like stucco. In reality, this stuff is nothing more than foam. Sort of like the stuff that is used to pack a television in a big box. The stuff is used mainly for vertical surfaces and covered with some kind of finish that is similar to auto body filler except that it will not eat into the foam the way body filler does. I want to see what these look like in fifty years. Since I originally wrote this line; I have seen one big exterior problem. This was from water stains. The entire exterior had to be entirely rebuilt.

These Mc Mansions are usually big homes. Somewhere around three to four thousand square feet and bigger. You would think there were twenty people living in them. My in laws raised six kids in a house that would fit into some of the great rooms.

Another problem is these are not made for low income housing. As one woman told me after they got one of these homes: "We can't afford to get sick for the next five years." Not my idea of fun.

When the housing bubble broke in late 2008, she ended up selling this place to pay for some of the bills they had accumulated while living there. I guess they expected to reap a big profit instead. Not my bills, thank God.

The developers also put these places in neighborhoods where all the homes look a lot the same, (Think development homes) they just do not call them that anymore. The builders do not want that image. The properties are usually a decent size in relation to the homes, only because the owners want to be able to tell visitors "We have a full acre here." So, just more grass to cut. It is in your problem to keep that landscaping looking good. Another expense.

Some of these developments come with "fitness centers" which is usually the size of my kitchen, and sometimes a swimming pool that is only slightly bigger than my kitchen. I know one guy whose development was pretty much built around the tennis courts. If you did not play tennis there, people looked at you like a leper.

One last thought, is that you can really impress your farty old relatives with a home like this. They will take a look at it from the street and think you must be doing well and treat you with either a lot more respect or contempt. It is your business how you handle this situation.

Chapter 6   MONEY TALKS

FINANCING THE CASTLE

A home will probably be the biggest money item you ever own unless you decide to buy a Lamborghini to park in the driveway. Let me tell you a bit about the money end of a house, I'll make your day.

To start with, most people get a mortgage to purchase the home. This is basically a big cash loan, which is paid back over a number of years, usually about 30 years.

There are all sorts of mortgages; there is a fixed rate type which has the same interest rate and payment amount for the length of the loan. This is best for those of us who do not like ugly surprises. There are balloon type payments which start off low, and at a given date the principal (the actual amount of the loan) is due. These can sneak up on people, sort of like death. This if fine, if you are expecting to be left a large pile of cash in a will. Just hope the person dies before the loan is due. There is also a variable rate mortgage with rates which fluctuate with the economy. I find them to be scary. This is just a fast overview, there is more coming later. What I want to deal with at this point is the loan companies and banks and their attitudes. If I had friends who operated like banks, they would not be my friends for too long.

Loan institutions have a strange way of looking at the average home buyer. You could be a self-employed electrician making $50,000 a year; and they will give you a bad time about getting a mortgage, simply because they have to rely on your word as to your income.

If you flip burgers for McDonald's for about $7 an hour that is okay, because you will have someone who will document that you make steady money.

True story; I know a woman who was a bartender she averaged $1000 a week. Could not get a mortgage. Took a job driving a school bus. Half the money; got the loan.

If you think I am kidding, call a bank and tell them you are self-employed. Make sure you are wearing your hip boots and have a shovel handy. I started writing this book several years ago but for things beyond my control it sat in a book shelf for about 17 years.

Since then; in the early years of the 21st century, banks got really loose about their loaning systems, and were giving people large loans with almost no documentation. That did not work out too well either.

The banks did not have the actual cash to back up their transactions so when the large housing bubble blew up in 2008, this got messy. This country is now up to its' ass in foreclosures or so it seems.

Also, foreign investments must present some kind of lure just like foreign movies. A bank will quicker write off a bad loan of $200,000,000 to a deadbeat third world country then loan a U.S. citizen $50,000 for a home loan.

TIME magazine did a story about these bad investments back in January 1983, at which time I decided to keep whatever extra money I had in a sack on my dogs' neck. If you can find an old issue, my letter to the editor is in the letter section. Really!

THE NON CONVENTIONAL HOME AND THE BANKS

Banks are not builders nor architects, bankers seem to have less imagination then a mushroom. The Wright brothers would have struck out with them, but by time American Airlines came along, flying was considered a decent risk.

If you decide to build an underground house using plans almost exactly like the plans used for a ranch, but built below grade, you may end up below grade. I personally knew someone who had this exact problem.

He and his wife presented the plans and were turned away like idiots. They returned a couple of days later with the same home above grade and got the loan.

Unless you have personally financed a bunch of non-conservative homes, the banks will treat you like a maniac. Of course if you have gotten this far on your own, you may not need the bank anyway.

WE WANT IT IN BLACK AND WHITE

When I got this house 31 years ago, banks wanted the whole world to look like a giant balance sheet. God forbid, you own a piece of property which is worth $55,000 in Cape May, NJ and pay $1000 a year in taxes on the dirt. They will disallow the fifty-five grand, the bank will say it is not a liquid asset, but is a liability.

If they thought you were the least bit of a risk they would ask for and want a: GIFT LETTER

Now for those of you who do not know what this is; it is simply a letter from someone who has property the bank can put a lien on and that someone says that he or she will GIVE you a certain amount of money to help buy the house. This is not a loan, it's a gift. "Hey, Pop, can you give me a small gift? Maybe eight or ten grand. Hello, Hello."

Damn phone went dead.

I ran into one bank that not only wanted the letter but had to show the money in my account so they felt it was safe. As a matter of fact; they wanted it in an escrow account, so I couldn't skip the country with the bread. Talk about nerve.

I told them to keep their crummy old money, and the house too. Went out, found another home and another bank. I hope the dumb ass loan officer who gave me the business buys a copy of this book and realizes he lost a mere $100,000 for his bank. Better still, I hope his supervisor buys the book.

Of course, everything the bank uses is done in at least triplicate. I have gotten to the point that when I sign something from banks, I turn the sheet over to see what is printed on the back of the sheet. Never mind all the nice clear stuff printed on the front. It's the stuff printed on the back in pink on yellow paper that will screw you.

The sad thing too; is that most people who work for banks say that banks are the cheapest outfits to work for, you would think with all the phony baloney stuff these people do, they could at least get a decent piece of the action.

One more item of interest is that if you get in touch with an "alleged" officer of the bank. This is all title. I knew someone who was given a promotion as a vice president of a bank in New York. I felt "Wow, I never thought this woman could get such a big shot job, she must be a lot smarter than I realized." This idea went in the trash can when I found out the bank had about 1000 vice presidents. It never hurts to get this persons' name (first and last) on the other end of a deal, you may be able to use if for some leverage; sort of like what people do with a silly title and a resume. Something is always better than nothing.

When you do talk to these people, keep a pen and pad handy, they are real sleight of hand types when it comes to getting a straightforward answer and if you keep notes, it will at least keep you from thinking you are going nuts.

MORE GREAT FINANCING INFORMATION!!!!

As best I can tell, the easiest way to finance a home is to have it left to you. The next easiest way, is to marry rich. Let's face it; most of us do not fall into either of these situations. Believe it or not; I actually knew personally, in real life flesh and blood, two people who have done it that way.

The fool who was left the house sold it and pissed the cash away playing the horses. At that time, he ended up renting for more than my mortgage. The other person used her brains and is still living like a big shot.

I did have an uncle whose dad gave him and the wife a home for a wedding present. That does not happen too often either.

INTEREST RATES AND THE TRUE EFFECT OF SAME

Back in 1980, the U.S. economy was running very high interest rates on homes. I remember hearing about 22% mortgages....keep that number in mind. In 1986, the rate dropped to about 9 ½ -10 %. Now taking a house at a price of $100,000 at both rates, and for thirty year fixed mortgages......Note the small difference.

$100,000 @ 22% 30 years.....Principal and interest $1835.99 /Month
$100,000 @ 10% 30 years.....Principal and interest $877.58 /Month

Now in my bankbook, that seems like a sizable chunk of change. In interest alone, we are looking at almost $12,000 a year difference. I know people who made less gross income than that in 1980.

Looking at the 30 year picture, you are talking about over a third of a million bucks. Now of course if you purchased the house back then with the high rates, either you loved the house, were on drugs or had a lot of money to start with.

BUT THERE IS AN ALTERNATIVE, WHICH IS CALLED:
REFINANCING THE CASTLE

Now as King or Queen of the castle, you may feel there must be something good about this refinancing stuff, and there really is, if you can wade through the mess.

The banks today are seeing the interest rates drop and of course they want a piece of the action. Now this might seem counterproductive, but think about this. If for example I took out the mortgage in 1982 with Bank A when the rates were about 14%. I signed a note for $31,000 on a local handyman's special. Payment on this is $367.32 a month.

This was not bad; considering I was paying less than some people I knew with apartments that were 1/3 the size of my home. So after Ronnie Reagan fooled around with the economy, said some magic words, a few prayers and some luck, the interest rates dropped to 9%.

Bank B is losing money all over town with the low rates, so they start to advertise 9 ½ % mortgages to bring in some extra bucks. Even at the low rate on a small mortgage of $30,400 (somewhere in that area, the interest is paid off a lot sooner than the principal) the bank can still make money on the deal. If this payment is still for 30 years, the bank will clear about $64,000 on the deal. Do the math kids. Three hundred sixty five bucks a month; times 360 months, minus the original $30,400 more or less.

This type thinking can work to your advantage. Take the same loan, refinance it for 15 years for a rate of 10 ½ % which was the rate back in about 1987 (This rate changes constantly).The loan can be taken out for $35,000 to cover the closing costs; the bank still makes a lot of money, but YOU the homeowner still saved about $65,000 over the length of the loan.

The new payment is $381.49 a month. This is about $15 a month more, for half the time. Talking about 15 years with the closing costs included in the deal. In a sleazy way you are beating the bank at their own game. Bank A is paid off. Good bye and good luck.

Bottom line here. We did this deal, but a few years later we still owed the bank about $22,000. At that time, they started with home equity loans with a rate of 2 or 3 % for a year, which would then jump to about 7 % at the end of the year. I jumped on this deal.

I went to one of the banks, took out one of these loans for the low rate, and paid it for about 10 months as if I was paying off my original loan. This would take a lot off the principal. These loans at 3% would cost me about $130 a month, so the three hundred something I was giving them was taking out another $200 or so extra dollars a month. At about 10 months I would go to another bank, and do the same thing. God bless the greedy bastards. We did this four times.

We got our last payment book; it came in the mail with our Income Tax refund check. I went to the bank and paid off the loan the first day. I thought the loan officer was going to cry. We robbed the banks without a gun. Paid off the house, start to finish in 14 years.

By the way, do not get sucked into that stupid stuff about the interest being a big deduction on you income tax.

This deduction business is entirely true at this time, but if you think about it. If you are paying 7% interest on the loan, and get rid of it, that is like having a bank account with a 7% interest rate.

On the other hand; I know someone who bought a home in 1970 for $22,000, got divorced and remarried. Kept floating home equity lines for useless stuff like expensive cars and a high end entertainment system.

They just sold the place and moved to Florida. At that point they still owed $114,000 on the place. These people were making well over $100,000 a year; so who knows where the money went. They are presently paying rent somewhere in Gods Waiting Room. This was 2009.

NOW COMES THE FUN PART, THE ACTUAL DIRTY DEED

The bank will put any kind of ad in the paper to get you in the door, after all; they are running a profit making business, and somebody has to cover their bad loans. You walk in the door; the soft music is playing *Hello*, by Lionel Richie. You bet your ass, *Hello*. The party is only starting.

At one time, all bank officers were middle aged men with either solid blue or pin striped suits. You could tell them from gangsters because they did not carry a gun where you could see it. Now the picture is starting to change. There are still guys like this, but now there are also PROFESSIONAL WOMEN in positions of power.

Actually none of these people male or female are all that powerful, but the bank likes to make them think they are. They have a title, business cards, a private desk, a phone and a pile of reference books. Used car dealers have the same stuff and usually make more money.

Some women still buy that old stereotype that they are not suited for professional work. The old pregnant in the summer, barefoot in the winter story. I like them to at least wear shoes.

So now some guy comes walking in the bank in his $50.00 Polyester Pete suit, and cardboard crippler shoes and thinks he is going to get over on this dumb broad.

He forgets she has an MBA, and had to fight to get where she is. She is smarter than he thinks. The woman puts on this routine like a secretary, hands him a stack of papers to fill out and sends him to another desk to try to decipher the paperwork.

This guy does not handle the money at home so he does not know small things like the present payment on his house, or the annual taxes or utility bills; so in desperation with his insides rolling, he comes up to the lady, mumbles something about a business appointment, and heads for the door. "Whoa. Jack; If you want today's rate, just sign here"......X...

He is in a big hurry by now and puts his John Hancock on the line. Now he can leave feeling like he got over on the entire banking world. Yeah, tomorrow buddy.

This guy feels he is basically making a good move, so he picks up some flowers for the wife on the way home, comes along with his suit of armor, and white horse and proceeds to tell the lady of the house what a genius he is today. "By the way we have a few papers to fill out. You want to do that? Your writing is much neater."

Have you ever noticed how forms are set up? Think about this for a minute. The block for name and address is big enough to fill in the family tree. The part with job history, credit account information, references and "Other Pertinent Information" is about the size of a postage stamp.

A credit card number is about 10 digits, and the space is big enough for about three. By time you get done filling out the paperwork, the bank knows enough about you to fill an encyclopedia. They crank all this stuff through a computer, and they even find out your dog's maiden name.

But being civilized persons, we fill out all the required paperwork and take it back to the bank. A word of advice: MAKE COPIES OF EVERYTHING YOU GIVE THE BANK. They have a way of losing the stuff that leans in your favor and finding stuff that is on their side.

Another item to beware of is the paper which wants some detailed information about your present job. Now if you are self-employed and have a lot of documentation to back you up, you may stand a chance.

If you are part of the "Underground Economy" you may have to fabricate some information. As long as it is on paper, in black and white and sounds like it makes sense, a bank will buy it. After all, look at the shit they sell to the U.S. public about themselves. I personally know of three mortgages which were processed through strange circumstances. Two of these were through the applicant filling out his own paperwork and having the bank call his own extension at work for verification. The other dude was on unemployment at the time.

One more important rule when dealing with a bank or a mortgage company. If you call up and ever get through; as opposed to a five hour busy signal. NEVER ASK TO HAVE THE CALL RETURNED, HANG ON EVEN IF IT IS FOR AN HOUR! This is so important I cannot stress it enough. It is akin to calling the Pope and getting through on the first try.

PERSISTANCE COUNTS

Lenders have a way of discouraging borrowers even though these people are their bread and butter. If you let a lender give you some nonsense about anything concerning the loan or the status of your paperwork, the creep on the other end will do his or her best to torment you just to make you squirm.

They know if you are going to get the loan within minutes of your application, but they are like a woman who wants to make you beg for a while before she takes you to bed.

It is really just about the same game, just a different type orgasm. If whenever you score a minor victory with the bank, you scream to yourself "Gotcha, You Bitch!" you will soon get the proper attitude to make it to the closing.

THE CLOSING

This is the part of the mortgage deal the borrower waits for with sweaty palms, reading daily interest rates in the newspaper, scrounging every extra buck available, lying, crying and dying just to get himself in debt up to his ears. If nothing else, when you get to the closing; bring along the kind of lawyer who could spring Bonnie and Clyde.

Your lawyer has to be just as sneaky and underhanded as the bank; even more so, as there is only one of him and the entire staff of the bank is his opposition. If your lawyer shows up in a K-mart suit; and a Bic pen, the bank will turn all of you into chopped meat. As far as I know, you cannot get a mortgage without a closing unless your mother owns the bank.

Don't be afraid to work your ass off to make this happen. When Janice and I got this home, we got the news on Friday that at the closing on Monday we were going to be about $700 short of the actual cash we had on hand. I had a furniture repair shop at the time. I told Janice, "I will be back in a couple of hours." I cleaned off a bunch of jobs I had waiting to go out, came back with about $400, she went to her bank on Monday right before the closing and took out a cash advance on her Visa card. We were in business.

On one of our refinance deals we actually had to drive to the other end of the state to pick up a $35,000 check to make that happen. This was one hour before the closing. Hard work pays off.

Chapter 7   WHO GAVE THE HOME A NAME?

This is sort of a strange item to put in here, but people do it, so here we go. I mentioned the Frank Lloyd Wright home of Falling Water in Pennsylvania. As an architect, he put names on a lot of the properties in which he either lived or built for other people. Fast note, when he did Falling Water, I understand his career was taking a hit, and this home revived it.

This is not about somebody's career, it is about naming properties. If you ever go to Newport, Rhode Island and visit the mansions there, you will see most, if not all of them have names. There is the Breakers, Elms, Marble House, Rose Cliff, Green Animals, Hunter House and others. There is one named probably after the owner, the Isaac Bell House. At one time there were hundreds of these homes there. Fires, taxes and maintenance costs have reduced this number.

Anyway, people do put names on homes. To my knowledge this is partly for identity, partly for snob appeal, and probably just to piss off the rest of the family who never thought to do it to their places.

Some people have no imagination for a name. Obviously a lot of these homes are named after some physical attribute of the property, but some were named after the owners of the families. There is a place in New Jersey called Walnford, which was named after the Waln family who owned it. For years I made jokes about this situation. I have always thought and still think it is a snob thing, but a harmless snob thing. And for years I would joke that I should call my house Pughaven. This of course taken from my last name of Pugliese.

A few years ago my brother Bob moved to Tennessee, somewhere out in the sticks where for excitement you watch paint dry. Since then, I decided to start using the name Pughaven North for my property and Pughaven South for his. This is totally goofy, but I do get a kick out of it.

Bedtime Horror Stories for Homeowners

Now there is no use having a name on the property unless you can show it off a bit. Being a cheap guy, I am not going to spend a lot of money on this, so here is what I did. In my art studio/shop I have several five gallon cans of clay I use for sculpture work. I made a piece out of clay which looks like a flat rock. I then printed out the words Pughaven North with my computer, with one of those programs where you can change the fonts and sizes of the letters. I made this in two lines on 8 ½ by 14 inch paper. I laid the paper over the clay and used it to punch holes through the paper into the clay and give me the design. I would then carve the lettering out using sculpture tools.

I would then use plaster to make a mold over this piece. It is basically a relief sculpture technique. After the mold is hard, I take the clay out of it, clean the mold, and cast the piece in concrete. I have the one for my house, and one for Bob's house.

I gave it to him when we visited one year. When the stone is buried level with the ground it looks pretty decent. Then again, this is the same thing I use when one of my dogs die and I need a grave marker. You may have seen the fancy stones you can buy for a garden. They have words like SMILE, or LAUGH. I know people who put these in cemeteries by somebody's grave. I am making one to go near my grave site. Mine will say.......NO MORE B.S.

I just visited the cemetery where I plan to get planted; turns out I am not allowed to use the concrete piece. No problem, I can put the lettering on the bronze plate.

WHO NAMES THESE PLACES?

Some time when you have time to kill; like we all have time to kill, take a ride out to the burbs. Any suburban area will do it. Take a look at the signs developers put by housing developments. We have one by us "Cotswold" What the hell is a Cotswold? Is it someplace you open your old army surplus cot and get some sleep? Check your dictionary; there is a real word with a definition.

Went past a place last week on a train. There was a 4 or 6 family condo unit stuck somewhere near Newark, New Jersey; not in Newark, maybe Rahway, not that it makes a big difference. The place has a sign in front "Riverview." Now I have been told that Newark, New Jersey has some of the best drinking water in the country. I am not sure. But where this "Riverview" place is situated there was a river. I wouldn't let my dogs swim in that dirty looking water. If I saw a stray dog swimming in there I would have to get him out of it just out of common decency.

Janice and I make jokes about these names all the time. There will be a place named something like "Wooded Acres" and the biggest tree there has a trunk the diameter of a three year olds wrist. The developers knock down all the old trees because it is easier and cheaper to build on the lots. My brother Bob has had two homes that are similar. One was in New Jersey, the other is in Tennessee. He has had these one at a time, he does not have the bucks to have both at once. Actually he is lucky to keep one at a time. That is not my point though. Both pieces of property had lots of trees on them. Old trees, mature trees, pretty trees. He will tell you, "I got this place because of the trees." Then he cuts most of them down, duh. He lives on a street named Woods Road.

Chapter 8 GETTING THROUGH THE LEGAL STUFF

CLOSINGS ON HOUSES

Back at my house, this place is more familiar to me so this is where I am going to start some of these stories. How about, I start with a closing; this is where you bring either checks or a paper bag full of cash and you and some legal type guys make a deal where you will own the house outright or pay it off for several years. I have been to four closings in my life. The first one was a closing on a small home in New Jersey. This was a former "summer home" that someone decided to use year round and eventually sold to me and my first wife Lorraine.

We had looked at several homes and eventually got this one for the simple reason we could afford it. This closing was simple. The previous owner was willing to take back the mortgage (he would be like the bank). We gave him a down payment of about $3000 back in 1975 and he let us pay off the rest of the mortgage over 8 years.

I remember the payments back then were $172.71 a month. I know people who spend that much on cell phones today. We had us; Bob, the previous owner, the real estate guy and a lawyer who probably covered both sides of the deal which is probably illegal anyway.

To make a long story short we were done in maybe a half hour and the dump was ours. Just being funny, it was a cute little home. The marriage fell apart after a few years and when we did the second closing the new owner showed up with a paper bag full of cash to pay for the place. We had paid $15,000 for the place and were selling it for $20,000 so that is how that deal transpired. We split the proceeds and went our separate ways. I don't care. It is ancient history now and the woman to whom I am now married has worked out much better, thank you. The first marriage lasted 7 years. We are at 30 years now and going strong.

Bedtime Horror Stories for Homeowners

    If this is your very first closing, let me congratulate you on getting this far. I wish you luck with your house. If this is a second of third or so closing, you have had some practice, so this may be easier. For you first time people, better to keep your mouth shut and let your lawyer do the talking, that is what he is being paid for. Besides, you don't know what the hell is going on anyway. The biggest loan you ever had before was for a car and almost anyone can pull that off.

    The attorney will explain all kind of good stuff to you. He will cover Termite Inspections, Surveys, Taxes, Insurance, Property Lines, Sewage Lines, Gas Lines, Telephone Lines and Bottom Lines. He will explain that the guy on the property was only checking out the size of the property, not looking in the window with his transit. Turning the dog loose on him will cost you.

    He or she will talk to you about FHA, VA, FANNIE MAE and making hay. You will feel like an enlightened person by the end of the deal. Then again, you may feel really stupid.

    There may be some tears during the closing as the seller feels like he or she is losing a part of themselves and you as buyer feel like you are giving birth to a child. Another reason for tears is that the seller has just realized he could have gotten a much better price, or the buyer has just realized that the $180,000 mortgage will cost him $600,000 if he pays it for the full thirty years.

    After some small talk, talk about the house; some legalese only lawyers understand, and some other silly words and exchanges of paper and lots of money, you will have survived the closing. Any closing I have ever gone to have been after 10 A.M. This is so everyone involved can get their morning coffee, the bank has its offices open for any last minute questions, and mainly so someone with the strength of a longshoreman can carry all the paperwork into the office.

This stuff is not to be taken lightly. When Chrysler applied to the U.S. Govt. to cover loans back in the 1980's there was a stack of paper supposedly 7 stories high, and it took several hundred lawyers several hours just to shuffle the paperwork back and forth.

Now, I am just going by what I've read. Lee Iacocca could have gotten a little heavy on the tale. The file at your closing will at least seem this large especially when you cannot understand half the printed forms and the others are printed in letters $1/100^{th}$ of an inch high. Like this. (Really, really, tiny, print).

You will notice that at a closing, people smile a lot. I don't really know why except that maybe everyone thinks they have just screwed everyone else really good and can't wait to tell their friends.

Seats are usually assigned for a specific reason. The buyers and sellers usually sit on the long sides of the table. This is usually a 10 foot table for four or five people. This size is needed in order to spread out all that good paperwork. Your dog would know how to handle this paper in about three seconds.

The proper clothing at a closing is important. The lawyer for the buyers should wear a dark Pinstripe and look like the driver of a Mafia Staff Car. As for the buyers, there are options. If you are barely able to afford the house, dress to kill. This will make the banker feel bad that he thought you were a low life. If you have the money issue under control, you can either dress as above or do the casual bit.

The casual bit is great in the summer where the person from the bank is in a stiff suit and your come along with cut offs, flip flops and a bare midriff shirt which has printed across the front in large letters: "PARTY NAKED" No matter what you wear, make sure it is comfortable, and you make the potty before the action starts, you may be seated for a while.

MORTGAGE INSURANCE

This is a deal the banks do to cover their butts. The reason is simple. Let's say I buy a home for $200,000 and I drop dead a week later. If I do not have someone there to pay for the mortgage, the bank is going to have a tough time getting their money. At some point the bank goes into the real estate business, and sells off the place. But this is like hiring a dentist to hang a door. It is not their type of business, it is probably annoying to them, and they do not have the proper tools in their possession.

This can make for an ugly situation. To solve this problem way ahead of the curve; most times when a mortgage is taken out, the lending company wants the borrower to carry an insurance policy to cover the bill. This is called mortgage insurance. This is also known as a decreasing term policy. This is the type policy where the payoff diminishes as the risk of the bank gets less. The bank tries not to let the borrowers know too much about how this works, borrowers might not be too happy about this.

The way this works. Take the $200,000 mortgage I told you about. The guy is carrying his weight lifting stuff into the house, and the poor slob has a heart attack and drops like a duck full of shot. So now the insurance company has to pay the bank the entire amount, especially if the guy has not made any payments at all. Here is the other end of the deal.

The guy takes the $200,000 mortgage for 30 years. Makes all his payments for the 30 years. He has one payment left, owes about $6 on the principal of the loan. This time, he is in the bathroom taking a good dump and drops dead from a heart attack.

The bank will collect a big $6. Not worth the paperwork. So that is the basic way this system works. Anywhere in between the first day and the last day of the loan, the principal of the loan will be different and the payout will be adjusted accordingly.

Bedtime Horror Stories for Homeowners

We took out a loan from one of the big insurance companies to cover ourselves. We both had other insurance policies on ourselves; but because these were not connected to the loan, they did not count. Now, there is an insurance agent connected to this deal. This is not like you can contact whatever company you are using and just fill out a form and send them money, too bad.

I would never make a dime doing insurance work. So the guy writes the policy, and sends us a copy to check to make sure it is accurate. We gave him a voided check so the company can take the money out of our checking account each month. I am not big on this arrangement, but I had enough arguments with my first wife for ten marriages, so I went along with Janice on this arrangement.

We got the policy. I think the names were wrong on it. The guy had a spelling problem. Goes back to him. Another voided check. He works it over and sends it back to us again. Some other screw up. I don't know how this guy kept his job. To make a long story short, we did this routine about 6 times in that many months, each time with a voided check.

One time he had the names spelled wrong, another time the address was wrong, the amount of the loan was wrong the third time, each time this was another transaction. Finally I realized this idiot had messed up so bad, we didn't have any insurance at all on the mortgage. At least we did not need the payments. Thank God.

Janice was the one who was handling the transactions; finally I got fed up with this. I told her in as kind a way as was possible. "Hey Janice, this guy is messing up, let me see what I can do." I didn't want to say "This guy is an idiot, and so are you for going along with him." I had no urge to sleep in my car. Janice was fed up with the mess so she decides to give me a shot at it.

There used to be a set of books in the library called The Standard and Poors Directory. It was like an encyclopedia of all the big companies in the United States. Gave you information about what they did, what kind of money they made and contact information.

I have no idea how I found out about this, but, but ...very useful.

I found the name and address for the Vice President for the insurance company. If you think about it, if you want some action from a company, a good way to do it is from the top down. The way you would want to look for a job in that company. Never did me any good looking for jobs.

I sent this VP a letter at his home address, apologized for sending it there and explained the situation. A week later I got a call from some secretary in the northern part of the state who helped me work out the problem. She asked me "Where did you get this man's name?" When I told her, she was amazed. I am in the Amazing Business. The directory is no longer in my library, or it didn't seem to be there the last time I looked for one.

It has been replaced by something else which was not anywhere near as helpful. If you can find one of these when you are in a bind, they are also dated year to year. They used to be current; it is a good set of books. Just because my library does not have these books anymore does not mean they are extinct. When we did get the mortgage paid off, we just took out plain old term insurance policies. Just enough to help us push up flowers. That is all we need.

Chapter 9
THINGS YOU MAY NEED TO OWN, OR KNOW TO SURVIVE HOME OWNERSHIP

- Go to Home Depot, K-Mart, Wal-Mart, Sears or any place that sells tools and other homeowner stuff. Buy at least one of each item. Even if you are not sure of what to do with it.
- Assorted adhesives, epoxy, wood glue, liquid nails, and contact cement: Read the directions, follow them.
- Camera and film: This is to document all the before and after work done in a house. Also useful for family parties, and to show Uncle Joe where you pissed away the money he asked you to invest for him.
- Answering machines: Get one where you can listen to the calls, keeps away pests.
- Insurance: Both Life and Homeowners. This is a good in case one of you buys the ranch before the ranch is paid off. Homeowners Liability Insurance is good in case somebody's clumsy kid takes a dive down the steps and lands on his face. It is better than giving the kid the house. Also good to have if you have a dog that bites.
- The use of the three above items camera, film and insurance are also useful when you have to document that you really did own a Belter Couch before the fire. Keep the photos elsewhere, preferably in a safe or safety deposit box.
- Wills: Don't be a fool and leave the house to the state.
- Books on home repair: A couple hundred should suffice.
- Candles and warm clothes: For when you forget to pay certain utility bills. Or the heat goes out.
- A pet, I prefer dogs but almost any animal will work.

- Credit cards: When you buy the house, everybody and his mother will want you to have their card. These are useful unless you get crazy with them and exceed the size of the mortgage. If you have a tendency to do stuff like this, do yourself a favor and don't get them.
- A good lawyer: You don't have to keep him on salary, but keep the phone number on file.
- A good accountant: Same system. This person will help you keep some of the bread Uncle Sam would otherwise take and piss away.
- A copy of this book: So if the going gets a little rough, you will know you are not alone.
- A wet and dry shop vac: Rigid is a good company, I think they come with a lifetime warranty. I will not go into detail, but these are good for cleaning a rug after your dog wets on it, also for taking water out of a toilet when you change the flush mechanism, and a million other uses. Use your imagination and the thing is very helpful. Most of these also have a fitting where the hose is attached and the air blows out instead of coming into the unit. Don't be a cheap guy, get a good one, and make sure you change the filter every so often. Read the instruction manual. Price on these was about $70 in 2009. Worth every penny.
- Pencils, pens, scrap paper: you will need these for Honey-Do lists.
- Refrigerator magnets: Companies give these away if you do not want to buy them, used to hang the above notes on the fridge or other steel surfaces.
- Mouse and or rat traps: Either humane or snap traps, I prefer the humane ones. The other ones can also injure your fingers. Do not pet the animals when you let them go.

- Bug spray: Let's be realistic, bugs love living there as much as you do. If you are the type who catches and releases them, you may not need this stuff.
- Cleaning supplies: Get the right stuff for the right jobs. Do not think you will do all the rugs with the above shop vac, get an upright one and save your back.
- Washer and dryer: Even if they are simple units, they are better than paying for a Laundromat.
- A sense of humor: This in general, is useful when you own a home. It will also help you get through life with all the other stupid stuff that happens.

HOME OWNERSHIP TERMS

TO MAINTAIN ACCURACY, THIS WILL BE IN A ROUGH ALPHABETICAL ORDER

A**HOLE: This term taken from the part of the body is used loosely by all parties involved. It may apply to the builder, any of his or her workers, anyone in the financial end of the deal, and last but not least either the buyer or seller of the home.

ATTORNEY: Lawyer, professional crook, shyster. This person can make or break you. Hire a sneaky one.

ASSUME: This is a term which applies to a type of mortgage in which the original owner decides to sell, and has a new buyer pick up the original mortgage rate with a few thousand bucks tacked on. Maybe about 50,000 bucks. This sometimes indicates that the first guy couldn't handle the payments and has decided to bail out and give someone else a shot at it.

ACCOUNT: This usually applies to some amount of cash in a bank somewhere which is supposed to cover some or all of certain expenses incurred in the process of a mortgage. The trick here is that the buyer has to show all the money, just so that the mortgage company folks know their tails are covered.

ASSET: This can be anything of value used to cover the above named account. Somehow an item such as a 1969 Chevy van does not seem to carry much weight in this department.

Bedtime Horror Stories for Homeowners

BALLOON LOAN: This is a sort of mortgage where the homeowner sort of gets away with paying for a big part of the loan for several years. All of a sudden it all comes due; sort of like death, you know it is coming, and are still surprised when it happens.

BUILDER: This is the person who is generally in charge of the actual construction of the home. This person is sometimes called a general contractor, and sometimes called a lot less flattering names.

BUYERS: This is the person or persons who get the ball rolling. Without these people, the whole idea of real estate sales would be null and void. These people are also called by a larger number of other terms including fish and sucker.

CROOK: A term sometimes used in referring to builders, lawyers, or bankers. Damned if know why.

COMMISSION: This is the money paid to the real estate agent and his or her agency. It is usually around 6% of the selling price and is paid by the seller. These people have to make their money somewhere down the line.

CRACK: What a person may do if he or she takes either the purchase or ownership of a home too seriously.

CASH AS IS: This a term used in real estate ads which can be translated to mean that if you buy the place; you will have usually gotten a home in an area in a bad neighborhood. Bring your bodyguards.

CASH: If you have enough of it, the situation sometimes becomes better...and sometimes worse.

CREDIT: Money you have stuck everyone else for to be paid back over a certain time period. Usually the more you owe; the easier it is to get further in the hole for a mortgage. Some logic huh?

CREDIT CHECK: One of the first things a mortgage company does to the buyer. This is so they can find out if you are screwing all the people listed on you application. This will cost you the buyer, about a hundred bucks. This is only painful when the bank denies you the loan because you beat the Record of the Month Club for a $10 Kenny Rogers CD.

CARPETING: Usually there are several grades used in display homes. The good stuff is on the floor, the el-cheap-o stuff is in the book; or the other way around. The builder will usually try to talk you into the better stuff. I suggest you do not get any in the kitchen.

CARPORT: A half of a garage usually found on older homes. This was built either because the owner could not build a real garage for one reason or another; or it was left behind after a fire in that part of the home.

CONDO: Short for condominium, an apartment with a mortgage.

DEBT: You know what this is, and I hope you will also know when you are in over your head.

DEVELOPER: A builder who usually builds several homes at one time. These people are sometimes associated with organized crime and occasionally have Italian surnames.

DUMP: A house which would cost more to fix up than it would to tear it down and start over. This type place usually smells like urine.

DESIGNER: This person can usually take an ordinary house and make it to appear to be something special.

DRAINAGE: This applies to a homes' ability to shed water away from itself through proper grading of dirt and the correct application of drain pipes and gutters. It does not take too long to tell if this is done right; one good rainstorm will let you know.

ESCROW: No; this is not some kind of bird. It is a type of bank account which ties up the buyers' money till the closing, so the mortgage company or the bank knows the money will be there when the closing occurs. This can tie up a sizable amount of cash on the buyer for several months. Too bad. If there is interest paid, it is about the same as a Christmas Club.

FINANCING: This is the money behind the deal.

FAUX PAINTING: This is a decorative type painting where a plain surface can be done to make it look as if it was actually something like marble, or stone. Also used to make murals on ceilings which look as if you can see the sky without actually having to put in a real skylight. This technique actually goes back several hundred years. Look at the Sistine Chapel.

GRADING: This is the difference where the yard can look like a yard or a practice pit for hand grenades.

HOME: This is the whole crux of the situation. The alternative is to stay renting or sleeping in the park or in a car.

Bedtime Horror Stories for Homeowners

HOMEOWNER: Someone who has decided that it is better to assume all the responsibilities and rewards of owning the property instead of just paying rent on it. This is a certain type of person, but it must be popular, just look around.

HOUSEWARMING PARTY: This is a party where all your friends come over to check out your new home (also can be used for older houses). They will bring you all sorts of useless items for the place, drink your beer and throw up on your rug and on your dog.

HAZARD INSURANCE: This is type of insurance taken out when a home is purchased in case one of the people at the above party gets drunk and falls down.....I mean doowwwwnn. They get like this and then try to sue you.

HARDWOOD FLOORING: This is one of the items designers try to push in a home, it hides the second rate sub flooring. If it is done properly, it is nice stuff.

INTERIOR DECORATOR: Something like a designer, occasionally thought to be a member of the gay community.

JUGGLER: You have seen them in the circus; wait till you try to figure out either the closing paperwork or your monthly bills.

KNOT: This is a mark seen in a piece of lumber. It is caused by the interaction of two branches on a tree. Sometimes wood is selected for the appearance of these knots, sometimes they just make the lumber in your house get bent out of shape.

LAMINATE FLOORING: This is a type of flooring that is basically very dense cardboard with a really tough plastic finish on the top layer. It can be installed by a homeowner with a chop saw and some patience. Some are tough as cast iron. Watch the fingers with that saw.

LUMBER: This is the frame or the skeleton of many homes in this world; just hope the person who selected and used it did okay.

MORGAGER: Ugly looking word for the lending institution which will come up with the money for your house. If you default, it becomes their house.

MORTGAGEE: The buyer. As long as you keep up the payments everything will be fine. Good luck.

MOVING MAN: This is someone you pay to beat up your possessions.

NOTHING DOWN: This is generally a sales ploy to help the first time buyers buy a new home. It works, but can increase the size of your payments and the size of your anxiety attacks.

OPEN HOUSE: This is another way to show off a home. It is used when the market starts to favor the buyers and a greater flow of potential clients are directed toward the home. Also used to unload dumps. Gives burglars a good chance to scope out the home.

PRINCIPAL: This is the actual amount of the loan used to purchase the home. It is usually about 1/3 the actual cost of an amortized mortgage.

PAYMENT: This will usually include the principal, the interest, and other items such as taxes and insurance. That is why you have to take a lot into account besides the price of the home. Piece of cake.

QUARTERLY TAX BILL: This usually applies to homeowners who do not have their taxes included in their payments. These can usually be stalled if need be, and paid with interest. The town does not really want to own your house anyway.

RESIDENT: This is the person or persons living at your address. In my house I'm allowed to have and open all the mail addressed to resident.

SEWAGE CHARGE: Without this and the accompanying sewers, we would still have outhouses.

TABLE OF AMORTIZATION: This is a printout which shows you what part of your mortgage gets applied to the principal and what part goes on the interest. You will notice that very little of the payment for the first twenty years of a mortgage (30 year) actually goes on the principal. On a 30 year mortgage of $30,000 an extra $150 a month would cut the mortgage from 30 years to about 11 years and save the homeowner about $60,000. This is 1980's house prices, it still works.

TAXES: Just life death, these are impossible to escape. Somebody has to pay the garbage men and the police.

THERMAL SCANNER: This is an infrared tool which is used to help locate poorly insulated areas of a home. Also useful to find live animals inside a wall. I recently was able to borrow one of these from the town library. Who knew?

Bedtime Horror Stories for Homeowners

UNDERPAYMENT: This is a situation where your mortgage company handles your taxes, makes short payments either due to error, or embezzlement and you are later notified and stuck for the difference plus interest. Tough shit

VACANT: Hopefully you will find your new home in this condition when you move in; no termites, critters, winos or gypsies.

WALLBOARD: This is another word for Sheetrock. This is the stuff 99% of today's homes have on the interior walls. These walls are later covered with other stuff such as paint, wallpaper, tile or graffiti.

X-RAY VISION: Too bad we don't all have this stuff like Superman. Repair work and finding your keys would be a lot easier.

YELLOW: One of the three primary colors of yellow, red and blue. These are the basis for all colors used to paint your home. If these are mixed with white or black, almost anything is possible. So much for colors such as Melon, Golden Harvest or Sunrise.

ZONING LAWS: These are the laws which will tell you if you can build a home in a certain area or if it is reserved for wildlife or 10 lane highways.

NEIGHBORS, GOOD, BAD, OR OTHERWISE

Unless you buy property out in the woods where the mail is delivered by air, you will soon discover the neighbors. Most people will at least try to start off friendly; they are still living here and don't need any problems.

GOOD NEIGHBOR

Most people fit into this category, even if you don't agree on everything with each other there are telltale signs here:
- This type guy introduces himself while you are moving in and may even volunteer to help.
- He keeps his dog in his yard till he is sure you like dogs, and then he introduces the pup by name.
- The woman next door gives you some cookies, plus the recipe
- When he plays a radio in his back yard he knows how to keep it loud enough to hear, but not so loud to make your teeth hurt.
- He changes his oil in the driveway and talks to you about that wreck you claim to be restoring. He does not laugh at your clunker.
- He talks to your children like they are intelligent human beings.
- He talks to you the same way.
- He tips you off to the local weirdoes.
- His property looks fairly neat, but lived in.
- He has friends and relatives stop by for visits. This person is willing to come over and feed your dog while you take a trip to Niagara Falls.
- He will try to advise you on problems in your house the previous owner failed to mention such as the six inches of water in the basement when it rains.

AS OPPOSED TO A BAD NEIGHBOR

If a person is a problem; it will not take long to discover this. Here are a few telltale signs:
- He walks his large dog on your lawn.
- His lights are out by 7 P.M.
- He owns a car nobody would want, maybe an old Kaiser.
- His property looks like A) An absolute mess or B) So neat even the grass is standing at attention.
- He and his wife can work in the yard all day without a radio, a drink or a word to each other.
- When he has a barbecue, it is in back of his garage.
- If his car gets hit, he will sneak it in the garage at night, and repair it with a rubber hammer and a low light.
- He never goes on vacation.
- He never talks to anyone in the area; nor does he ever get any company.
- He personally knows the building inspector, and all the police. They know him as a pain in the ass.
- His dog bites some kid, and he gives the mutt a Milk Bone as a reward.

THE OTHERWISE NEIGHBOR

The otherwise type neighbor is the type person who will wave as he passes in the car, but makes no big effort to meet you until you make the first move. This is sometimes the result of a bad neighbor he has encountered in the past. Remember; you can't expect to be hanging all over each other, and everyone develops friendships in different ways. It helps to get to know the neighbors, just to know who is in the area. This way, you know who is friendly, helpful or a stinker. They are also checking you out.

IF YOU WANT TO BE KNOWN AS A DECENT NEIGHBOR

- If you want to be known as a decent neighbor, exhibit some intelligence. People do not appreciate loud music and parties all night long when they have to go to work early in the morning.
- They don't like it when you save garbage for one big collection at the end of the year.
- Chain saws eleven o' clock at night are a No No.
- If you have a kid who will glue himself to the neighbors' house, keep him away from the house, and if he does make it, at least apologize and scrape the glue off his house.
- If you beat your wife or husband, do it in prime time so the neighbors think it is the TV.
- When the guy next door is out of work, don't come around bragging about getting a raise or a better job.
- If the neighbor has babies, even if you hate kids, at least show enough interest to see if it is a boy or a girl. Learn the kid's names and write them down if you have to.
- If you are the type who likes to sunbath in the buff, use some discretion.
- Don't throw beer bottles or other garbage over the fence. I had someone throw a big piece of watermelon skin into the yard once, so I sent it back the same way. The woman asked me what I was doing and then realized her kid threw it first. He heard it from Mom then.
- If the neighbors' house catches fire; call the fire department first, then take photos.

MORE POINTS ON BEING A GOOD NEIGHBOR

- If the dog next door gets loose, just catch him and tie him back up, don't be a jerk and call the dog catcher.
- When the woman next door locks herself out with the alarm system roaring full blast; and she is in her short negligee, at least offer to help her. Don't stand there checking her out. After you help her, *then* you can check her out.
- If the kid next door sneaks his girlfriend out of the house at 3 A.M.; you do not have to rat him out. His mother probably knows what is going on already. Moms' seem to know this stuff.
- If you hear the smoke alarm across the street going off, it might be polite to check things out instead of waiting for the flames to come through the roof.
- If you get sucked into buying one million dollars of life insurance, you do not have to turn the whole neighborhood on to the salesman.
- If the guy next door hit the lottery for a ton of money, don't get sore, it could have been you who won, if you weren't too cheap to play.
- In short if you want to be a good neighbor, let the Golden Rule apply.
- Communicate on the same page. The woman next door called me one day and said she wanted me to come over there and jump her. I had my pants down to my ankles before I realized she was talking about her car battery.

THE HOME WE ALMOST BOUGHT

When Janice and I were looking at houses; we did not look at lots of houses, maybe got inside 20 of them. In a buying situation, that is not a big number. At least not in my mind. We were pretty much open to a home that would be big enough for us and the dog. We had no kids, no plans to have any and we never did. That is fine with both of us.

We took a look at a home in Bradley Beach, NJ. This is a nice little shore town. It has beaches, a downtown, pizza places, movies. Decent place, crime rate is not bad. So we got to look at this one home there. I guess because it was in our price range, and was in really nice condition, we were impressed. We put $100 down on it to start the deal.

Now that I look back at the house, it was tiny. I bet it was no more than 500 square feet. The guy who owned it had put large mirrors in a couple of rooms which visually made it look a lot bigger. I do not know if he did this for his own use or to sell the place. There was no basement; just a crawl space with a small open area on the outside entrance part, sort of like I had in Beachwood. I felt like we were going to have to take the furniture apart to get it into the house.

Another thing; the guy who had the place had allergies, had a strip of grass that was about two feet by ten in front of the house. Everything else was poured concrete. Maybe I could paint the concrete green. There was a big heavy rail fence (the kind of fence you see on the side of a highway) running along the side of the property, a driveway, and a fish restaurant on that side.

So after we had given the $100 to the agent, Janice and I went to a diner to have lunch and talk things over. At this point we were still pretty excited about this deal. We had lunch and called our families to tell them we had bought a house.

Bedtime Horror Stories for Homeowners

About two or three weeks into the deal, we get this story. There is no clear title on the property. This is like trying to sell a car with no title. Who actually owns it? So we had the lawyer check this out.

The lawyer was some guy who a friend of ours had recommended. Patty had used him for some kind of deal, she said he was great and catered to her. I think he was just trying to get lucky with her.

So anyway he starts looking into this problem. Aside from the title business; the part of the property near the heavy fence had the chain link fence on the city property. Another problem.

So after about two months of silly negotiations and so on, we decided to drop the deal. By this time we had given them only that $100. We wanted out.

So the lawyer gives us this crap "You have to buy this house." All we have to do is die and pay taxes and we can skip the tax thing if we are willing to take a chance on going to jail. The dying thing is not an option.

We told him, "Drop the deal, and send us our $100 back with a bill for your services." Well it took him six months to do that. I could have built this house in six months. When we did get the bill, Janice was really pissed. She paid it; $100 a month for six months just to pay him back for trying to play us out. In between we found our present home.

At some point someone did work on this place. They added a second floor which was a good idea, better them than me.

THE VERY FIRST DAY IN YOUR OWN HOME

You will notice one item as soon as you move into the home. The woman knows almost by instinct, "Garbage Day". A woman can hear a garbage truck when it is started at the other end of town. She would never think of inviting the garbage man in for a cup of coffee or a cold beer; something about social status, but you can bet she knows when he will be there for the trash.

A thing about social status. I have been told a garbage man in New York City makes more money than a school teacher, and he does not even need a college degree, even if he has one. I don't know this as a fact, just passing on what I was told.

The garbage men are in fact, very important people to know, probably more important than the mailman; they help you get rid of the trash mail the mailman delivers. Think what your home would look like without these guys. A tip for you, kids.

When you decide to dump a ton or two of old plaster or tree limbs, get your body out there to help the men load it on the truck. Then tip them a few bucks for coffee. They are usually very appreciative of this type behavior.

It pays to stay in good with these guys. Suppose you lost your $100,000 a year job tomorrow, wouldn't it be nice to know that there was *someone* who would talk to you without looking down his nose!

You will get to know these fellows really quick when you move into the house. I don't care if this is a new home or an old home; there will be a lot of garbage going out in the first two weeks.

One of the things I did when I came home from my closing was to get a tight grip with two fingers on some fake brick wall covering made of plastic. I just held on as I walked through the kitchen, and the stuff came along with me. My house was pretty clean when I moved in but I still threw out some goodies.

Bedtime Horror Stories for Homeowners

Many people want to move in the day of the closing, and sometimes the house is ready. Most likely there will be a couple of days of cleaning up, redecorating and organizing first.

Now don't sit there whining. "It's my house; I want to move in today." GROW UP; THERE IS A GOOD CHANCE YOU'RE GOING TO BE THERE FOR A LONG TIME. MAKE THE MESS BEFORE YOU MOVE IN.

If the place just needs a fast paint job, just do that. The heavy decorating work can wait. You will never get the place completely the way you want it anyway. My wife said we would have the place perfect in three weeks, that was 30 years and $45,000 ago, and we are still doing things here. It never ends.

I remember moving into one of two houses which I have owned; the first move was over about 9 P.M. in a rainstorm. I had a big ten bucks in my pocket and had supper at Dunkin Donuts. We found the electric fuse box the next morning. A neighbor bailed me out with a spotlight and an extension cord.

The one thing I remember most about moving into my second home is that the move went so smooth it was scary. No breakdowns, no fights, no kids. No screaming, no fighting. After the move I remember lying in bed with my girlfriend Janice who I married six months later. She said "God this place is quiet." So to make her feel at home I farted.

You may feel the same way especially if you move away from some maniac who plays his stereo as if it were the sound system for a rock concert. Believe me you will get used to it.

YOU ARE NOW A HOMEOWNER

After the move you will have time to read over all the small print on the stuff you signed at the closing. You will not understand it any better, but at least you read it. You will also find a number of strange things will happen. Everyone you know will be giving you junk for your house. This was stuff they were going to get rid of anyway. You just saved them a trip to the dump.

You will realize there are a few things which you should keep from some of this junk. An old power mower beats tearing the short stuff out by hand.

You will soon discover that there are several items that you could use that nobody gave you. When my friends buy a house, I give them a one gallon paint can full of assorted nails, screws, hardware, plumbing washers and other assorted junk. It is amazing what proves to be useful.

Suddenly you will discover the true value of a hammer, a level, and a broom and also the value of shutting off light switches and keeping the thermostat at a reasonable level. Heat is suddenly an expensive item.

It will amaze you how the stuff that fit easily in a one bedroom apartment is suddenly filling an entire house.

Unless you are an artist, you will wonder where all the empty walls came from.

Your cat may be upset and start shitting in the sink. You may also get that upset.

Until you get used to them, you also will realize there are people looking at you from other houses. These are your neighbors.

Chapter 10 HUMAN PESTS

VANDALS, BURGLARS, RELIGIOUS FANATICS AND SALESMEN

These people all seem to fall into a general class: PESTS. Really, if you think about it; these people can cost you money, time and peace of mind.

VANDALS

These are usually local kids; they can be as young as five or as old as about 20. Half their problem; is that they are bored, the poor babies. Now some people would like to help these kids and that is fine with me. Where the hell are their parents and their upbringing?

If these kids were taught to do something useful with their time, they would be better off all around. Now if you feel you were put on this earth to help these kids, give it your best shot. If they respond, you are both doing better. If however this does not work; here are a couple of stories about vandals and how they were handled.

Many people have a problem with kids running through their property. If this happens only once in a while, it is no big deal but this can become a local cow path where the property and the owners suffer for it. The yard soon becomes a garbage pail, your privacy is a joke and if you say something you are a mean old S.O.B.

Most people I know who have this problem put up a good strong fence, maybe 6 feet tall and that solves the problem. Stockade fence is good for this, open pole fences are useless. My father had a house which bordered a cemetery; all the kids used the graveyard for a playground including yours truly. As long as we didn't do any damage, or cut through peoples yards nobody complained.

Some kids were lazy though; and instead of walking a couple hundred feet to the entrances, would take all the shortcuts through the yards. Dad got sick of this routine, he tried to be civilized and just put up a fence.

As a final measure, he simply painted the backside of the fence with a heavy coat of slow drying tar. After a few kids brought some of the stuff home on their hands and feet and fixed up Moms' carpets this business stopped.

One person households have a problem with vandals, especially if the person living there is elderly. I have heard some pretty ugly stories of kids harassing old people and so far the only recourse is either to call the cops or act crazy.

Now most kids today are not afraid of the police anymore, but they *are* afraid of crazy people. This is because crazy people play by their own rules. If for example you live in a two story house, and see some smart ass painting his name on the side of the house and are able to drop something like a pillow or a magazine, better to use a pot of hot dirty water, or possibly puke on him. He will get the idea.

One guy I knew had a problem with teenager's hot rod-ding in front of his house. This stopped when he threw a garbage can through some guys' windshield.

I had a problem with three juvenile delinquents; I mean poor misunderstood teenagers. Seems I got into a small argument with them one night. Well we seemed to end this with some talk and I thought it was over. Bullshit.

For about six months these guys would throw garbage on the property, steal things on me, and hot rod on the street. I called the cops a few times spoke to the kids a few times and also talked to their parents. Well, all the civilized stuff did not work, so I started using their type thinking. Yeah; I'm stooping to their level. Too bad.

I took to hanging out on the front porch with a pitchfork, but my timing was bad. After they had ripped my mailbox off the post a few times I wrapped it in barbed wire, and put tar over that. Of course I painted it the original color so as to look normal.

I would wait for them to whiz down the street with the cars and throw small logs under the wheels hoping they would kill themselves.

These methods sort of worked, but did not make them believe I really meant business. Then I went to a sport shop and bought a bear trap. To be polite; if this thing slammed shut on your leg, it is now half a leg. Even though I thought it would be nice to really catch one of these guys, my lawyer advised me against this idea.

Instead, I used a little psychological warfare. At the time, I had a wood stove with a lot of logs. I simply took the trap all over the area and especially to the homes of these kids and played it like Mr. Nice Guy. I acted as if I didn't really know who was causing the problems by my house and offered to help anyone else who had a problem.

"By the way, look what I got to take care of these kids." At which point I would produce the trap, and a two or three inch diameter piece of firewood. I would carefully set up the trap, drop the wood and ZZZZZAAAAAAAPPPPP!!!! I would have two pieces of wood, and splinters. I simply explained this trap was going on my property, under the pine needles and the kids were fair game. Suddenly and forever, the problem was gone. Amazing.

BURGLARS

Now here is a different type problem, much of which can be avoided with a little common sense. If you buy a new TV; don't be a dummy and leave the box sitting on the curb for three days, dump it as the garbage truck is coming up the street.

It doesn't pay to flap your mouth in public about expensive photo equipment or anything else that can be fenced easily. If you are selling a house, avoid open houses; I know if I were planning to hit a home, the open house would give me all kinds of good information. A little common sense goes a long way.

A loud dog is helpful, knowing your neighbors and looking out for each other is also useful. I mean if you are so scared of being hit, go live under a rock. If someone wants something bad enough, he will take it.

You could try hanging mirrors inside all the windows so the guy would scare himself to death, or put bars on the windows or a hundred foot deep moat around the home. Even a fish tank full of Piranha inside all the openings might be a good system.

A machete under the bed is not a bad idea, and neither is a gun if you do not have a wild temper. Don't do what one of my neighbors does. He has a sign on the front door. It reads something like. "Don't try to rob this house, we have guns and are not afraid to use them." I wouldn't let the bad guys know I was armed even if I had a machine gun in the house.

And remember if you do shoot someone, put a knife in his hand and say it was self-defense. Then again, if you have a really good food processor, you can always have a years' supply of dog food. Make sure you refrigerate it. The bones are OK too as long as they are not too soft.

Three fast stories. I have a brother who has a home in Tennessee. His adult son went to a gun show and came home with a trigger lock for a weapon. It did not occur to the son to unload the shotgun before he tried to attach the lock. He blew a 10 inch hole through the wall by the front door.

A guy I used to work with was a sort of electrical engineer type guy. His solution was to electrify all the aluminum siding on the outside of the home. Not enough to kill anyone, but enough to get their attention.

Another friend of mine who had a pistol, decided to try using his basement for a target range. This is not a big basement. He thought he hit his wife when he shot the gun and she started jumping around the basement screaming. She did not have the ear muffs on to stop the sound.

The guys who run alarm companies have told me burglars come in the windows and go out the doors. Keep that in mind.

Bedtime Horror Stories for Homeowners

RELIGIOUS FANATICS

Unless you live on the moon, you have been talked to by at least one of these persons. I seem to have the kind of face which tells these guys I need some sort of guidance or something. Even when I go on vacation, I'm approached by these people. The truth is that I have a hard time telling someone to get lost.

Even if I am not really interested I usually give the other person a chance to give me his pitch. I have even donated to causes I did not really understand because the guy had a good story.

Anyway, you can usually tell a religious fanatic. It is 90 degrees out and this guy is walking through town with a black suit, a briefcase, sometimes with children, and none of them even look warm. I would offer the guy and the kid cold beers if I thought they would take them.

Now these people are smart. They come around on weekends because they know they have a better chance of catching someone at home. This is also when I do a lot of work around the house. They usually knock on the door about the time I get done tearing out a wall and need a cold beer. As I sit on the porch floor, explaining to the dog the next part of the job I hear this small knock on the door.

Shit, they have caught me in the open. Quick, maybe I can tell them I don't speak English, or act deaf and dumb. Maybe the dog will scare them away. I could tell them I am illiterate. Well here they are; halos' and all.

This time I got snagged, but I'll tell you two excellent ways I have given these people the slip. Actually I have to give my ex-wife credit for one time. I'll tell you her story first. This happened when I owned my first house which was a summer home I converted to a year round residence.

One day we were planning to go somewhere, I don't remember where, but I know we were getting dressed up for it. Probably a wedding, one of the few reasons I wear a suit. I am standing out on the front porch in my jacket and waiting for her to get ready.

This lady used to like to wear a lot of makeup, so it is like waiting to get the car painted, so I had time to kill. I must have had a vacant look on my face when all of a sudden, along comes this guy in a suit and his halo and starts to talk to me.

Out of general courtesy, I started to listen, hoping Lorraine would get her act together and we could get going. Well after about fifteen minutes of this lecture, it was evident this guy was planning to talk till the next day and I had gotten caught big time. Lorraine was in the house and realized the situation. She also wanted to get going.

Now if you plan to do this stunt, make sure you can handle it. Lorraine was always an exhibitionist so this was right up her alley. About the time my brain is going into the dormant stage, she walks out on the porch in a black push-up bra and matching panties and says to me "We better get going before your wife comes home."

I thought this guy was going to break a toe getting off the porch. He took off like we were going to get hit by lightning and he did not want to be too close. Even after we split up, we would laugh about this incident.

Now the religious types are not always on the prowl, some of them are neighbors'. You have to stop these people as soon as they get started or you will never hear the end of it. Whatever you believe or think you believe is fine with me, just don't go nuts trying to get me there.

I have a friend in Pennsylvania who has a neighbor across the street. Now this story actually goes right in with the borders and visitors part. Her neighbor is maybe 60 years old, and is always preaching religion to Diana. It is not the same religion as Diana's but the woman got Diana to visit her church a few times. They wanted Diana to switch to her church also but that did not happen.

Somewhere in the mess, the neighbor's brother needed a place to stay for short time. He was coming out of some kind of drug rehab deal, and Carol, the neighbor talked Diana in to having him stay by her for a short time. This lasted several months.

Bedtime Horror Stories for Homeowners

Diana of course; got emotionally involved with the guy; sort of like bonding with a dog, but at the same time he was dating other women, and coming and going as if he was living with his mother.

Meanwhile Carol would quote religious stuff to Diana to try to make her think that everything was fine and dandy. This brother eventually moved out, but this pair; the sister and brother, have been a problem for over a year. Diana finally took my advice and stopped getting involved with either of them.

Diana has a sister; I think her name is Linda. She [Linda] comes home one day to find some religious nut trying to convert her kid. This kid is grown up, but I guess he did not want to appear too uncaring, so he let this woman talk to him.

Linda gets here just as the nut is going into high gear. The woman says to her "Do you feel you are living a good life?" "Of course." Linda answers. "ANNNTTTT" (Like the sound of a buzzer on a quiz show). The nut is trying to imitate a buzzer. "No, you are not."

A few seconds go by; the nut says "Do you think your children are leading good lives?" Linda answers. "Certainly they are." "ANNNTTT" again the fake buzzer sound. "No, they are not." a pause...."Do you expect to go to Heaven?" before Linda can get her "Yes" all the way out of her mouth, the nut says "And your kids?" "Do you expect them to go to Heaven?" Faster now, Linda answers. "Yes, I do." Again "ANNNTTT" "You are wrong."

At this point, Linda has had enough. Says to the lady. "Do you expect us to join your religion?" The nut says "Yes" Linda says "AANNNNNNTTT" "You are out of here" Gave her a dose of her own medicine. Threw her annoying butt out of the house.

I have a neighbor who has turned out to be a nice guy and his family is fine also, but when I first met him, I could not carry on a conversation with him about *anything* without getting some quotation from the Bible. If I talked to him about my coffee mug, he would have some verse to bring up about this. I figured I had a problem neighbor on my hands.

Fortunately he has backed off considerably and we get along fine now. But, I've got to tell you what I did to the poor guy the day he was moving in. I couldn't let the God thing go.

The day he was moving in was a beautiful summer day; 75 degrees, blue sky, clear. You could not pay for weather like this. Now I decided to have some fun with him. I play guitar and one item I have is an amplifier with big speakers, sort of like a DJ would own. It has 150 watts. That is enough power to make all the windows in my house rattle, or at least the old windows that were here when I moved in. So the day he was moving in, I knew he was coming in about 9 A.M. so I put the speakers in my bedrooms which are upstairs. I kept them a couple feet back from the windows. I have a tape with the sound of thunder on it. I use this for Halloween parties. I also have a reverb system that makes me sound like I am in a cave.

I waited till Don (the new neighbor) is trying to get a big padded chair into the house. Now I have been in his house and know how it is laid out, so I know that he will have to make a sharp right to get the chair into the living room. He is outside the house, trying to get this chair into the doorway, and I start with the thunder over his head.

You could hear this for about 2 city blocks. I know, because I tested it earlier. Now I let the thunder run for about 30 seconds, backed down the volume a bit and get on the microphone with the reverb.

"YO, DON......GET THAT STUFF IN THE HOUSE BEFORE IT GETS WET." (You didn't know God was Italian? Vatican / Pope?)

Then I fired up the thunder again for about a half minute. He is looking up at the sky which is clear as glass and I am laughing so hard I almost wet my pants.

I came downstairs about 20 minutes later and he asked me if that was me. I had to come clean and tell him the truth. I also told him anything crazy goes on in the neighborhood it usually leads back to me. We did get a good laugh out of it.

I DON'T LIVE HERE

This is a stunt I used one day which saved me a lecture and a half. I was standing in my driveway talking to my neighbor Ray, when he motions there was someone near my house. I should have realized the fact that he motioned and was quiet that it was someone I didn't really want to have visit.

He motioned to me and then disappeared into his tool shed. This guy is no fool. God will get me for this one. These two old black ladies are knocking on the side door and the dog is going crazy. Noah the dog was not all that big, about 40 pounds but he was extremely convincing.

He is bouncing off the storm door with about 100 teeth showing and barking his tail off. The ladies knock a couple more times, turn around and notice me. By now I've had a chance to get my wits together. I tell them that I was here to collect some money from the owner of the house.

I concocted the story how I had done some carpentry work for the creep and he was supposed to meet me here and all I got was an empty house and this rotten mutt. "And don't go near that dog, he is a nasty S.O.B." With that, I said I was leaving, and would try to catch him later. Got in the van and split on the double. With my luck, these ladies will buy a copy of this book and be back next week.

One guy told me the story about a friend of his. This religious guy came around to visit this old neighbor. The neighbor is about 90 years old. Says to the old guy, "God has a message for you." To which the old guy replied, "My name is Harry Smith, and I have a message for you. "Get the f**k out of here."

Make sure you read the part in chapter 18 about religious wars in the hood.

SALESMEN

The above techniques for the Vandals, Burglars and Religious Fanatics can be used on sales people. But a quicker way to get rid of them is this approach. Say yes to anything they are selling. You need a $1000 vacuum cleaner, a car, a magazine subscription. Say Yes...Yes...Yes...and then send the guy on his way.

If you decide to keep the item, fine. You just made a deal. If not, many states have a three day cooling off period where a consumer is allowed three days to cancel the deal. Check out your state for this.

This law is due thanks to companies such as an alarm company I know of which would sell you a system on a Friday night and have the crew out there on Saturday morning 7A.M. to install the system before you had a chance to change your mind.

VISITORS AND BORDERS

This is a strange item to put in this book, but one I feel belongs here. We all have been in this mess at one time or another. We all know someone who says they are going to visit, and *never* do. Give you an example; I have a cousin who lives about 20 miles away. His barber is 3 blocks from my house. I can walk there, or take my bicycle.

He goes to this guy because he supposedly gets these great haircuts. Mind you this cousin is no movie star to start with. He has a large nose, and a gut. No matter what gets done with his hair, it is not going to do that much good.

He will call me from the barbers shop to let me know he is there. Big deal. I get my hair cut on the other end of town. He is also there at 6:30 A.M. even though the place opens at 8 A.M. The funny thing is that there is usually a line in front of this shop. The barber has these guys trained like puppies. This is not the part I wanted to tell you about but just give you some background.

Bedtime Horror Stories for Homeowners

Whenever cuz wants to get together; it goes like this. "Come on down, we are here." Sure they are. These people never go anywhere. They buy $50,000 cars with a navigation system and never drive out of town except to visit his brother once a year at the other end of the state. He will have a car for 3 years and trade it in with maybe 17,000 miles on it. Hell, I do that much driving in six months.

When we do visit, it is because we are sick of hearing him whine like a baby. His stupid TV is on 24/7 and he will look over my shoulder to watch some dumb ass show while we are trying to visit. Meanwhile, he can be driving through my town and not even come near my house.

Not like I live in a dump. If anything, mine is bigger than his, and a lot more visually appealing. Maybe it is my dogs who want to sit near him that freak him out. That is one guy.

When my father was alive he had a brother who would call up and say, "Hey Jimmy, we are in the area, want to get together." It was only after a short conversation that Pop would find out that the brother has been in the area for a week and was leaving the next day.

Dad used to say that if my mother died first, he was going to keep a black book full of people's names that pissed him off so he would have a record of who was pulling this stuff.

I have an aunt who pulls the same stuff. She will visit the town fifteen minutes away and then when I invite her, she always has some stupid excuse why she can't make it. Like she has to re-arrange her underwear drawer.

Now I go to the other extreme. I have a friend who has a 4 bedroom home. She should dump it and get rid of her son in the process. This guy is in his 40's with a good job. He should have a place of his own where he can bring girls to do the dirty deed.

At one time I met a guy I will call "Glen" who had a house trailer. I introduced him to a lady who I thought might work out with him. In about 10 days, he had sold his trailer; moved in with her, and was telling everyone they were married. That is strange enough.

He was sort of overbearing, and she finally threw him out. She tells everyone it is a medical problem that when she gets intimate with someone it gives her physical pain. I personally think the only pain there was him. So now he comes to me with his tale of woe. Now if you can believe this, he supposedly owns two pieces of rental property his parents left to him.

Either that, or he screwed them out of it. So now he was looking for a new place to live. I suggested to him to get a home equity loan and pick up a senior citizen house somewhere. Good thinking.

Now he has never had to float a loan for a house seeing as his were left to him, so he is basically clueless. At this point I feel sorry for him, and try to help him work things out. So I suggest to him. "Why not move in by my friend?" I will call Jackie and they can work out some kind of rent till he gets situated. "Oh you are so wonderful; I would give her $750 a month just for a room." He was so grateful; you would think I was also finding him a new girlfriend.

At this time Janice and I would visit with these two and play Rummy Q which is a game the senior citizens play. My mom showed me the game years ago.

So we would go there every week and play this game. Meanwhile; Jackie has not gotten a dime from Glen. We told both of them they should discuss the money issue one of these days. Now, Jackie has three small dogs she runs in agility trials, and since these poor mutts are in cages most of the time, they are frustrated and bark a lot.

Glen says this is like living at the SPCA. (If it is that bad, well move out. Duh). One night we got over there to play Rummy Q and Janice casually mentions "Did you two ever work out your money?"

To look at Glens face; you would think he was hit in the head with a ball peen hammer; a big one, a very big one. He got really quiet and copped an attitude the rest of the night. The following weekend he skipped out while Jackie was at a dog trial. She has never gotten a dime from him. We now refer to him as "Skip" as in "skipped out." I hear he got remarried, I hope the woman is wearing gyp proof undies.

Chapter 11 MODERN CAVE DWELLERS AND OLD HOMES,

GOING UNDERGROUND

No, I have not been sitting at this machine too long! There are people who truly live in underground houses. The cave people knew what they were doing; they just were not as formal as we are today.

Now before you turn a thumb down on underground houses, think about this. Have you ever been to a shopping mall which has parts of stores built into the hills of the parking lot? Those stores have an underground location and they don't feel wet and buggy and all that nonsense. If the taped music is shut off you would also notice a fairly quiet room.

People who have done some decent research into this style house have come up with books on them and they are usually a well-built home with concrete walls and roofs. This entire structure is usually built into a south facing hill with the south side having a lot of glass for solar gain (that is heat from the sun).

The concrete floors and walls absorb this solar energy and help heat the home. This is on top of the fact that about ten feet below the ground, the temperature stays at about 55 degrees all year, winter, summer, cold, hot or otherwise. Simply put, the earth is a poor conductor, so when the air temperature changes on top, it stays pretty much the same down there.

I honestly do not want to go on and on about just the energy efficiency of this type home, better you buy a book on them and get all the facts straight instead of here. But I will say the system does work.

If the original underground temperature is 55 degrees, it is not going to take much energy to kick it up to 70; you will have no reason to even think about air conditioning.

There are no conventional roofing materials. The roof is usually concrete and protected by a rubber membrane and four feet of dirt, this baby is going to last a long time.

I had the good luck to take a look at a place like this in Colorado a few years ago. The guy had bought the place and got all the specs on it when he did. He only had about a foot of dirt over the roof, but the front of the place was tilted 12 degrees back off vertical to help absorb sunlight, he had solar collectors with water on the roof where the water went through radiant heating tubes in the concrete floors and was stored in a 500 gallon tank at night.

His biggest expense was the electricity needed to pump the water. He could have been lying to me, but had no reason to do that. He said he was heating the place for about a quarter a day. I could live with this. The size of the place was about 1500 square feet.

Most of the homes I have seen like this; are built sort of like a long ranch house with the long side facing south, with a lot of glass on that side. This is only a general idea and not to be taken into every detail. Now if you decide to get involved with a home like this, let me give you a few ideas.

First of all, research the hell out of the houses; make sure you know a lot about the construction of them. Remember; if it leaks after it is built, the outside walls are not going to be easy to repair. By the way; concrete *is* porous so make sure you have a good drainage system and a waterproofing system on the outside. Make sure this works or you will have the indoor swimming pool you always wanted, a few drops at a time.

Either you should be born rich, or know someone who will help you get the house off or under the ground. Financial institutions are sort of wimpy with new ideas, and to an average bank, this is like reinventing the wheel. Make sure you check out the local building codes, it is going to be tough adding windows after the place is buried up to the roof.

Make sure that everyone who will be living there will feel okay, when the place is done. If someone feels like he or she is living in a hole in the ground, it's going to be rough.

Last, but not least, try to make a list of the good and bad points of the home. While some people like a place that is as quiet as a tomb, someone else may feel it is just that. While you may get a kick out of mowing the roof, your wife may like to look at it from a window instead from inside the home. You can always keep a couple of sheep on the roof to keep it groomed if you think you need a pet.

It is really nobody's business but yours; but is your family and friends going to give you a lot of ribbing about living underground? If this happens, leave your heating bill lying around sometime when you invite them to visit in zero degree weather.

One more point, make sure your property is marked off or fenced to keep campers from setting up on your roof. With my sick sense of humor, I would play loud music under their tent all night and let them think they have discovered something special.

HISTORIC HOMES

Let me give you my take on these places. They are old buildings. Get it! Old houses, old barns, old grist mills, whatever.

As much as some historians may rant and rave about these places, they are not as special as some people like us to think. My house is old, I would say close to 100 years old and I can appreciate that. One reason is that it did not cost me a ton of money, plus it does what we need.

Some of these old places have managed to get on the historic site list. I forget the exact title, but basically it means someone has acknowledged that the place is old, big deal. My brother in law has a house like this. Huge windows, original siding, 11-foot high ceilings and heat bills that are like the national debt.

The other group of these historic homes is the ones that park systems and the government pick up and turn into tourist traps, or so they think. We have a few of these in New Jersey. My county alone has at least three of them, which are passed off as historic farms or homesteads.

There is one here that has so few visitors, that one guy who worked there told his wife that big thrill of the day was having the cat food delivered. The place was so quiet, that when visitors would show up all the "historic site interpreters" (*translation...* "Tour guide/janitor/ maintenance man/groundskeeper") would rush out to meet these people just so they could run the spiel about the place. It is sort of pathetic to watch this group in action, especially if one of them is really serious about the stuff.

And talk about being picky about the place. It was clean as a whistle. And why not? What the hell else is there to do when nobody visits? Was this because of the poor marketing efforts or lack of effort? I don't know. I was told they had the cleanest bathrooms in the state, and probably the most bored help there too.

Then again, I was told the manager of the place lives two city blocks from the park. The guy, who told me this, said the manager does not have a life anyway. Now remember, this again is *his* humble opinion. I don't know all the details; I just pass along what I was told. So if you love this stuff, enjoy it.

The other side of some of these old buildings is that sometimes they get converted to retail stores or restaurants. If they have lasted 100 years, I am sure they will make it through another 100.

The people who convert these to commercial use at least insulate them and put energy efficient windows in the buildings. Some of the people who own the "historic" homes will not do this, because they are afraid of losing the "historic" value of the home. The only thing I see as history is the owners' cash. Their money will be history due to the owner paying huge energy bills.

A short note here about my house. As I stated before; it is old and when we moved in here, walking around inside in the winter was like being outside. We have done considerable renovation work here which includes new double pane windows and lots of insulation. Now if we want, we can walk through here summer and winter in our underwear and feel fine.

Chapter 12

GETTING WET AND NAKED, THE WEDDING DAY

This was an exciting day; we were ready for it, at least in our minds. Janice and I had lived together for a couple of years before we got married. I had one bad marriage in my baggage. Janice did not, but she had some old boyfriends in the past. Neither of us were stupid, so we wanted to check each other out before we did the legal thing.

I remember when we did the closing on the house. Jan's mother said to the lawyer something about us getting married. He said "We can do that in the next room." Well it did not happen that day, but about six months later.

I think what made up our minds was when my father died on Valentine's Day 1983. We figured maybe it was time to stop fooling around and make it a marriage. So we made plans for May. I am sure there were people who thought we were pregnant. We were not, never were. We have survived fine without kids. Our dogs are our kids.

We made some plans, set up a room at a local restaurant, got the church thing worked out. The priest realized the speeches about how to make a marriage work were moot as soon as he saw we had the same address and phone number. We would not lie to a priest. We don't do that.

Then we went to JC Penny and got Janice a nice dress in the prom department. She could not see blowing $1000 on something she was going to wear once. I agreed. The veil? Talk about a rip off. These were going for about $150. Crafts store special. Lace and a barrette, ten bucks. I was in a crafts store the other night and see they sell these now plus a lot of other stuff to help run a wedding, about time.

We wanted to have Noah; the dog, to be the ring bearer. The church said Noah was not an assist dog so that was out. I guess I should have worn dark glasses and a cane.

We designed our own invitations. Very novel, very readable

Bedtime Horror Stories for Homeowners

See this type lettering? This, you can read. Script lettering? Get lost. I hate the stuff. It takes me an hour to figure out who is getting hitched. "*This is a sample of script type lettering.*"

We even had these reply cards for people who could, or could not make it. They were done in a comic style. They had multiple replies you could check off like "Yes" or "I can't make it because I am going to an orgy." or "My dog is making his Communion that day." Or the always simple. "Other" You get the idea. We wanted to have fun.

The day started off fine, the weather was decent. We were not getting married until 11A.M., so we had time on our hands. This was good for me as I had been doing wallpaper in the kitchen the night before. I am not real fast with wallpaper. I got finished at six in the morning, got about two hours sleep and got with the program.

Jan's sister Gloria was the bridesmaid. She got down here I guess about 9 or 9:30. As long as she was ready when the action started I didn't care what time she got here. When she arrived, Janice was cutting the front lawn. She was in a tee shirt and cut offs. There is a small patch of grass we call our lawn. It is so small I have done it with a weed whacker.

Gloria drove up, parked her car and almost had a hemorrhage when she saw Janice cutting the grass. "What are you doing, you are getting married at 11 o'clock?" She says in disbelief. "What does it look like, I am cutting the grass?" That was the end of that discussion.

My brother Bob showed up later. He figured, he is not getting married. What is the big rush? The antique cars arrive, two of them. I forget what kind of cars they were, but one looked like it came out of a mob movie. The other one had a jump seat.

My neighbor Ray was hanging out in the driveway. His driveway ran parallel to mine. I came out of the house all dressed up with a tux. He is amazed, he has never seen me all prettied up like this. "Hey Paul, where you going all dressed up?" "To a wedding, Ray." I guess I barely knew him and Gloria at this point, so that is the reason we did not invite them to the wedding.

When I told him it was ours, he was amazed. He thought we were already married. Not like you wear a shirt that has printed on it "Living in Sin." We got ourselves together, did the church thing, got some photos and headed for the reception.

By the way, somewhere along the line the weather crapped out and got cloudy. The guy who was shooting my pictures screwed up an adjustment on his camera. Shot about 6 rolls of film, got about 4 shots that looked any good. I shot a wedding for a friend of ours one time, came out fine. Way too much stress. Screw it up, and they may be mad at you for years.

We did get enough photos to fill an album. Got them from other people, blew them up, and took the pics out of the wedding album from my first marriage where we never filled out the information. We ended up with an album. God did get me for this. We are looking for another album. Mice ate the cover off this one. We got one from a professional photographer so I gave up on repairing the first one.

The reception was nice; people came back, more beer, more party. People stayed over that night. We didn't need the honeymoon deal. We had been screwing for three years. We are married 30 years now and Janice is still putting up with me. We plan to grow old together. Janice has three sisters and two brothers, and when I tell you I got the pick of the litter, believe me.

WATER PRESSURE

A drain is tough to fix, but there is one big advantage in a drain over a water line. There is no pressure on a drain. The water goes through with gravity, and only leaks when someone is pouring water through it. Simple.

You have never had a good time with water until you work with a water line under pressure. Now that is fun. What I mean about a pressurized line is this; a pipe with water is pretty stable till someone turns on a faucet. Then the water is moving. OK, we all brush our teeth I hope, so you know what I mean.

Now the water pressure in my neighborhood is about 80 pounds per square inch coming in from the street. To give you an idea of what this is about for you guys who are not too sharp on math, here is the picture. Let's say you weigh 160 pounds, and the tip of your finger is one inch in diameter. That means if you could stand on two fingers, there is your 80 pounds per square inch. Even if you were REALLY STRONG, you probably could not support that kind of weight. So maybe that gives you some idea of what I am talking about.

Though in reality, I actually did see some guy do this on TV once. ONCE. I am in pretty good shape and the best I can come up with is a few one handed push-ups, big deal.

Well, anyway, I think I made my point. Now here is the reason I went through this one minute physics class. I want to tell you about my water main experience.

THE MAIN WATER LINE FIASCO

About six months after we moved into the house, Janice and I decided to get married. We all had a good time, had a lot of people back to the house after the ceremony and the reception. Unfortunately my dad had died the previous February 14th. He would have had a good time.

After the wedding we had decided to go to Washington D.C. For about 5 days. I will not go into that trip. That alone would make a good story. The reason I even mention this is that when I go away for more than a couple of days; I usually shut off my main water supply. This habit goes back to when I lived at home.

We had gone away for five or six days and when we were gone a ⅜ inch water line that fed the toilet broke and flooded the first floor of the house. You cannot believe how much water this is until it happens.

Better to believe me, than to have to live through it. At the time, we had to punch holes in the basement ceiling just to release the trapped water. The clean-up took us longer than the vacation lasted. So back to my present house.

As we were leaving, I explained to Janice my reason for closing off the water and went down the basement to close the valve. Of course, with old houses, come old plumbing and valves. I turned the valve clockwise till it went off with a soft "Ping!" I didn't even have to check it, but I knew. I HAD SNAPPED THE VALVE.

I can't exactly explain how I knew it, but I guess it's about the same as when a woman has her period; she knows it without needing any visual clues. Well big as life, at least the valve was broken in the off position so I felt I didn't have to worry about a leak. To hell with it, I'm going on a trip; I'll fix it when I get back. So for a few days we went off on the honeymoon.

We were campers at the time so we stayed outside Washington D.C. in a local campsite. We got home on a Friday night if I remember right. It was raining hard; we were tired, grubby and sick of driving in the bad weather. We also needed the bathroom. In case you do not know it, your toilet is flushed by your water supply.

Well, me being a gentleman, I let Janice have a shot at the pot, and I went in the yard with the dog. He had his trees and I had mine. We only had enough water in the tank for one good flush so Janice got that one. I even suggested we stay at a motel, but Janice wanted to sleep in her own bed. At least we had some water left in the icebox in the van to make coffee and get washed up. I was a big sport and took her out for breakfast the next morning.

After breakfast, we returned home to unpack and get the water going again. The unpacking was easy, I let her do it. Now I had planned in my mind how to repair the problem with the water valve. See, the valve is located on a ¾" pipe which enters the basement near the steps. It is about four feet from the floor, between the wall and the hot water heater. Well, I had stopped by Herb to pick up a new valve.

He sold me a beautiful brass compression fitting type valve. With this type valve there is no soldering, All that has to be done is to cut out a section of pipe a little shorter than the length of the compression fitting, slide the sections of the valve over the cut ends and tighten the big nuts into place. Sounds pretty simple, and it is simple. The new valve I installed between the original valve and the rest of the house. That idea was so I would not have to worry about the water pressure when I installed it. Now the new valve went in like nothing, all I have to do now was to get the old valve open to start the water flowing again.

The reason I did not shut off the water at the street was I was afraid the old valve there would also snap (it did at a later date, and has since been replaced) and to get the water company out there to shut off their valve at the curb seemed to be too much a pain in the butt.

So, in order to keep some of the pressure off the valve where I was working, we opened all the valves in the rest of the house, including the outside hose. After all, with everything open, how much pressure could be left in the main line? I'll tell you how much. I still feel like I am going to drown when I tell this story.

All I did now was to remove the old handle and the nut on the outside of the valve and screw the broken shaft out of the valve. Nothing happened, at least not for about three seconds. Next thing, is that the water pressure blew the little piece of valve left in the pipe straight out of the hole. So now there is water coming out of every pipe in the house including the one level with my chest. Not being the type person who panics easily, I decided all I had to do was to force the broken stem into the valve and put the nut back on. In theory, I was perfectly correct. Of course, theory in this case means nothing. Something about draining the swamp and being up to my ass in alligators.

By now Janice is looking down the steps watching this water flood her basement and giving me a shower. "What should I do?" she asks. "Get my board, surf's up!" I try to maintain my sense of humor at times like this. Well Janice decides to call the water company at this point. Have you ever tried to call the water company? Really? The first number she gets is a recording giving the company hours and some other phone numbers.

Of course, between the time the phone answered and the voice starts, there is music playing. Now you must remember, nobody calls the water company to just talk to someone. There are only a couple of reasons people call the water company, either to report a leak or to bitch about a bill.

You know the music is going to be something soft like Ray Conniff or something else of a soft soothing nature. In the callers state of mind; Jimmy Hendrix or Led Zeppelin would not be conducive to resolving the problem. So there are a few bars of this soft stuff DA DI DA DI DA DA, DE DA DE DA.

Meanwhile Janice can visualize her house floating down the street. By now, she was looking for life preservers. After about 30 seconds of this nonsense, the recording tells Janice where to call to report a leak.

Now, the water company has a lot of water, so most leaks are not that important, as long as it isn't a fire plug. So when she calls the leak reporting number, she gets more soft music. At this point Janice has mentally kissed the house and me goodbye.

BACK AT THE SCENE OF THE CRIME

While Janice is playing with the phone I have been trying to get the valve repaired. The only problem here, is that when I place the broken part into the opening, it causes the water to spray out in three hundred sixty degrees. It looks like the spray heads that are used to cool off kids in the summer.

I had to go after the valve about four times before I could get the thread to catch at all. Meanwhile I felt like I was going to drown due to the power of the water spraying in my face. At some point, I did manage to get the valve back together. Thank you God, I appreciate the help.

Actually; it only took me about five minutes to do this, but five minutes goes pretty slow in this type situation. We got off pretty light; a small flood, some wet beams and a good excuse for getting my clothes off in front of the horny young wife.

Chapter 13   YOU BALANCE THE CHECKBOOK,
              I WILL RIP OFF THE ROOF

There are several skills that you as the homeowner might want to have. Some of these are more important than others and take more technical training. Let me explain. When I met Janice, I had spent several years doing renovation work so I at least had some idea of how to fix things. Janice was a nurse; health care she knew, most of these other skills she is sort of learning as we go along. I've got to give it to her, she is a worker. No matter what kind of job she does, she does it well. I will give you an example.

THE BACK YARD

One area that was a disaster when we moved in was the back yard. Somewhere along the story here I probably mentioned that Janice had an ability to clean up the yard; not just with a rake but with a machete. It is my machete, but she is the one who used it the most on the yard. When I started working on the inside problems here she must have felt that with her limited technical knowledge there was something she could do. Now the back yard was always there, but as Janice put it "I didn't know I had a yard, all I saw was weeds"

This was due in part to the fact that the home had been owned by a nice old lady whose husband had died a number of years ago and she was in no shape to do any heavy work herself and only had limited help from her family. There were fences on the sides of the yard, and a garage in the back which belongs to another neighbor.

To look at the yard from the kitchen window, it looked as if the yard was about 10 feet wide and 20 feet deep. The weeds had taken over; this was their territory. At least till Janice showed them who was the boss.

She got back there with a rake, a machete, some garbage bags and work gloves. If anyone was hiding in the bushes they were as good as dead. I am not big on landscaping. God put the plants there; let him take care of them. Janice changed all of this for us. Due to her hard work, we found things there that we did not know even existed there. Jan found and tore up single handed the old foundation from an old garage, a half dozen fence posts, about a mile of vines, 2,000,000 stickers and the sticker bushes that they belonged to.

Janice found wire, rope, old pipes, lumber and bricks, she dug up two small stumps but instead of killing herself trying to pull them out, we used the trusty old van and a chain. She has made the grass grow again, defined the property lines, helped me put up some stockade fence and a tool shed and generally made the yard look a lot better.

Now to read this, you might think Janice is built like a gorilla. Quite the opposite. It is just that she uses her brains when she does the work and is a good worker. Nobody will ever be able to call her lazy. Plus she helps cut the grass and plants flowers, what a woman!

MORE SKILLS

If you owned the dog before you met her, don't expect her to clean up the mess when he goes on the rug. If you are the cook in the family, and the other half is the cleaner-upper and you can settle this system, go with it. It will make meals a lot easier. If neither of you can do either decently, better eat out a lot. You can always turn the kitchen into a game room.

If one of you is good at handling money, and the other one spends his bread like it is water; you know who better run the checkbook. If neither of you like to do any work at all, you probably didn't buy this book or the house in the first place. If you both have a lousy sense of color or design, find someone whose home impresses you and hire them to decorate your place. Or do as a friend of mine does; look in design magazines and copy what is done there. That is not always the cheapest way out, but it does work.

MORE ON MAINTAINING THE CASTLE

There are a number of skills you may want to acquire when you buy a home. This is not because you want to work with your hands, or because it is good therapy. It is a matter of survival. It is simple economics, money and time. Have you ever tried to get a plumber to come over and stop a leaky faucet? It would be easier to get the Pope to come over and bless the house, or give the last rites to your dog. (You didn't tell me your dog was Catholic). There are a lot of jobs any $100,000 a year executive or his family can learn. One of the simplest is:

PAINTING

The only thing that makes this any easier than anything else, is that there are items like water based paints and rollers. Water based paints use water to help make the paint. It is easier to clean up than oil based paints and even though this paint has an odor, it goes away quickly and is really not too bad on the lungs.

There is one item that I ran across years ago which is called Goof Off which is used to remove dried water based paints. If you use this stuff make sure you have a lot of ventilation or do not use it at all.

It seems sort of harmless in the little yellow can, but the stuff will make you feel like you had a heart attack after it gets into your system. Better to wipe the wet paint with a soapy rag and water.

Now through my many years I have noticed one thing about men. Many men hate to paint. I guess if a guy is doing it for a living, he can justify the work, but at home? Most guys would rather do almost anything else. Mix a two hundred foot concrete sidewalk by hand? No problem. Paint the five by five foot bathroom, no way.

I think I know the reason why this situation exists. There is nothing macho about painting a bathroom or any room unless of course there is a 20 foot high ceiling involved. This would take either a scaffold or a really tall ladder.

Now the old guy can sit back with his beer, and talk about how he was 18 feet off the floor and the dog decided to join him. Too bad the dog is 90 pounds and shakes like hell four feet off the floor. Of course this guy is not going to tell you how his ass is taking a bite out of his Jockey shorts while he is doing the job. Aside from jobs like this, a lot of men consider painting to be woman's work and most women are pretty good at it.

The reason behind this is pretty obvious. Most clean-up work is done by the lady of the house. Guys do not realize this; they seem to think things like dirty dishes and dust just take care of themselves like magic. Now, if a woman makes a mess while painting, she is stuck with it. The only time you may get a man of the house to paint is when he can impress someone with the job.

This may be as simple as trying to show off to Junior that he can climb a ladder to the edge of the roof, or show off to the young hottie living next door. (God; what a stud, or possibly, look at that old fool up there on that ladder). This brings us to another exterior job that may require attention.

ROOFING

If your wife knows how to do roofing and does not mind humping ninety pound bundles up there; by all means let her do the job. On the other hand, if she is superstitious and will not clean the house in any week with a Friday; maybe you will do the cleaning. Most people do not really like to get up on the roof of a house. It's not bad if you are talking about a low pitch roof or one which is only one story high.

Most of us can live with that. I know some people who cannot even stand to watch someone work on a roof. Now someone who does this work for a living has either nerves of steel or some other metallic body parts, is possibly a little crazy or has convinced himself that it is just as easy to die on the ground as it is to die three stories up.

Unless you have acquired the necessary skills, guts and confidence, do yourself a favor and stay off the roof. Leave the roof to the pros and the birds.

CONCRETE PATIOS AND SIDEWALKS

Most men really do not know a hell of a lot about concrete. Many people call it cement when cement is only one ingredient in the mixture; you also need water, rocks, or sand. If is not mixed into the correct proportions, you will have a patio the cat can dig up and use for a litter box.

A lot of guys get a big kick out of pouring a concrete patio or a sidewalk. There is a lot of real macho shit involved here. You have the concrete truck, which is the size of a dinosaur, it is loud, and makes the ground shake. You have the preparation work with the forms which are all nailed together with large nails and heavy hammers.

The guys get all sweated up, just like a pro athlete and drink beer while pouring the stuff, and cuss a little while trying to make it go in the right places. The guys can ogle the women, and act like they are some kind of big muscle man and the homeowner can act like a big sport and tip the truck driver $20.00. Plus when the concrete is hard the guy can compare it to at least one part of his anatomy. My wife compares it to my skull.

ELECTRICAL WORK

Now here is a talent which can make or break a homeowner. The guy or woman can really look like a hero or a fool in the time it takes to make a spark. There is also a simple reason for this situation. Mainly; many people are scared to death of electricity. We have all seen movies involving lightning or a trip to the electric chair. This makes a big impression on us.

Bedtime Horror Stories for Homeowners

The trick here is to use logic when you attempt this type work. Standing in a puddle in the basement and wiring a fixture with the power still on is usually good for a punk type hairdo, like hooking up outside lights in the rain. When, or if you decide to take a shot at this work, remember to shut off either a circuit breaker or a fuse before you attempt the job. Shutting the switch off does not always work as there may still have power in part of the line and this might give you a good surprise.

As with many jobs around the house, it pays to do this one dressed to go out if need be. If you have to be rushed to the hospital or set the house on fire I'm sure you do not want to do this in your flip flops and Mickey Mouse boxer shorts. It pays to either take an Adult Education course on this work, or learn it from someone who knows what they are doing before you pick up a nickname such as Sparky or Zaaappp. If you are standing behind someone who is doing this type work, it may seem funny to make a noise like BZZZZ when they touch two wires together, I am sure they will love you forever for this.

TILE WORK

It's not necessary, but it helps if you have a name like Vito or Tony and do this work. It seems Italians have a natural ability to take a box full of tiny bits of ceramic pieces and make a floor with them. Most of this work is pretty easy once you get the hang of it, but tile men try to make you think they are brilliant when they do it for you.

The floor tiles usually come in a one foot square sheet which is attached to a backing. The entire unit is glued to the floor, and when the glue dries, the floor is grouted with a material which either looks like plaster or cement depending on which type grout is used. Most of the fancy design work has been done at the factory and this is a good job for helping a man get out of the doghouse. In a few hours he can install a new floor where there was an old crummy looking linoleum floor and say "I did it by myself."

If you are doing larger tiles; like 5 or 6 inch, make sure you use a backer board instead of plywood for a sub floor. This will help eliminate cracks after installation.

Wall tile is similar, but basically it works the same way except vertically. The main trick here is to strike a level line for the bottom line of tile, make sure you stay on that line and continue the process in whatever direction leads up.

There are tools used to cut tile, one looks like it would be used to trim elephants toe nails and there is another one which looks sort of like a glass cutter. They are used in either cutting straight lines or chipping out small sections. The best part of this work is it is bisexual; mainly both men and women can do it without too much problem.

PLUMBING WORK

God may have created both lighting and water but it was man who has done his best to domesticate them. Water is essential to the survival of all life and we all have become used to the idea that you turn on a faucet and out it comes either hot or cold. The system usually works that way, but there are occasional breakdowns.

These usually occur when your mother-in-law is coming for a four day visit. About the time she rings the bell, a cold water pipe decides to leak in the wall. You know which wall, the one you just finished paneling and trimming. Needless to say, this is going to be a fun job.

Now no matter who uses the water in a home it is always the man who gets stuck fixing the pipes. Not that he knows any more about them then the rest of the family, it is just that he feels that most men figure that at least if they do the job it will get done right, yeah sure.

A few other theories are that some guys get off handling pipes of various lengths; something with their manhood. This kind of work also lets a guy use cuss words he has forgotten he knew or invent a few new ones.

When he is under a kitchen sink wedged between the Ivory Liquid, a can of bug spray, pots and a leaky pipe, cuss words are almost a religious experience.

Men usually thrive on the grimy and skuzzy. They don't often admit this but plumbing work gives them an outlet to play with a lot of really messy stuff.

This type also get a big kick out of showing the wife and kids a two inch pipe which is 90% full of God Knows What and giving them a lecture about washing grease and coffee grinds down the drain. The grosser the mess, the better he likes it.

When working on sewer pipes, a lot of guys will find a bunch of not quite digested tampons blocking the pipe. This usually gives the guy a good excuse to tell the woman she is not allowed to have her period anymore. Like this is really going to help his sex life. If nothing else, he may tell her to throw the damn things out in the garbage. This should at least keep the local dogs busy trying to figure out who is in heat.

To do this type work you usually need items like a pipe cutter, a torch, solder, flux (some kind of stuff that looks like petroleum jelly and helps clean the pipes before the solder is applied) a few wrenches, including a basin wrench (that is the one which looks like it has a birth defect), a bunch of pipes, fittings, angles, pipe cleaning brushes and a sense of humor.

If you decide to go the PVC route, you will also need the proper cleaner and cement to make the joints and a hacksaw to cut the stuff. Just remember PVC has no conscience; once in place it is pretty much like a diamond, forever.

When working on this type job, no matter what the instructions on the toilet fixer package says, they lied. The job will be messier, take a lot more time and no matter how careful you are, don't wear decent clothes. You will get wet.

THE JOB LIST/ HONEY-DO LIST

Some people keep a list of odd jobs posted on a piece of paper. Usually the wife makes up this list to keep the husband busy when she is not home. Some lists are just a bunch of small scraps of paper kept in a big jar, it is like a game. Today you pull out a piece of paper, and that is the job of the day. This can be a real challenge. It is sort of like playing the lottery or Russian roulette. Sometimes you win, but only sometimes. Generally speaking, you pull the job to re-roof the garage on Super Bowl Sunday. This is fine if you do not follow sports.

Another way to look at this. You may also pick that same scrap of paper the same day the hot young woman next door invites all her girlfriends over to sunbathe in the nude in the back yard. It's a tough job but somebody has to do it.

CARPENTY WORK

Now most men growing up in this country (USA) have had at least one year of shop class. Manual training. Woodworking. At least most guys who grew up before 1980. So a lot of us seem to think this prepared us to repair anything made of wood. Good luck. I can tell you, I taught in a vocational school for a year and a half (Carpentry 1 & 2) and even the best students were going to be in for surprises when they got out in the real world.

Due to all the books and magazines which tell us how easy this is to do, most of us have a lot of guts when it comes to tearing out a wall, or adding a room. Wait till you open that wall, you will love it. It all looks so easy and simple. Some of it is. It is only simple mechanical logic. This type of thinking is fine with most of the simple work, but when you get into taking apart anything with support problems, you have to use the brains before you use the tools

Bedtime Horror Stories for Homeowners

You will soon discover there are different sizes and types of nails, screws, bolts and other type fasteners. You will find out about the real size of lumber as opposed to the nominal size given the pieces. You will discover wood in an old home that cuts like butter, or be hard as steel. You'll know it when you find it, believe me.

You will soon develop an appreciation for being able to take a hot shower at the end of a day of working in an attic in July. After breathing insulation all day, you will drink a cold beer outdoors in January, in Vermont. And you will enjoy it.

There are many kinds of wood with different looks and characteristics; you will find which will work for you, and against you. You will discover how to use shutters for cabinet doors, or how to juggle walls around to make a room at least look bigger. You will learn the value of a big mirror.

You have not lived till you tear out an old ceiling and eat about 100 years of old dust. Great stuff. After you remove all the trim from an old window to change a window chain and you find out there is an easier way. There is a small removable door inside the window frame. Your piano playing will certainly suffer after you smash a finger with a good heavy hammer. You will also invent new cuss words.

You will either have a good helper within your wife when you make a big mess, or find her and the dog sneaking out the back door when you call her name.

Suddenly there will be times when an eighth of an inch will mean nothing and times when it will ruin a job. It's all in fun a hundred years from now, when none of us will really remember the mistakes. But someone will have grandchildren who can spot them.

Splinters will take on a new significance, especially when you can't find the little sucker to remove it. Try sticking a piece of tape over the splinter and pull it off, it works sometimes.

You will find new definitions for the words *pain* and *tired* after a good day or two working on the house. You may also find you have talents you never knew you owned.

Chapter 14   YOU PARKED WHERE?

GOOD AND BAD PARKING SPACES

I have lived in houses most of my life, and this being the case I have discovered a few strange things that happen outside the home. The automobile is a fact of life in our world. This can create some problems as well as being a good way to go from point A to point B. Take for example a friend of mine who lived in a house where there was a street that sort of aimed for the front of that house.

It was not a 90 degree type ending, but more like 30 degrees off the front of the property. This may not seem like a big deal until you find out that she has had 3 cars torpedoed right in front of the place. Seems people would drive down the street, somehow thought that the street continued in that direction and found out too late that her car was not moving, but in fact, was parked.

I have a neighbor with a similar problem. He has lived there for at least 20 years, had a bunch of kids and a bunch of cars. He lives on a street which has a double yellow line down the center. Except for years, the line was not really centered. His side of the road was about 35% of the road and the other 65% is on the other side of the road. This road has since been repainted.

When people drove down his side of the road, this situation created an illusion that made people think all the parked cars are just in the line of traffic. He has lost at least 7 cars. His kid lost a jeep when some guy in a Mercedes slammed into it and drove it about 30 feet into a pole.

So far, nobody has been hurt or killed. Still an ugly situation. This is something to look at when you look at a house. His next door neighbor decided to take some of the property on the side of his house, got it dug out and paved and turned it into a parking area which will hold 3 to 4 cars. That deal set him back like $24,000.

Another thing to consider when you park your cars on the property. Take a look at what is over your head. Do you have gutters, TV antennas or tree limbs over the parking area? If you do, I can almost guarantee that there will be bird poop on the car every morning. We had this situation when I lived at home; I had an antenna over my car.

Every morning, I had a speckled racing stripe down the car. We moved the antenna. The house I live in now has a lot of trees around it. This is fine except for the birds that live in these trees and decorate my cars. Lucky for the birds, I am an animal lover. I stopped feeding them at this location; that helped a lot.

Even when you think you have a good spot, it can backfire. We had a neighbor years ago whose driveway was directly in line with the street that came down toward his house. Got a brand new Cadillac, this is before you needed insurance to take a car off the lot. He was smart enough to be covered.

He drove the car home. Parked it in the driveway. Had about 6 miles on it. Went inside to get the family to show them the car.

Before they even got out the door............POW.....ZOOM.........and I don't mean Jackie Gleason and the Honeymooners. Some drunk driver came straight down the street; thought the driveway was part of the road. Creamed the Caddy. So much for homeland security.

Chapter 15   DO I LOOK LIKE BILL GATES?

HOMES I COULD NEVER AFFORD

When you look for homes there are a lot of things to consider. Location is always important. This was a situation that I faced at one time. When I was looking at homes with Lorraine; the first wife, I looked at a lot of houses, more than Janice and I looked at. Simple reason. We had very little money, crap jobs and not a real good future at that time. We had our limitations.

So I was looking at a map one day, and see there is an area in North Jersey where it looks rural, probably old farms and other assorted dumps. I did actually look at an old log house at one time, and an old church. So looking at this map, I decided to look at property in Bernardsville. I knew NOTHING about this area except for what I got off the map. Turns out; it is rural all right, that is because they have huge pieces of property there, with homes to match.

When I went to real estate agents, they usually had this small book of black and white Polaroid photos. (For you young readers, these were photos that would print in 60 seconds in the camera). These were never real good shots, but at least gave the buyer some idea of what the home would look like. There are still books like this, but since it is almost impossible to even find a Polaroid camera anymore, I guess they use a digital camera and a printer today.

I showed up at this real estate agent like I really have a plan for the day; and ask him about property in the area. When I told him the price range I was looking for at the time, I thought he was going to laugh. He was a gentleman and kept it in his mouth. At the time, we were looking to spend fifteen to twenty thousand. You could not buy a garage in this area for that money.

Turns out the area was populated by people with big money. He was kind enough to show me photos of one house. This photo book was more like a wedding album, 8 X 10 inch color photos. Front view, sides, back, aerial views, I think you get the picture.

Bedtime Horror Stories for Homeowners

At the time, he showed me a house that was two stories high, with a long driveway, a four car garage and a lot of other stuff I could not afford. By the way, back then this was $250,000. Probably six million today. I told him if I ever got rich I would be back.

Some agents are just whores though. I am convinced of this. I had one guy trying to sell me a house in an expensive area. At the time it was maybe $70,000. Beautiful home; had a kitchen where you could cook for a crowd. After spending all that money, who would have any money left to buy food? "Just put down a deposit, we can work it out." "Sure, and I can take six jobs to pay for the place. Go play in traffic you moron."

Had another guy; I was in between marriages, living out of a van that I had converted into a camper. He wanted to sell me a condo in Georgia to the tune of $100,000. Right. I was doing caricatures of people while traveling. Probably making $125 a week. Another of these "we can work it out" guys. Maybe I should have given him the other clown's phone number.

There was another situation in which I got involved. This was a deal where the builders had put up a bunch of development homes and people would go try to buy them. This was about 1975. I was in the market, so I decided to go check some out. This was when I was still in my first marriage, and when I had more of a temper, not like I am so laid back even today.

I was not amused that these guys left me hanging in the wind with a deal gone bad. Turns out the mortgage had not been approved and we were supposed to be moving in three days. We had been living out of boxes while planning this move. To get my deposit money back I had to meet with some guy near Freehold, NJ. I forget his name. I am sure by now, he has forgotten mine. When he walked in his office, I am sitting there with my big dirty boots on the top edge of his desk; I am slouched down in an office chair, smoking a De Nobile cigar, Guinea Ropes, as they are called, with two black dogs.

The dogs are lying down on the floor on either side of me. I also had not shaved since Saturday. This was for the image. I am not all that big, but I wanted to give him the feeling he was dealing with Clint Eastwood when Eastwood played in the spaghetti westerns. Basically I wanted to scare the poop out of him. I was there for my money and no crap.

He walks in, sits down, he does not look all that comfortable even though it is his office. I state my case. "We had a deal going, the deal shit the bed; I am here to get my deposit back. Period." He is only one cog in the gears of this company but it is his decision to make the money come back to me. Bank Check, Remember?

I reminded him I had given them a Bank Check which was supposed to be as good as cash. He is shook a bit, but has to act like he has some kind of authority. He asks me to call the bank to make sure this check has cleared. He has the number. "You can talk on the phone here; I will go in another office he says." Like I am a six year old and does not know he is listening in on an extension phone. I make the call, the bank clears the funds. I say to him on the extension. "O.K. Dude, You can get your ugly ass off the other phone now."

He said it would take an hour or two to get this through the finance department. Wanted to know if I had anything to do that would keep me busy for a couple hours. I did, I was going back to Beachwood to check out the area a little better.

I told him. "I will be back here in two hours for that check. If it is not waiting for me, I will tear this place apart, starting with your face." Niles gave him one of his "I am gonna tear you up" looks. Noah was willing to just get out of there and mark the bushes.

I came back in two hours almost to the minute. I could not find him, but I did not care...the check was there, it was good and off I went to cash it and drop off the $3000 with Bob in Beachwood.

Chapter 16

THE PEOPLE NEXT DOOR, YOUR NEW FAMILY

NOISY NEIGHBORS

I suggest you talk to the people in the area when you look at a home. Here is one real good reason to do that. Noisy Neighbors. I don't mean the guy who runs a lawnmower on Saturday afternoon or the people who have one loud party a year.

These people are just making normal type noises. They are fine; we all make some kind of noise; we can't expect to live in a place that sounds like a graveyard.

The kind of people you want to avoid, are the people who do things like play a stereo at full volume for hours on end, the kind who scream for no reason at all or run a chain saw at midnight. These are the kind of idiots I mean. People like this should find a home maybe somewhere in Nevada, 50 miles out in the desert. There are locations like that there. Been there.

I bring up these examples for a simple reason. I have known people who do these things. The guy with the chain saw. I am not saying who he is. If he reads this book he will know who he is. He thinks nothing of running a gas powered saw at midnight and then calls the neighbors' dirty names because they called the cops. Give me a break.

When we moved in here, there was an older couple, a guy named Bucky and his wife Sophie. They were in their 60's at the time. Nice people, grew a huge garden, would have enough food to go from one year to the next. Always nice to talk to. Bucky and I would have a beer over the fence every so often.

As time went on, Bucky had health problems so they worked out a deal on the house with their kids. Not kid kids, these were adults and Bucky and Sophie moved into an apartment. No maintenance worries.

So now the sons decide to sell the property since they had their own homes and did not need this house. So they sold it to some guy who wanted to go into the rental business. For a while we had a family of four; two adults, and two young girls. Nice people. They eventually moved. Then he tried college kids. The guys were sort of noisy. I thought that was going to be a problem, but after the cops broke up a couple of wild parties they were cool.

Then we had college girls there one year. That was nice; they were quiet, friendly, cute, and nice on the eyes, at least my eyes. Then in came the family from Hell.

Talk about LOUD. These are the kind of people who make you almost wish you would go deaf. They had 5 kids. Two of the kids were teenagers and the other little brats were all about 5 or 6 years old. Now I don't say they are supposed to sit in the yard with their fingers crossed, but it would be nice if they got a clue. That was my job; I had to give them the clue.

This bunch had an above ground pool in the yard. Lots of people have one. The guy across the street who also had 5 small kids had one. His kids were so quiet; you didn't even know they lived there. But with the ones behind my back yard, it was as if there was a war going on there all the time. The whole bunch of them would go out in the yard or in the pool and just scream all day. This included the adults. I think they were on welfare, because nobody ever went to work there. I work at home, so I know when people are home around here.

Aside from that. Middle of the night...we would hear loud screams from the house as if someone were being murdered. I was ready to give the killer a couple more knives if he could finish them all off in one trip. No such luck, it was only them. We tried to talk to them; wasted effort, called the cops a few times, that was useless. The stupid cop, who showed up, sided with them. Some dumb thing about, "Well, they should have *some* kind of fun." "Fine flatfoot, want to buy this house, I am ready to move." This kind of response. Now I don't roll over too easy. I fight back.

Bedtime Horror Stories for Homeowners

I had considered going over there with a meat cleaver and taking out the pool. Actually I was half the way there when I changed my mind. Had considered using a sling shot to blow the liner out of the pool. A gun would work better, but I was worried about a stray bullet hitting some innocent person. If it hit one of the renters, that would not bother me.

They were so loud that I was in my home; in my living room, which is about as far from them as possible and could not talk to people there because of the volume.

That day, I freaked out and walked out in the yard and as loud as I could, I screamed "SHUT UP...SHUT UP." This did not stop the noise, they just knew I was getting pissed off and they were way too ignorant to give a damn.

Then I got another idea. I tape recorded them making a racket. Just a Radio Shack machine, nothing special. Cheap microphone in the back yard. I then used an item I recommend for situations like this. A commercial sound system.

I am also a musician and have a 150 watt sound system with speakers like you see DJs' use at parties. I don't play loud; I don't have to for the type music I do.

I had brought this unit years ago when I was working with a singer and we had a keyboard and mikes and all that stuff. She and I broke up, but it was my system so I still have it.

So I did what I felt would get their attention. I ran the tape through the tape recorder with one of my big speakers in the kitchen window. Only ran it at maybe 25% of its power, you could still hear it a block away.

To see them hanging over the fence...they looked as if someone had hit them in the heads with baseball bats. Want to see stupid expressions? It was basically the same look a dog gets right before he gets hit by a truck. And then as soon as I got their attention, I got on the mike and yelled. "THAT IS YOUR NOISE YOU STUPID ASSHOLES, NOW SHUT UP."

Five minutes later the cops were at my door wanting to know what I was doing. I told the cop. "Hear this shit? This goes on 7….8… 10 hours a day. Every day. I should go over there and just kill them all. I will do it with my bare hands so I don't give gun owners a bad name."

He tried to make some sense to me; said maybe we could talk it out. The last time I tried the talking bit, I got this answer. Get this. "We're loud, cause we are Puerto Ricans." That has to be one of the dumbest things I ever heard. The guy next door to him was that race. He moved to this area to get away from people like this. He has told me that right to my face. He said. "These people give the Puerto Ricans a bad name." I also have other friends of that race and they all said this bunch was bad news.

About two days later, after the sound system incident, I had a talk with the father over at his house and we sort of ironed things out. I told him if he wanted to sneak over to my house some time. We could sit and listen to this together so he could appreciate it.

He basically was not a bad guy, but had no control over the kids. After we talked, he did get them to cut it back a bit. But they would occasionally get loud again, which was pretty annoying.

We were out that New Years' Eve; came home about 3A.M., and Thank God. The house was up for sale. A few years ago this house would sit for years. The market was dead in this town. Luckily, at this time the market here was hot and the place sold in 2 weeks. To make a long story short, the idiots moved away. I almost gave myself a hernia doing back flips. I will have other noise stories, but I was so happy I just had to stop whatever I was doing and type this one out ASAP.

Turns out, I did get hold of the actual owner of the place. He lived at the other end of the state and had no idea of what was happening here. The renters had been dragging him out on rent for all the time they were there. Say the rent was $1000 a month for a number. They would give him maybe $400 the beginning of the month and fool around the rest of the month to get the other $600 to him. He finally got fed up with it and sold it out from under them. Thank God.

In my mind, I can see it now. All the people in the neighborhood are standing there. We watching these losers pull away with the moving truck.

We start out sort of low; not sure of ourselves, and get gradually louder.

We sing........................

"We hate to see you go. We hate to see you go. We hope to hell you never come back. We hate to see you go."

And in unison......we give them the finger.

The funny part is that I would run into the father of this group. Maybe in K-Mart or Home Depot. He would come up to me. "Hey, how you doing?" Of course I would be civil to him, but in my mind I was saying "Fine, since you morons moved out."

NEIGHBORHOOD WHACK JOBS

When you move into a neighborhood, I always suggest you talk to the people who live there. I did this and it saved me a lot of problems. I found out about the sewers, the trash pickup, the kids, the dogs. A lot of good stuff.

Now at the time, there was a problem living in town which did not exist in this particular area. This is the neighborhood Whack Job. This is the new version of the village idiot. We all know someone like this. I hate to compare them to idiots, because I feel this is an insult to idiots. We have a woman like this in the area; not a bad person, but a pest.

This is the kind of person who does not have a life. She can count her friends on her fingers and does not need both hands. There is a reason for this. She will come around looking to talk to you. Nothing special to talk about and I mean NOTHING special. Mostly to run down her whack job family and the people in town. Always telling me. "The people here are not friendly." "Nobody likes me!" "My family never gives me any help" etc, etc, and on and on.

For a while I felt sorry for her, tried to give her ideas on how to help herself, suggested she get a boyfriend, or a pet. And of course none of these ideas were going to work. "Men are Pigs, What am I going to do with a cat?" Who knows? "Get a sheep, whatever."

This woman would for no good reason at all, come down the street and ring the doorbell. Made me curse the doorbell company for making such a good product. This would usually happen when we were taking a nap, which would set off my dogs who would bark until I either answered the door or she would leave.

I could see her by the front of the house; stretching her neck trying to look in the windows to see if I was here. I should have mooned her. I even gave her some guys' phone number to try on for a boyfriend. He is almost as nutty as she is.

Not quite as bad. I called him yesterday and told him maybe he is better off without her as she is too weird, even for him.

This is to protect a guy who will put my four way flashers on in my car if I stop in an empty parking lot to get out and take off a jacket. She figured out my phone number and what finally made me tell her off is when she called me up at 11:30 at night to see if my friend was up here. This was on my answering machine.

"Hi, I thought if Rod was up here maybe we could hang out or go for a ride somewhere." Where are we going for a ride at this time of day? Maybe go look in people's windows to see who is getting ready for bed? The only reason I didn't pick up the phone and tell her off is because the portable phone was at the other end of the house and I was not interested in getting out of a warm bed to go look for it.

Then the next day, she had the nerve to call twice to see if I could call Rod to see if I could call him for her. She wanted to have him meet her somewhere so they could go out. She has his phone number, but says she feels funny calling him.

Meanwhile she has no problem asking me five hundred personal questions about myself and my family. After she called me at 11:30 P.M. I tried her number at 6:30A.M. Because this is what time we were getting up to go to work for the second day that weekend. The bitch would not pick it up. She called me twice that day when I was out and had the nerve to tell me that she had seen my car there, and how come I didn't call Rod for her.

Just to show how nutty she is, she called back later that day. I told her off and said she should get a life and get out of mine

Let's see how good this sticks; she is much like a stray dog that will follow you home. I would probably keep the dog. She would be dropped off at the SPCA. Bottom line; for a while after I told her off, she kept coming around. Still being a pest. All of a sudden; I have no idea why, she started ignoring me. This is a good thing, and to top it off she has disappeared from the neighborhood. I have no idea where she has gone. But then again, I don't look for trouble.

CLEAN HOUSE / MESSY HOUSE

I will never get an award for keeping a house perfect. I am not a total slob, but I am not Felix Unger either. I have a cousin Steven who keeps the house like that; he also waxes under the hood of his car when he cleans it. He has too much time on his hands.

We live in a decent size home; there are two of us and at this point two dogs. Sometimes it is only one dog when we lose one. The place is big enough for us, a little tight on storage space, and sometimes it is easier to hang a shirt or a bra on the end of the brass bed then to bother dragging it to a closet.

Things do get put away, but they get put away when we feel like it. We are the adults here, so it is not like Mom is here getting me to clean up my room. When we have company, of course, we make sure the place looks nice and neat. My good friends have seen the messy rooms too. Get over it.

Now some people are just too messy. I mean not only messy, just downright disgusting. I got involved with a kid years ago who was in some kind of program with the probation department in a New Jersey town. He didn't do anything too bad, but his mother could not handle him and he ended up on probation. Somehow I got involved with this program. I would take the kid places and show him a life that his mother could not, or would not. At least with me, he could find a place to sit in my house.

I am not sure how people get this messy. If the home they were renting was 600 square feet, there was a mess a foot deep across almost every square inch of the home. Now if they moved into a smaller home, the mess got smaller, but deeper. A bigger home, a bigger mess.

Talk about crud; you could look under a couch and see half a sandwich under there from who knows when. I would never let my dogs in the place. I was afraid they would eat something that was left over.

Bedtime Horror Stories for Homeowners

I would also not sit on anything or put down something where I could bring home roaches or some other crummy bug.

I used to hang out with a guy who I remember rented an apartment. This was about 1980. One bedroom; big enough for one guy. When he moved in, there seemed to be enough room for him. He was an artist so he had some art supplies; anyone who does art work knows how this stuff multiplies. He also was a record collector. Vinyl, Tapes, CD's. He could start his own radio station if he could get the license.

Eventually he got a home. The house started the same way and ended up the same way. He had a completely empty basement when he moved in there. His mother died a few years ago. She had old furniture. Not valuable antiques, but old furniture.

I am not sure where one type furniture ends and the next begins, but I know he tried selling some of the furniture and got nowhere. It is now piled in his basement. In his attic are magazines piled to the ceiling. I guess the good part is if there is a fire, they will act like insulation and keep the flames from reaching the roof. His place is so cluttered; you have to walk sideways in order to get from one place to another. His home is not the only one I know in this category.

I told you about the woman whose home is so cluttered that her kid had to practically carve a hole in the garage to park his car. At this time there is a canoe hanging over the car at this time. I could not visualize either of these fat people even getting into a canoe.

A few years ago she wanted to drive from New Jersey to Florida to pick up some stuff in a home down there. Again; this is old furniture, floor tile, rugs, that kind of stuff. We did the math. It would cost more to retrieve this stuff than it was worth. Let it stay there.

The room where I am typing this book, used to get cluttered all the time. Janice thinks of this room as a dumpster. If she does not know what to do with something, it goes here. I just bring it back to where ever she picked it up and put it back. Most times the things are like a movie on a DVD that is mine.

Bedtime Horror Stories for Homeowners

I have about 6 movies, she has about 100. You will notice all of hers stay by the TV in the bedroom, mine do not count. I also watch much less TV, maybe two hours a week.

The stuff I don't understand however is paper. I am sure it multiplies in file cabinets when I am sleeping. As I type here, I am convinced there is a sound in the file cabinets. The paper is having sex somewhere in a desk. That desk could be empty today, and tomorrow it is full.

We also put a lot of stuff through a shredder. This is to avoid identity theft, and to get rid of old records of transactions that the IRS might use to put me away. Just kidding.

Janice knows we have a shredder. She may even know how to use it. But, Heaven forbid she should actually put a piece of paper in it. Nope, she will just drop the paper on the floor to a point that if I do not shred it, the paper would just pile up to the ceiling.

In between my chapters I have been shredding paper. I got to a point where the overheat light on the shredder went on a few weeks ago. I just got so inspired I just shredded some ancient pay forms as I was taking a think break here.

I also have a friend who just refuses to clean up his condo. Never opens a window. I am convinced that the air in the place is the same air that was there the day it was built.

He has a bathroom where he used to smoke. He has quit after many years. The smell in that bathroom is so bad that if anyone ever buys the place, they will have to tear all the sheetrock off the walls and ceiling to get rid of it, and to be quite truthful, I am not sure if that will even work.

Plus, he buys these make believe air purifiers that are supposed to make the place smell good. The crud on those things is so thick, that cleaning them would be a waste. Better to throw them if you could stand to touch them. Wear rubber gloves for this job, industrial type gloves.

Bedtime Horror Stories for Homeowners

Now in my house our dogs help us make messes. They are experts. Just give you a couple of examples. We had Babe and Barney. Babe was a little terrier mix, looked like a short German Shepherd. Barney was a Shepherd/Collie Mix, pretty dog. For openers, of course he could not help it; Barney shed enough fur to make another dog each week.

If we did not vacuum the house at least once a week, the house would look like a dog. OK, but that went with the territory. We got both these dogs when they were puppies. We all know pups like to chew and do damage. Well, they were always doing something to wreck the house. I remember coming home one time and the door on the side entrance would not open.

I walked around to the side window to see what was going on. These two had opened a brand new bag of dog food; the food must have been two inches deep behind the door. That was one deal. Another time we figured we would lock the dogs in the bedroom. Smart guys. Yeah.

When we got home; the bedroom looked like someone had put a hand grenade in the pillows, there were about a million feathers all over the room. If I remember right, the dogs got into the trash can and spread all that stuff all over the room. They also shredded a doll Janice had from when she was a teenager.

She found a piece the size of a top of a soda bottle. That was all that was recognizable. Someone had also shit in front of the TV; maybe they did not like the show. Later into the years, we got Sammy who was probably the smartest dog I have ever had. He was a Lab/Golden Retriever mix.

I understand the Seeing Eye is now breeding dogs like this. He was also smart for himself. He would go through a wall for food if he thought he could do it. He was a big dog and a counter cruiser, tall enough to take stuff off counters if he stands on his back legs. I was doing some kind of repair work on a phone. Sammy waited till I had taken the receiver off a telephone and laid it on the radiator cover.

When Sammy got done with the receiver, *nobody* was going to repair it. He had chewed the life out of it. I came back and here is this piece of white plastic with wires and a little speaker hanging out of it. I actually took that thing to the park where we did our doggie play dates to show the other dog owners. Wait, wait, my heart, my heart. Janice actually put some paper through the shredder.

I think every dog we have had in the house has worked on the dining room set at least once. Our dog Lacey, Boxer/Pit mix seems to like it. She likes to chew the top end of one chair that we keep near the landing. First she chewed one side of it. Repaired that with Rock Hard Putty, which does get like a rock. So next time, she worked on the other side and the center of the chair. I did the Rock Hard Putty thing again, now I had to repaint the fake grain into the repair.

Now there are people I know also who go the opposite direction. They either have a house that is so big that there are places and room for everything, or they are just such neat freaks that it kills them to have anything out of place.

My cousin Steven is one of these guys. I mentioned him before. Then again he does not have a life. When he had his house in Brick, NJ the place always looked perfect. The only annoying thing is that he would run his wide screen TV with the sound system so loud you could hear it in the street. I am not kidding; he had some movie on about tornadoes. I happened to stop by. I thought the noise was a vacuum cleaner.

I dated a girl in college, same type. You could run the camera crew from Better Homes and Gardens through her Moms' home almost anytime day or night. I have never met someone who had such an obsession with cleaning.

After considerable thought; I have come to the conclusion that most people have a certain amount of mess and the messy ones outnumber the clean freaks. So anytime any of you clean freaks want to come over here and shred some paper for me; I will save you a pile.

NAKED WARRIOR BREAKING UP A FIGHT IN THE STREET

I am not a fighter, at least not when it comes to street fights. If I get sick, I fight to get better. If I feel someone is trying to screw me on a money deal I will fight them for the money; but street fights. I gave up that crap 40 years ago. That is a fast way to ruin yourself.

One night, Janice and I were sitting in the bedroom watching TV. I do watch it sometimes. We heard some screaming and yelling. At first I thought it might be the TV, but since it did not fit into whatever the show that was on, that idea didn't work. So now I looked out the window.

In front of our house, across the street, some guy is beating on a woman who is sitting in the drivers' seat of her car. I do not know if they were married or what, I don't really care. I also think a guy has to be a jerk to be beating on a woman. I tell Janice about this. I now try to dial 911. Problem is, I wear glasses and without them, the numbers on the phone were too small.

For what they were worth, the numbers could have been written in Chinese. I said to Janice, "You call the cops, I will be right back." Now I can be a little impulsive at times; I am also naked at times. This was a time when I was both.

In my bedroom I had a long steel pry bar. Instead of going to a gym I would use this heavy bar for arm exercises. It is maybe 40 pounds, enough to do some good. Well with the impulse thing going strong, I pick up the big bar. It is about 5 feet long, with a round end on one end and a big square end with a point on the other end. I do not bother putting on clothes, I am pissed and in a hurry.

I now run downstairs with the bar, go out the front door, holding this bar over my head; straight up pointed toward the sky, and letting it all hang out. I yell at the guy. "HEY YOU, IDIOT!" He must have figured that a naked guy with a steel bar was crazier than he was. Got back in his car and took off. I went back in the house. Just as well, the cops showed up about 20 seconds later.

Bedtime Horror Stories for Homeowners

THE DITCH, THE SLAB, AND THE GAY GUY

This is part of the story about waterproofing our basement. We had done pretty well digging our ditches; I wanted to have them all open so we could cover the walls with tar all at once. So far the dirt was nothing, but now we hit a problem. Part of my foundation was surrounded by a concrete slab. This was used by the side door as part of an entrance. The water was sneaking under the slab and going through the wall. It was an ugly job, but we decided to tear up the slab in order to waterproof the walls.

Now let me tell you a bit about my neighbors'. They are, for the most part all families, they keep regular hours, and nobody is all that noisy. At the time I tore up the slab, we had a new guy living in the neighborhood. This gent is supposedly gay. I couldn't document that, but I am not blind either. And to tell you the truth I don't really care, he can do what he wants with his life.

Well, this guy has a very successful business in the area and probably bought the house just to have a place to live and party. He happened to buy it at the right time and sold it just as well, made about twenty five grand over about a year and a half due to the price appreciation in the area.

I will say the man did some beautiful work in the house and kept the property very nice. His landscaping perked up the property, and for the most part he was a nice enough neighbor. He only had one drawback. His parties. See this guy has a lot of money in relation to the rest of the neighborhood and uses it to do some serious partying. He definitely wants to preserve the local wild life.

He would go out with his friends, and come home 12, or 1A.M. in their rented limo. Most times they would be a little loud, slow down after a half hour and go home or go to sleep. The back of his property faces the side of mine and his parties focused on a hot tub in the back yard. Well, this time the crowd arrived at 3A.M. They are half loaded and ready to drink some more.

Bedtime Horror Stories for Homeowners

At first I ignored the noise, but after an hour I got a little annoyed. First I did the civilized thing. I called the police. Give up that idea, he probably has a lot of pull in the area, a no show police force.

This was a Friday night and I was off the next day, meanwhile Janice the R.N. was taking peoples' lives in her hands, at work at 7A.M.

I called his phone number a few times and got some satisfaction after he pulled the phone out of the wall. I could hear him bitching about it in the yard. Tried another police call. Another No Show.

By now it is 5A.M. We have the windows shut, the air conditioner is being used like a white noise generator, I'm freezing my ass off, Janice is mad as hell, and the dog is going nuts. We're all having a great time. I eventually took a walk around the block and threw a couple of rocks through his front windows. The party continued. At about 5:30A.M. I couldn't sleep so I started bolting a trailer hitch setup on the back of my van. I had my job cut out for the day anyway. I had to pull up the slab.

By 6A.M. Janice is up to go to work, I've got the police on the phone again; this time I use a different approach. "If there isn't a cop here in five minutes, I'm going over there and killing people." Three minutes later, there are two police cars in front of my house. When the local asks me what the problem was, I simply answered "Hear that racket over there, it started about 3A.M." I was told about all I could do was to sign a complaint. I don't really like to complain, but I felt a show of force would cool off the party.

Well no signed complaint, but as I am walking back to the house, I'm talking to the teenage kid next door who has been listening to this party all night. The gay guy had the balls to complain that I called the fuzz on him; gave me a big song and dance about how he had brought a lot of class to the area, and on and on. I was hoping he was coming over the fence, I was mad enough to go after his ass. It ended with some verbal dueling for the time being. Janice has her coffee and is off to work.

Janice worked on weekends on and off so when I am planning to make a big mess, I usually try to do it when she is not home. Its' bad enough I get involved in it, so I try to keep her away from the real bad ones.

Well, this Saturday she took off for work; and I took off for the tool rental place for a real heavy duty, adult size jackhammer, not the little electric one I used in the basement.

For any of you who have gotten drunk on wine, you know how you feel. You want to sleep, and when you wake up, the hangover is a bummer. Visualize about ten people in this condition after this guys' party.

I finished up the trailer hitch, have breakfast and go to the rental place to pick up tools. The whole area has gotten nice and quiet. I gently back the van into the driveway, have a fast cup of coffee, and ever so gently, commence to remove the concrete slab. I did this with a COMMERCIAL JACK HAMMER AND A COMPRESSOR AS BIG AS A COMPACT CAR.

The cops were at my house in about ten minutes; meanwhile my buddy across the street comes over with his old clothes, sound deadening earmuffs and a big smile.

Of course when the police told me I had to shut off that compressor, it was left running full blast, while I explained it was after 9A.M. "AND WHERE WERE YOU GUYS AT 4A.M. WHEN THE PARTY WAS GOING ON?" I continued. "LET THE CREEP SIGN A COMPLAINT IF HE WANTS." I yelled. "THE SLAB HAS TO COME UP, THERE IS A SIDING CREW COMING HERE ON MONDAY MORNING AND THIS MESS HAS TO BE OUT OF THE WAY. THIS EQUIPMENT SET ME BACK $65.00 FOR THE DAY, LET HIM COME OVER HERE AND SETTLE IT LIKE A MAN. SCREW HIM."

With that, the cops got the picture, hit the road, no complaint was signed and we ran the machine till lunchtime. I guess the new guy figured the noise was over at twelve.

After lunch, I tore up two more sections of sidewalk as an afterthought. I had a headache for two days, and I was not even drinking. After that episode, the parties were a lot less frequent and a lot less noisy.

Within six months the new guy took his money, his class, and his friends out of the neighborhood and sold the place to a couple with a dog. Nice quiet people.

By the way, the party and the compressor were totally a coincidence; I had scheduled the tool two weeks earlier, never knowing the party would happen. Thank you God.

THE NEW SLAB

We had a fun time removing all the broken concrete from where the old slab had been. Janice worked right along with me to pile it in the yard. The pile grew to about six feet in diameter and three or four feet high. There is not much market for used concrete.

We thought maybe Janice could take a small piece to work in her purse every day and drop it in the garbage. That would take till we were about 100 years old.

Also, the trash collectors are not obligated to pick up construction trash. A dumpster would have been a good idea. Can't think of everything. Here is a thought if you ever get into this situation. We dug two big holes in the yard and made a dry well out of the stuff. My gutters and leaders now drain into them. See, I told you there was something to be learned from reading this book.

We used some of the pieces for this and some of the smaller ones for fill when we did the new slab. Now I have to tell you something about concrete suppliers. If you think plumbers, electricians, and carpenters are independent, I dare you to get involved with a concrete supplier. I have spent much of my life in construction work and can tell you from experience that unless you are building something like a hospital where the concrete flows like water; you are in trouble.

From the viewpoint of the concrete company, a small load of mixed concrete does not pay. It is almost like kids who buy gasoline a buck at a time, it costs almost that much to pump it. Of course when you are the person doing the concrete work and it does not make sense to mix it by hand or with a small mixer, you need a concrete truck.

Now concrete is sold by the yard; not like cloth, but by the cubic yard. For you people who either never learned it or forgot it from school; a cubic yard is a measure of solid, gas or liquid which measures three feet long, by three feet wide, by three feet high.

So when concrete is poured, it is measured that way. One yard of concrete will do a slab with a nominal thickness of 4 inches and outside dimensions of 9 X 9 feet.

The 9 X 9 measures to 81 square feet, which multiplied by 4 inches or one third of a foot, equals one cubic yard. Enough math lessons.

If you are inclined to figure this out for yourself, enjoy yourself. So what may look like a good sized patio may be only about two or three yards of concrete.

Of course the concrete people do not want to be known as party poopers, so they have a system to sell small quantities of the stuff. It is lovingly called the LESS LOAD. This means to us that if less than about 6 yards of concrete are ordered, there is an additional charge tacked onto the order.

Now you can complain all you want, but that is how it is done and as far as I know is accepted as a fact of life. Small time contractors have the same set of rules as homeowners and have to use this in their estimates to cover their prices. The last time I ordered concrete, the price ran about $50.00 a yard, plus a $50.00 Less Load Charge.

There is also a time limit. So many minutes per yard is allowed to pour the concrete. I think it was allowed about 5 minutes a yard. After that it will cost you extra for the time the truck is at the job site. This all seems to stack the odds in the favor of the concrete companies, but remember they have their expenses.

They have to pay the driver, who is not making minimum wage and the actual operating expenses of the truck must be taken into account. I mean you are not gassing up a Toyota pickup here. Concrete trucks probably get about 10 feet to the gallon. It might be better than that, but not a lot better. Plus the tires on those trucks have got to add up.

One of those tires cost as much as some cars I have owned. Also you have the cost of the materials to make the concrete, the office people, insurance, and the company owners. So they have their problems too. Plus like any other business, they would prefer to make a profit. So much for their problems, let me tell you about their attitude ...that is where to find the real action.

YOU WANTED IT WHEN?????

Concrete companies are most helpful when the construction business is slow; they will be helpful just to cover expenses and keep their small customers. Who knows? Maybe someday some of these small businessmen will get lucky and hit it big time. Most contractors have a memory like an elephant when it comes to remembering people who treated them badly.

But when the building industry is busy, if you want a small load, have fun. If you call a week ahead of time for 4 yards, at 9 A.M. and you have yourself and two helpers there at 6:30 doing prep work, you may still be doing prep work at three in the afternoon waiting for the truck.

I cannot say all concrete companies are like this, but I have had it happen, meanwhile it is costing me about $25 an hour for the help to stand around drinking coffee and beer and getting lazy. By the time the truck gets here, these guys may have to be retrained. Overall it can be a real fun time. There is also a weather condition which must be considered. You cannot pour concrete very well in the winter. There are chemicals which can be added to the mix to keep it from freezing, but a lot of people do not even know about the stuff, and it does have its limits. Besides that, who wants to do this kind of work in cold weather?

Rain also poses problems. If it is raining while the concrete is being poured, the rain may dilute the mixture and you will have a pile of small stones with a light coating of gray stuff. This mess cost you $300.00? So now you have the Readers Digest course of concrete pouring information. The course will continue as I tell you about the new slab.

The sun shone for two weeks straight after I tore up the old slab. Good beach weather. The temperatures ran about 75 degrees. The mess came up; we leveled off the ground, did the waterproofing part, and set up the forms. (The forms are the pieces of wood used to hold the concrete edges straight; you don't think that shit comes out of the trucks that way.....do you?)

We were pouring the slab on a Saturday. My brother Bob and his wife Marilyn were coming up to do the job with us. Bob was a professional landscaper; B&M Landscaping, Brick, NJ

I have had a lot of experience in the work, and Marilyn has done a lot with Bob. Janice didn't really know much about the work, but she is a good worker anyway. There is a certain degree of anticipation involved in this work due to the permanent nature of the finished product.

I was awake at 5A.M. IT WAS RAINING. Not to be one who gets easily excited, I figured we could sit it out for a while, the truck was expected about 11 o'clock. At about 7:30 I called Bob who suggested I try to put some sort of tent over the area to be poured. We were actually pouring two slabs; one by the side door and the other was to replace my old wood floor on the front porch. This slab is being used for thermal mass in a solar heating system. There will be more on solar heating systems later in the book.

Remember the vinyl siding job I told you about? It had been done about a week ago. That went fine. So with brand new siding on the house, I was sort of limited on how I could make this cover on the side of the house.

I hit the Shop Rite at 7:45A.M. I snagged a couple hundred feet of clothes line. My next stop was at a lumber yard to buy some plastic. To make sure I had enough, I picked up a roll sixteen feet wide by a hundred feet long. Wrote a check. Janice covered it three hours later.

Meanwhile the rain is coming down even heavier. We could have called off the whole idea, but there was a lot of preparation work and Bob isn't just sitting around waiting for me to call him for help. Aside from that, I'm sick of walking through a yard that looks like a combat zone.

In my mind, I knew what I wanted to do with the plastic, and the rope. I just had to get the stuff up where I needed it. We took the roll of plastic out of the box, stretched it through the living room, the dining room and the kitchen, added a few feet and with the touch of a brain surgeon, cut it off with a utility knife. The trick here is to make it long enough on the first shot.

We took the clothesline, rolled it into one edge of the plastic, and taped it in one place with duct tape. So now we had the equivalent of one side of a big tent. Next, I took the whole mess outside, threw one end of the rope up to Janice who is getting soaked hanging out the front window of the house, and tell her to tie the rope to the headboard of the brass bed, and then get to the back bedroom and wait for me by the window.

I then took a ladder, placed it on the back edge of the roof by the back bedroom, dragged the plastic and the line up to the back window. Janice took another short shower here pulling the rope in and tying it to the radiator. These are both second story windows.

We then managed to grab sections of the rope and pull it into two side windows directly over the proposed slab location. Then we nailed the rope in to the inside window frames of the four windows, starting in the front and working our way back. Using this system we did no damage to the new siding and only minimal damage to the inside of the window frames, we also effectively secured the plastic to the side of the house.

Of course; what had to be done now, was to stretch the plastic out over the slab area so we had some room to work. Being a camper since childhood paid off this time. I simply tied sections of the plastic with more rope, used long pieces of wood to hold the tied section off the ground and used the chain link fence to hold the loose end of the rope. The toughest part of this, was holding the plastic up to the wood without getting a soaking every few minutes.

Every five minutes, I would move something which would cause about two gallons of water to slide down the plastic, down my sleeve, and down my pants leg. I remained wet that day till about five o'clock. Lots of fun, I would have made a good fish that day.

By the time Bob and Marilyn arrived, the plastic was secure. I was wet; but at least slightly relaxed, and just waiting for the truck. Bob's reaction to the plastic was. "What are you, some kind of nut?" "See any water under there?" I asked. "I'm not all that nuts."

We checked the forms, which I had moved while doing the plastic, reset them and waited for the truck.

THE TRUCK

We had a distinct advantage that day as far as the truck. This was due to the crummy weather. Most people had called off their concrete deliveries for the day. Now, for those of you who have never been close to a concrete truck, they are a lot bigger close up in real life then they appear on the other side of a highway.

I can hear a concrete truck 5 blocks away; they have a distinctive sound just like a garbage truck. They are just as large and have the barrel moving all the time to keep the concrete mixed.

I imagine the old cave men must have had the same feeling in the pit of their stomach when they ran into a dinosaur. They were about the same size and inspire the same awe.

The truck we were supposed to get was to be a metered truck where you don't get hit for a less load. They mix it as it is delivered and only charge you for the amount you use. I think the rate for the concrete is slightly higher, so we sort of broke out even.

Bedtime Horror Stories for Homeowners

I hear the truck on Broadway, then on the stretch from Broadway to my street. It starts as a low rumble in the distance which gradually increases as it gets closer. The excitement level increases accordingly. I'm surprised I didn't wet myself.

"MONBACK"

If you decide to become a concrete worker, there are certain words you must learn. Some of these can be picked up on the job; one phrase is taken from the ranks of the garbage man. That phrase is "MONBACK, MONBACK!" This translates to "Come On Back." Without this phrase, you are out of luck. Many concrete trucks have to be backed in somewhere. Another good one is "KEEP IT COMIN'."

This is the way the driver knows to keep pouring the concrete. Probably the most important one to know is "WHOA, WHOA." This is the same as telling your dog to stay; it is the way to stop the concrete flowing. This command also requires a sense of timing as there is always concrete left in the chute and even though is does not look like much; it can be enough to make or break a job.

It also helps if you can whistle loudly. I have an aunt who can stop a cab in New York City from a half a block. That whistle is just about perfect for this work. In case you wonder why all the phrases are in capital letters, it is because you have to use these words at a loud volume so the driver can hear you over the roar of the truck. Even though I have worked with a lot of concrete trucks, the size of them always fascinates me.

When they are backed into position it is like parallel parking an elephant. The tires are about four feet high, the barrel is about sixteen feet high and they always make a lot of noise. I don't know if all the noise is necessary, or if it is just something to keep people in awe.

We are lucky that there was a lot of room in the driveway, of course we had all the cars and the van out on the street, and the dog is locked in the bathroom so he cannot come out and try to shake the truck by the tires. This also keeps him from walking through the finished patio.

Janice had never been anywhere near a concrete truck, so this machine really impressed her, I think she really wanted to keep the dog company, but didn't want anyone to laugh at her.

Bob is really good with the screaming and yelling part of this job. He has always had a good voice; some people have even called it a big mouth. God knows, I don't know why. He was a coach of a kid's soccer team, and with his mouth, the opposing teams left the field shaking. He's got it made with concrete trucks.

So when this truck rolls up the street. Just in case the driver has missed the plastic on the house; the tools leaning against the wall and all of us standing in the rain in work clothes. Just in case; Bob gives him a "WHOA!" The truck stops short, the tires are shaking either from the vibration of the motor or from Bob's mouth. The driver is used to loud people, he NEVER SHAKES.

Most of the guys who drive these trucks not only how to drive the monsters, they can park one in a spot that was vacated by a VW and they usually know a lot about concrete work. Even though they all give the image of Johnny Badass, they are just doing a job just like anyone else. They do have an image to protect.

I don't think the concrete companies will hire anyone who wears glasses, or looks like they would have a problem pushing the truck if it got stuck. Even if the driver is 5'2" tall, he will either weigh 170 or better, or if he is not that heavy, he should look as if he eats nails for breakfast.

As if this is the driver's first job, Bob is up on the running board next to the truck door. The first thing Bob sees is a clipboard. This has a release form which in effect says that if the weight of the truck destroys your cesspool it's your problem. Can't blame them either. This form covers almost anything which could be damaged by the truck or the driver.

Simple set of rules, sign the form or mix it yourself. We have all been through this routine before so it is no big deal, besides we are both responsible type guys.

Bedtime Horror Stories for Homeowners

This form protects the concrete company from lowlife lawsuit starters. Bob tells the driver where and how he wants the concrete poured. There is more to this work than just having the concrete fall on the ground where it will just settle in place. The driver looks at the plastic, shakes his head and backs up.

THE DRIVER

The guy who drives this truck fits his image perfectly; he was most likely born in a concrete truck. He is about 6' tall about 240 pounds. He has a beer belly, but aside from that, the man is big and solid. He has the usual flannel shirt. These shirts are all made in some sort of checkered pattern. I know, I own lots of these and they all look like that. The guys who drive these trucks always show up wearing this type shirt, even if it 90 degrees outside.

They also have the jeans that sit low on the hips, and the motorcycle wallet. One of the big gompy type wallets which stick out of your back pocket and are chained to your belt loop. They usually carry enough shit in these wallets to document their entire life, which includes a nude shot of either their wife or girlfriend, sometimes both in the same shot. They also wear heavy work shoes.

These guys were onto this type shoe years ahead of EPA dress codes for people in hazardous occupations. Their friends and families told them this is the shoes to wear to make sure you can still walk when you get old, like 40. This guy wears like a size 13EEE.

He has hands that can palm a medicine ball. Regardless of his rough appearance, he is there to do the job and does it right, and he is a pretty civilized type guy.

A lot of this size is important for this type job. A lot of construction workers and foremen have this big macho image they have to uphold, so the concrete company cannot send out a wimp to deal with these people. Also the physical nature of the work makes the drivers stay in shape. The chutes are about 50 pounds each, and steering a truck like this takes a certain amount of strength.

I am not sure if all these trucks have power steering, but with the weight of the load, in a tight spot, it could still get tough.

This guy's name is John. No chance he would have a name like Brian, or Daryl. Guys with names like that usually go into something like music, or art or medicine. John gets the truck backed into the driveway toward the back of the form.

NOW THE ACTION STARTS

John has three chutes hooked on the back end of the truck in about 20 seconds. This comes to him like breathing. Now he is on the tail end of the truck spraying water on the chutes. It's been raining for 7 hours, and we still need more water on the chutes. He hits the lever that starts the barrel rolling to remix the concrete.

Basically when the concrete is put into the trucks; it is sand, stones, cement and water. It is usually mixed a little dry to preserve the strength of the mix and water is added at the job site.

The truck is loaded at the company and as it rides to the job, this huge barrel rotates to get the right mix going. Some chefs in high priced restaurants are not this careful about their dishes. Alpo ala smooch.

By now Bob's adrenaline level is rising, this is a great time to show off how good he is at his work. When the concrete starts to flow down the chute, he starts to salivate, his eyes widen. He sucks down his last Marlboro in one great breath. Now he will kick ass and take names.

We grab the end of the chute nearest the form, and aim it at the back corner nearest the house. Makes me glad I taped plastic all along the side of the house to about 8 feet high.

The concrete comes alive as it slides down the chutes. We move it back and forth to cover the dirt at the back of the form. Even in rainy weather like this, the concrete will not wait for you to take your time with it. Bob is running across the edge of the form, with the end of the chute.

Bedtime Horror Stories for Homeowners

I'm pushing the concrete with a rake like God making a mountain, and the women are staying out of the way for the time being.

We do this for about five minutes; the slab needs only about 2½ yards of concrete, so we don't want to overload it. In about another minute, Bob gives another "WHOA".

This keeps us from going swimming in the stuff, and gives us a chance to see where we are high or low on the forms. Bob has a great eye for things like this; he drives like he is blind, but can spot a crooked sidewalk from around the corner and across the street. Bob sends Marilyn for cigarettes from his truck. Marilyn comes back with the butts from the truck. Bob squats down near the edge of the form and points out a low spot for me. Marilyn throws the butts across the wet concrete to Bob. He has great hand/eye coordination; he should have been a professional ball player. He whips the smokes out of the air, and with the same motion he points out a high spot.

Now Bob is yelling at the truck again. Even if John were deaf he could pick up on the vibrations and Bob waving his arm like a weed in the wind. More concrete comes down the chute; Bob does me the honor of aiming it toward the other side of the form. I swing the chute across the back edge, the concrete flows right where I put it.

Bob waves the truck toward the street. John hits the switch to kill the feed, Bob is pointing me toward the porch and Marilyn is chasing a couple of 2 X 4's. Janice brings out a tray full of coffee. We all drink the coffee while we work. John didn't want any. Too bad, his loss. We know the truck is timed, so we basically want to get it done and on its way. Bob tells me to start on the porch, while he gets a jump on this slab.

Now, my porch had jalousies all the way around. They started at about 30" high and go to the ceiling. When we moved in, they were frozen shut due to the fact that the old lady living here never used them. Armand who lived across the street grew up right down the street and never knew these windows opened till I opened them.

I don't really know how long the jalousie windows had been in this house, but when we first opened them, it was like opening a tomb. They were all frozen shut, the gears worked, but the levers were all weak and we broke a couple before we got the hang of the system. When we cleaned the glasses, we gently took some of them out and washed them.

We did not remove many of them, just the ones that were too dirty to clean in place. I have always been a little careful with glass and at five or six bucks a piece for this type glass, I didn't get too funny. Well, the truck had to get in here. We did not have time to take the glass out gently. It went more like this.

Janice stood at the end of the porch and I would push the glasses out and have her stack them. They were all pretty much the same size, so that was in our favor. Instead of being civilized and removing them gently, it was more like pulling a band aid off a cut. The faster, the better. I would push the frame part of the window to almost horizontal, hit the bottom edge of the glass with my right hand, grab the glass with my left hand and damn near throw it at Janice.

We pulled about 100 pieces out of the front of the porch in about that many seconds. We only broke one piece. This gave us room to get the chute into the porch. The storm door was already off the house, so we were in good shape. The porch still had all old siding inside, so we didn't care about messing the walls up a little.

There was also an old window which we were planning to replace, so that was as good as gone. The slab on the porch is being used for heat storage on a solar heating system so it is thicker than the slab at the patio. The slab on the outside is four inches, reinforced with heavy wire. This slab on the porch is full of broken concrete of the original old slab and has an inch of foam insulation under it. It is about 8 inches thick in the front and about 14 ½″ thick at the back.

We left the original floor joists in the slab to help strengthen the framing of the walls when the concrete arrived.

John probably returned to the concrete yard and got a good laugh telling about the maniac who filled his porch floor with concrete. Of course nobody really cares, they all made money on the stuff. I laugh when I hang out on the porch in the winter and it is 20 outside and 75 on the porch. I figured that by 1990 I should be able to heat the house with the light bulbs.

Now, Bob is leveling the side slab, I have a long handled shovel and I am spreading concrete over the porch floor while doing a balancing act on the old floor joists. As soon as the concrete is spread on the floor, Janice paid the driver and I went on the side of the house to work with Bob. John, at this time stopped for a fast beer, wiped his mouth with a bandanna the size of a bedspread and is on his way.

Meanwhile, Bob is doing the long stretch out and balance routine with the cigarette hanging out of his mouth. His eyes are watering from the smoke, his shirt has pulled out of his pants, he is soaking wet by now and he has knocked the hell out of the concrete. He has it almost level. He and I now use a long 2 X 4 to level it a little better and he then grabs his 3 foot float to really make the job look good.

This tool looks like a long handled broom shape except instead of having a broom on the business end, there is a piece of thick aluminum about 10 inches wide and three feet long. The handle is about 12 feet long with the extensions. Once someone gets the hang of this tool it is not too hard to use and gives great results. Bob handles it well; I usually make a mess with it.

He gives the slab the hairy eyeball, yells something at Marilyn and we attack the porch slab. While we are smoothing the slab in the porch which is already getting hard, Marilyn went after the edges of the first slab with an edging tool.

This is a small tool which gives a rounded edge to the concrete and helps prevent it from chipping. She has had a lot of practice with the tool and whips it right along like a pro. Bob had her on a job once with a helper who was using the tool. He made the helper watch his son while Marilyn finished the job right.

The porch floor is starting to set up already, but Bob has another tool he uses for this problem. I don't remember the real name of this tool but he refers to it as THE POUNDER.

This name pretty much tells the whole story of the tool. It has a flat piece of metal across the bottom which is made like a box with a couple hundred holes in it. Above that, are two handles which come about waist high. To use this tool, you grab the handles, look down to avoid creaming your feet and commence to bang the concrete with the plate on the bottom. The water in the mix is forced through the holes and the pounding action causes the stones in the mixture to level out.

This is a simple operation, and in theory it is, but try it sometime. If you are in good shape you should be able to use the tool for about 10 minutes at a time, if you are a wimp, you will either grow some muscles or end up hurting. It's a good job for someone else to do.

I had been using the pounder for about 20 minutes as the concrete was setting up and doing okay, Bob has come out to the porch, starts yelling, and suddenly the concrete starts to level out a lot faster. Either he has inspired me or scared the concrete into place. Maybe a little of both. He has now grabbed the tool, is yelling magic words at it, beating it on the floor joists and telling the floor who the boss is. "Get down there you S.O.B., you dirty rotten.........Mother.......).(^%$&&(#@.......You get the picture.

When all is said and done we ended up with two great slabs, the entrance on the side now has redwood expansion joints, these are pieces of wood left in the slab to make up for expansion and contraction of the concrete with the weather. I understand redwood will not rot out. From what I have seen, this is not the truth. I eventually replaced these with plastic 2 X 4's. They never rot.

By now Marilyn has sore knees; Bob makes some dirty remark about her love life and takes the tools away from her so we can clean them. Bob refused to take any money from me for the job, just said that sometime he would have some dirty job for me to help with.

After we finished, we all took showers. (Not together you slob, my tub is not that big anyway). Bob comments this is the best shower he's had in months; he is not too thrilled with his hot water at home and enjoyed the adjustable shower head. Ah, the joys of simple pleasures, probably falls right behind relieving a gas pain.

I asked Janice "What did you make for dinner?" I asked. "Reservations" We had dinner at a local Mexican restaurant. Bob got his first taste of Mexican food. "You really eat this stuff?" He asked as he wipes out the rest of his meal. I nod. "Yes" and drown the meal with a cold beer.

Just one short note here. Remember I mentioned the compressor and the jackhammer? I had rented that locally. When I went back with the machine, I told them about the guy with the party the night before, they all thought that was hysterical. Since then I have rented a few tools from them. For about 3 years every time I went there, they referred to me as the maniac with the jack hammer, because of the way I killed the neighbor's hangover.

JERKY JOHN AND DAD

This is one of the people who fall into the bad neighbor categories. Personally, I think he had mental problems. I mentioned him in another story. He was the ex-boxer who we figured got smacked in the head too many times. To his credit, he kept his property really nice. That was also the down side. He was the kind of guy that if some kid brushed his bike on the roses, the cops were called. And this was back in the late 50's before kids got nervy. Besides John was a big guy.

He seemed to think that the world had it out for him. Bad attitude. He would accuse my father and me and my brother Bob of looking out the basement windows checking out his wife's legs when she was working in the yard. Never happen, the woman has legs like an old table. Now his daughter; her legs I would check out, she was hot.

When we first moved in John would at least talk to Dad, but this came to a screeching halt after John decided to build a wall to keep his driveway from eroding down the hill into our driveway. Dad even volunteered to help John build the wall. He decided to do it himself.

Our driveway was a decent width at the front, and the wall was not a problem there, but the wall kept getting wider as it went toward the back of the property. Problem is that this was all his property, and he did not want to hear about selling Dad a foot or so of it so the wall would be away from us.

The wall went up, Dad got a new truck. I remember it was a beautiful green International pickup truck. It was the only new truck Dad ever had. When he picked me up at school with it, the day he got it, I almost cried it was so nice.

So now Dad has this new truck, and a garage at the end of the driveway, and Johns' wall the length of the driveway. The wall made it impossible to get the truck to the back of the driveway without scraping it on either the house or the wall.

Needless to say, Dad was not too happy with this. There was part of the house which stuck out about two feet at the back end of the house. This was done to make one of the bedrooms a little bigger; this is how we found the home. Dad eventually decided to take the two feet off that part of the home to be able to use the driveway for the truck.

Fortunately, since he did carpentry work, he knew how to do this. We did get it done. Actually put in the new foundation without letting John know it was being done, built the new wall inside the old one and when the time came, Dad just tore the outside wall off the house. Just like magic. We filled in the dirt in the driveway and were back in business. This was the start of the ugly relationship between Dad and John.

If Dad would put a couple of sticks in the ground to stake out a garden, the building inspector got called because John thought we were laying out a room somewhere. If we had a truckload of wood in the driveway, he would bitch to someone.

If he saw anything he thought suspect, the inspector was called. I remember Dad built a set of steps for a local mechanic; we leaned them against the flat roof of our carport to see how they looked. John called the inspector because he said we were putting a second story on top of the carport.

This guy would walk down the street and give people a hard time because he thought their grass was too tall, or the house needed painting, or their garbage can was beat up. A little flaky.

Nobody in the neighborhood liked the guy, but there was not much you could do about him. If he would see my father out in the yard, he would walk around the driveway whistling, just to annoy Dad. If he saw the other neighbor Bernie in the yard on the other side of the property, he would do something annoying to try get to Bernie. This guy never had company, never went anywhere, and never did anything that looked like fun. I sort of felt sorry for his kids. They were fine but they had to live with this nut.

Bedtime Horror Stories for Homeowners

When John used to walk around whistling, it used to get my dad angry but he could not think of anything that would annoy John till by accident, he fell across something. Have you ever seen how old Italian contractors blow their noses? They hold one nostril, tip their head, and blow. The other nostril then clears itself. Personally, I think it is pretty disgusting. Well, Dad would do this every so often when he was outside and did not have a handkerchief.

John saw him do this once and almost threw up in the driveway. So every chance Pop got to do this to John, he would do it. This kept John in the house more often.

John was a churchgoer; he was in the church more often than the Pope. Dad would go to church for weddings and funerals. So of course, John felt Dad was no good. On the other hand, my father was the kind of guy who would help anyone, any time and John would screw you as fast as look at you.

These two guys never got along after the wall incident and my father said that if John ever went on vacation and he knew about it ahead of time, he would call in every concrete company in the area and fill Johns' basement to the ceiling joists with solid concrete.

Dad said he would put a tape player in the guys' basement with an endless tape with someone yelling "KEEP IT COMING, MORE, MORE." Nice fantasy, never happened, too bad.

As I said John would get the building inspector down there for anything. I remember Dad wanted to close off two windows on the driveway side of the home. He made two panels out of plywood, covered them with siding to match the house, and painted them.

One Sunday when John was in church, Dad pulled the two storm windows off the side of the porch and installed these two panels. Probably had this done in about 20 minutes? John came back and knew something looked different, probably took him a week to figure out what Dad had done. Dad said that if John ever died before he did, he was going to throw a block party to celebrate. We moved before that ever happened.

Chapter 17 DOG TALES

DOGS AND NEIGHBORS

If you decide you want to have a pet, just try to be a responsible pet owner. I go so far as to encourage you to adopt from a shelter instead of paying a ton of money for a dog that may end up in the shelter anyway. I have had shelter dogs for over thirty years and so far have had pretty good luck with them.

My cousin Steven was the kind of pet owner that would really annoy me if I lived near him. They had two small dogs. One was a cocker spaniel. That was Buffy. The other guy was Bengi, and he was a little white dog. No big deal. The problem is not with the size of the dogs. The problem is that he would walk them on everyone else's lawns, let them crap there and never clean up after them. One neighbor even had a sign on the lawn. "NO DOG WALKING." Steven does what he wants to do. At this point both dogs have gotten old and died so at least he is not doing this anymore and has no plans to get any other dogs. Meanwhile, his lawn looked like a golf course. He spent more time and money on that stupid grass than anyone. And God forbid, you should even walk on his lawn. Not that I would. It was full of chemicals. A good way to get cancer or cooties or something.

My neighborhood is full of dogs. I have two, and within a hundred feet there are eight more. One neighbor had this old mutt, a female who was not a bad dog. Problem is she used to tie the dog to the house near the fence because the dog used to take off on her. I had told her to put a harness on the dog. She didn't listen, the dog jumped the fence and accidentally hung herself; bummer, not my favorite dog, but I still felt bad when I heard about this.

If you are going to have a dog, and invite the neighbor's pup over for a play date, make sure these two are going to get along. My neighbor Chris has a dog Tela' who used to play with my dog Lacey. Somehow Tela' hurt her leg a couple of years ago, and now has developed a problem where she and Lacey do not get along any more.

We all watch out for each other's dogs in this neighborhood. Now if I am going on a long trip and have to leave the pups home for a few days I get this dog sitter to come in to take care of them instead of putting them in a kennel. The guy is expensive, but my dogs are always fine when I get home.

There are times we may go to visit someone and get tied up, we have all the neighbor's phone numbers and will call and ask someone to throw our dogs out. We do the same thing for them when the situation comes around. We all know where we hide keys, and we all get along with each other's pets. This is a decent system, and has worked out well for everyone involved.

If the neighbors' have dogs, expect a certain amount of noise, that is normal. If your dog is noisy, expect that also. My dogs see someone walking down the street sometimes and actually get annoying. If there is a dog walking by they do not like, they get even worse. If you have a dog that has a bad attitude and attacks other dogs, use your head and check before you turn the pup loose to go in the back yard with another dog.

A fenced in yard can be a real asset, but I never go out and leave mine in the yard. Simple. People steal dogs and use them for bait to train other dogs for fighting. Use some common sense. A fence does not always do it anyway.

My brother Bob had a dog named Sparky who used to be kept in a pen. The dog should have been named Houdini. He was out more than my brother. The pen was not built that well either. That was part of the problem. Bob had about 4 or 5 German Shepherd dogs at one time in this pen with Sparky. One day they all got loose. One got shot by a cop for going after a rabbit in a pen, one got hit by a car, two fell through ice and drowned. Sparky found his way home. If you build a dog pen make sure it is going to work.

I had a dog named Nils in Beachwood who was a fear biter. He was dangerous because he would bite someone for no reason at all.

He never did a lot of damage, but I did not need this. I ended up putting him to sleep at six years old. I got him from a private owner, not a shelter. I had this great dog pen we built, it had a concrete floor, 2 X 4 supports and heavy wire sides and a closed in top which was made of wire. It was attached to a back porch which was set up so the dogs could not get out.

When I was selling the house, there was a door that led to this back porch. This dog could open a door by turning a knob. I also had a bolt on the inside of the door with a sign "Do not open the door, the dog will bite you." I was not sure he would bite, but why give him a chance?

Then some dogs take heat for a bite that never happened. When I had Babe; a small terrier mix who looked like a miniature German Shepherd. I had a kid go past the house with his bike. Babe ran out of the driveway and barked at him. Never got within 10 feet of him. His foot slipped off the pedal and the pedal came around and hit the back of his leg. He thought he got bit. He and his mom were back a couple hours later to find out what happened. It worked out fine when I told them what had gone on.

Another thing you might want to address is this. Dogs get fleas. They all get them at one time or another. Now this is not always a problem, and most of the problem can be prevented. I had a situation one time that was interesting.

A neighbor's dog had fleas, and he was hanging around with my pups, this was years ago. Well, before I realized it, my two dogs had fleas. My home started to look like a flea circus. If I sat on the couch, they would jump over me. (The fleas, not the dogs). I would get in bed, and the fleas were there.

Of course I was not going to let this be a long term arrangement. Not like I could get rent from them. So my next idea was to get in an exterminator. The house had to be bombed. The way an exterminator does this is to close off the windows and doors, put these aerosol cans in the house, and open the cans. The fog kills the fleas in the house.

As for the dogs, I was on my own. I came home from work at lunch time. I had some kind of desk job at the time. Had to put on some old clothes, and give the dogs baths before I got them back in the house. The shampoo would take care of the fleas on the dogs. So in the end; the house was clean, the dogs were clean, I got to see what dog shampoo tasted like, and we were all happy campers.

Now we had another situation with a neighbor's dog when I had the home in Beachwood, this was sort of funny.

There was a guy we sort of hung out with at the time. He was a few years younger than I am, and we would go places together. One day we decided to go out to some park with all the dogs. We were taking two, and he was taking one. His dog was Diablo,... Diablo, AKA Dobbs. He was a Great Dane who weighed more than most adults. All black, a beautiful dog, but really big.

So we are working on getting out of the house, and he decides he has to go get some butts. I tell him. "Leave Dobbs here, go get your butts and come back, it's too hot to leave him in your van"

This is the same dog he left in the van one day, with the windows open. He came back and found two fingers on the seat. I guess someone thought they were going to get a free van. Try to explain that to the ER people. "You lost your fingers where?"

So he takes off with the van, and the pup is in my living room. Dobbs was young, maybe a year. I guess he either got spooked or something. First, he takes a dump on the living room floor. Lucky for me, it was a painted wood floor. OK, I can deal with this, get the snow shovel and clean it up.

I just get that done, and all three dogs now decide to start playing tag in the house. The yard was not fenced in so not like I could throw them out. In the living room I had a coffee table I had made from an old wire spool. One of those big spools the phone company or somebody uses. The dogs started running all over the house. Now this was a small home, 26 feet square, and one story so there is not too much room for them to play.

They start running all over and finally jumped over this table.

At this point it started getting really stupid; so I picked up a newspaper, rolled it tight and hit the table with it. That got the dogs attention. They all took off for my bedroom where we had an old iron bed. This bed was quite a bit higher than most beds. Well, my two dogs slid under it in a heartbeat. They were about 40 or 50 pound dogs. The big guy thought he did the same thing.

In reality, all Dobbs got under the bed was his head, and neck. The rest of him was just sticking out behind him. His butt was as high as the top of the mattress, and he thought he was safe. He realized his situation, after I swatted his back end with the newspaper. All I did was tap him with it, I didn't want to hurt him or make him panic. If my dogs could laugh, I am sure they would. He spent the rest of the afternoon trying to figure out how I found him.

Another neighbor I had one time lived behind me when I still had an apartment in Paterson, New Jersey. This lady had a German Shepherd, big female. Well; she went into heat. The dog, not the neighbor. I did not know this, but my dogs did. So one time when I opened the door to let them out, my two bolted like Sidewinder missiles and went over her fence to check out the female. I was young at the time, so I was on these mutts like a shadow. I had them back on leashes in about a minute.

Now the woman comes out and starts giving me a speech about my dogs trying to hump her poor baby. I told her I was sorry, but I was sure there were other dogs trying to do the same thing. Since my two dogs were the only ones she had seen, I was a liar. Fine, I put my 35mm camera on a tripod in the back window which faced her yard.

Every time I heard my dogs bark, I would go push the button, take a photo and advance the film. In about 2 days I shot the entire roll of film. The dogs would let me know there was another dog there, and the camera did the documentation work. I showed up at the end of the week with a contact sheet showing her all the dogs who were visiting her "baby."

This came to a screeching halt after a big Shepherd hopped her fence, and she came out to see him and her dog locked together butt to butt, like dancing cheek to cheek, wrong cheeks. I told her to throw some cold water on them.

She is out there with a little pot that I would use for making instant coffee or tea, gently pouring it on the dogs where they are joined. "No.....No...Get the hose or they will never quit, you are just giving them some lubrication." After we hit them with the hose, they split up and the stranger dog took off over the fence.

When I lived at home, we had a neighbor who was a little soft in the brain department. He had been a boxer in his younger days. In my humble opinion he got hit in the head too many times and loosened up his brain. Well he was about 6'6" and 250 pounds. He was a big guy. Now maybe it is me, and I don't know why, but he had one of these little foo foo dogs. Some little mutt that weighed all of 10 pounds, she was almost as big as one of the guys' feet.

My father had a contracting business and had a helper working with him at the time. The helper was walking up the driveway. The two driveways ran parallel to each other; Johns' was uphill from ours. For some reason, the dog flipped out when he saw the helper guy and decided to jump in our driveway. Now if you can visualize this, John had built this crappy looking concrete wall the length of the driveway to keep erosion from pulling his blacktop driveway down the hill. His wall was maybe 14 inches high at the front and 20 inches at the back.

So when he saw the dog jump in our driveway, he would have liked to go pick the mutt off the ground, but he and my father did not get along so he would stay on his own property. There is more about this guy in another story. So John asked the helper to pick up the dog for him.

Now, the helper knew the relationship between John and my dad, so he played the chicken part. "I'm sorry Sir, I am afraid of dogs." This left John lying on the ground hanging over the edge of the wall trying to grab his mutt.

It was actually pretty funny watching this big guy trying to catch the pup that is running around his hand and barking at him. He did finally convince the dog to get close enough to grab the little shit.

When my brother had Sparky, the Houdini dog, that mutt used to get loose so often that is was almost a waste to have either the dog pen or the house to contain him. He went through a glass window once to get at a neighbor's dog in heat, I saw him jump a fence and push someone else's dog over a line of bushes. He was a fun dog.

My mother had a neighbor who had a big dog; I think he was a Doberman, nice big critter. He had the owners trained, every night he got a bowl of ice cream. No ice cream, no sleeping.

My dad was working on somebody's house years ago. Now dogs are funny, most of them like to go for a ride in a car. Dad opened the door of the house; the dog is out like a rocket, takes off down the street. I don't care if you have the world record in the 100 M, a dog will outrun you. Almost any dog can do this unless the mutt is really old.

Well, Dad and his helper Nicky tried to catch this mutt for about 5 minutes. They were not doing too well. Dad never had good luck catching dogs. The owner finally came out of the house when he saw what was happening. Says to Dad "Open the truck door; he loves to go for a ride." The mutt was in the truck in seconds.

I had a similar situation. Working on some ladies house; it is raining, the big Shepherd is sitting by the door. I figure he has to take a leak. The yard is all fenced in. I open the door expecting him to come back as soon as he is done, fat chance.

He took the fence and was gone. So now I had no choice but to come clean and tell the woman what had happened. Seems this happens all the time. She asks me to come along with her. I needed a break anyway.

We get in her car, a big Lincoln town car. I do not know what this car costs, but it is more than you will see me spending on wheels. We bolt out of the driveway, down the street.

A right, a left, the car is sliding on the wet ground. I am seeing my life in front of my eyes. Six blocks later, she brings the car to a screeching stop. Opens the back door and like magic; in hops her dog. Drags about a pound of water and mud into the back seat; she is not even concerned. Her baby is safe.

Getting back to Dad for a bit, he got us some kind of small dog when I was a kid. From the photos, I would guess a Jack Russell. These are working dogs, lots of energy, they need a lot of training and activity; keep that in mind if you ever get one. One of their jobs is killing rats on farms. These are not lap dogs. Dad was under the belief that he knew how to train dogs. To this day I am convinced he did not.

He decided one day to take Lucky to the field in the cemetery behind our house. Nice spring weather. Clear, warm, a good day. The grass is wet with dew. Now Dad did not bother to wear sneakers. I am not even sure if he had a pair. This was way before this country decided that sneakers are the footwear of choice.

He was wearing his slippers. Even if he was a fast runner, slippers are not made for running. He now takes Lucky off leash, like the dog is going to listen to him. Sure, like the dog is going to learn calculus in college this year. He is off like a dragster. The dog; not Dad. Runs across that field chasing birds, squirrels, mice whatever he could see or hear or smell. Dad was the least exciting part of his life. "Dad, Who?"

At first Pop was amused. That did not last, he wanted to go home and eat. He had only had one cup of coffee and was about to pass out from lack of caffeine. So now he takes to calling the dog. "Lucky, Lucky.....Good Boy...Come here." "Come boy, here Lucky." Now if you have ever tried to catch a dog, you know what they do. They come within five or six feet of you, and stop. They know how long your arms are and how fast you can run. Dogs are not stupid.

Dad tries another approach; Lucky gets close, Dad takes off one of the slippers, holds his foot off the wet grass. I have no idea what he was planning to do. Throws the slipper at Lucky. Maybe he thought the dog would bring it back like a retriever.

Since there was almost no bonding there, Lucky is off to the races with the slipper in his mouth. Dad is now pretty annoyed, he is chasing the dog with one slipper, the other foot is a half inch shorter because there is no slipper on that one. He is doing a limping run after the dog.

He chases the dog for about five minutes. At some point, I guess Lucky either got it, or felt sorry for the man, but he came back with the slipper and gave it to him.

Dad had him on the leash in less time than it took to call the dog a bad name. He also had to walk home with Lucky with a wet foot in one slipper. Of course when he came home and told us about this, we all laughed till we almost threw up.

One thing I have noticed; this comes from having dogs for the past thirty or so years. A dog will always come back to a stranger faster than to the owner. I have been told that this is because they figure the owner will put them back in the house or a leash. I only grabbed my neighbor's dog the other day like this. We saw a black blur go past the house, actually Janice saw him. Yells at me "RIDER JUST RAN DOWN THE STREET" The kid next door who is about 16 and owns the dog got nowhere.

She knows I will help round up any dog, and besides that, I like this pup. He is about two years old, some kind of mix. All I had to do was step out the front door; called him once, and within seconds he was there licking my face. "Go back to the kid, you crazy or something?"

Janice had a woman who used to work with her. This lady had three Irish Setters. Pretty dogs, not real smart. She had a table in her dining room that was so scratched from them jumping on it, that if she wanted to refinish it, we figured we would have to take ¼ inch of wood off the top for openers. She had a running contract with a local glass company to come in at least once a week to replace low windows in her home where the dogs would break them out to get at the mailman.

We had another friend whose dog destroyed a big wooden chair so badly that we had to replace the part people would sit on. He was a Great Dane, Max was his name.

I remember taking my dog Noah over to her house for a play date with the two dogs. "Is he housebroken?" She asked "Sure; of course he is." Noah walked into her hallway about 6 feet and lifted his leg on a table. "Maybe not." Marked his territory.

Two more fast Noah stories. One time when we went away for a few days we asked my neighbor Ray to keep an eye on Noah. This was during the summer. We were going to be gone for maybe 3 or 4 days. Noah used to like to go sleep in the basement in hot weather. The basement stays about 55 degrees all year, so when it was 90 out, he had the brains to go there and chill out.

Ray had stopped by during the day to see how the dog was doing. By now the dogs hearing was pretty well shot. We could sneak up on him even if we were not being sneaky. It happens, no big deal. Noah was sleeping at the bottom of the basement steps when Ray showed up. Ray walks in the house.

"Noah, Noah." No answer, no nothing. So now Ray is a little concerned. He liked the dog and felt we had left him in charge. Then he decided to look down the basement, the door was open. He put on the lights at the top of the steps, there is Noah. Out like a light at the bottom of the steps. This dog scared the hell out of me a few times; he could sleep through a war. Well Ray didn't realize Noah was losing his hearing; he is calling down the steps at the mutt, no response. Now he goes down the steps, walks all the way down.

Noah is still as death. Ray leans down by the dog and shakes him. Now Noah shakes his head, and shows some life. Poor Ray thought Noah had died on him and was doing the whole scenario of how he was going to tell me my dog had died on his watch. I knew I had an old dog and of course would not hold Ray responsible if the mutt just crapped out on us. We all have to go sometime. I think Ray almost died from fright. Maybe Noah was having an out of body experience.

One more story about Noah and the basement. The dog hated thunder. I don't care if it was in another country; if he heard it, he was shook.

When we would have a storm, he would hide under the bed and shake. It was so bad he would actually shake the bed. One day when I was putting in my first sump pump, the thunder started. I think I was home alone with Noah. Of course it didn't bother me. I kept digging my hole in the corner of the basement. This was this hole for the sump pump. This holds a big plastic tube with holes in it with stone on the bottom. "BOOM." The thunder hits right over the house.

Noah was still young at this time his hearing was still OK. He shot down the basement steps like the devil was chasing him. Hits the basement, flies past me and jumped in the hole in the corner. He was going to get as far from the noise as possible. I think this is enough dog stories for right now.

DOG BEDS AND OTHER SILLY STUFF

I lied, here are more dog stories. There is one good reason to own a home. You can get a pet. Might be a dog or a cat or a goat, but whatever it is, there is no landlord telling you there is a no pets clause in the lease. I have never been much of a renter. Most of my life since I left home has been in homes I have owned. There have been only two so far, but that is fine. Some people spend their lives collecting rent receipts. I know people like this.

It may sound silly to a person who has no interest in pets, but whenever I looked at properties I kept the pups in mind. Now I call them pups till they die. I have had 14 year old dogs and still call them pups. I remember two homes in particular that I looked at, one had a yard as big as the inside of a Honda Civic, call that a yard? Give me a break.

Half that yard was occupied by an oil tank. That place came right off the list. Another place we looked at had concrete on most of the property, seems the current owner was allergic to grass. He had a small strip of grass in front of the house. So small you could cut it with barber clippers.

You will find out some strange things about pet owners. I know a lot of them who have dogs. These people will let a dog tear up trim on a wall, scratch up a wall and not get too bothered with the animal. They also let dogs sleep on the bed. I remember hearing that something like 85% of dog owners have the dogs sleep on the bed.

This must be true; mine do that, and the dog beds which cost us about $100 apiece sit vacant. The dogs do sleep on them also, but I think they look at my bed as a bonding experience. To their credit, when I fool around with Janice they stay off the bed. As soon as we are done and relax, the mutts are back up there.

DOGS FALLING THROUGH CEILINGS

This may seem like it could not happen, but here are two short stories about dogs falling through ceilings. The first story is about my house in Beachwood. This was a home that was small; 26 feet square, originally built as a summer home. The ceilings here were made with something called Celotex.

Now, Celotex was used big time back in the 1950's for homes and offices. It was more common than fleas on dogs. You may have seen this stuff somewhere along the line. The tiles are usually one foot square, and are installed in the ceiling like a grid work. The material is a sort of fiber/cardboard type stuff. I don't make it; I can't tell you exactly what it is, but it works.

It is strong enough to do the job, but not strong enough to stand on when it is installed. Mice can walk on it, the rest of us are out of luck.

This Celotex was installed on 1 X 2 inch furring strips which were nailed either on an existing ceiling or on ceiling joists. A furring strip is a piece of wood either 1 X 2 inches or 1 X 3 inches. The ceiling joists usually are heavy framing, anywhere from 2 X 4's to 2 X 10's depending on how the building is constructed. The furring strips run perpendicular to the joists. If that big word confuses you, think back to high school math classes or look it up in a dictionary.

The Celotex is stapled to the bottom of the furring strips, and when there is nothing but ceiling joists above this, the ceiling joists may have insulation in them which is light and will not damage the ceiling. This is the proper way to insulate an attic, keep this in mind.

Actually I am going to tell you about the other home first, because of the insulation issue. A friend of ours called me in for a repair job one time. One of her Irish Setters had gotten into a storage space in the second floor of her house.

Part of this storage area had a plywood floor, but there were sections where there was nothing but ceiling from the room below. sheetrock ceiling, wet sheetrock ceiling, soggy sheetrock ceiling. Now here is an educational moment for you.

If you ever insulate an attic, put the insulation on the ceiling joists at the bottom/floor of the attic. Do not staple it to the roof framing unless you use an air spacing system to keep it away from the sheathing. If this insulation is installed on the roof framing without an air space, condensation will form between the insulation and the sheathing. Eventually this will cause either the sheathing to rot, or make moisture in the attic or both. The moisture in the attic is what caused the sheetrock to get wet. This takes a long time to accumulate, sometimes several years.

By time the dog got into this space, the sheetrock was spongy, soft and weak. The poor dog walked on the sheetrock thinking it would be a nice place to hang out. And he did just that. He hung out. Out of the ceiling, broke right through it.

He got lucky; they were able to take him out of the hole in one piece without him getting hurt. I got hired to repair the ceiling. I suggested she take all this insulation down from the roof framing and do it the right way. She could either hire me to do this, or give her son a six pack of beer and a dust mask and have him do it. She didn't hire me, so I guess the son did it.

That was a construction mistake, mine was a dummy mistake. This was the first week I lived in Beachwood. This was my first home. I had two dogs at the time, I had Noah and Nils.

They were good sized dogs. Noah was about 40 pounds, Nils was about 55. Considering the fact that I had done construction work for years, it still amazes me that I did something this stupid.

I was putting stuff up in the attic in the house. I had to climb up a ladder to get there, not steps. This access hole was above where I would eventually put a washer and dryer.

I was up there arranging crap on the floor/ceiling joists. I did have some plywood down in a couple of places. The trick here is to either walk on the plywood or on the joists. If you do this, you do not put any weight on the ceiling and no problems. I knew this, and keeping this in mind, I should have just continued what I was doing. Nooooo, I had to grow a crop of stupid.

The dogs were in the kitchen near this opening, and they are whining. They look at me with the big brown eyes and whine some more. Lorraine says. "Oh, they feel bad; they want to be up there with you." I should have just said, "No, get lost." But for whatever reason, I decided to have them come up there, as if they would know where to walk.

I seem to give my dogs a little too much credit for brains once in a while. This was one of those times. So like Mr. & Mrs. Really Dopey, we lifted the dogs up into the attic. Not a good move. At first, they just sort of sniffed around, walked on the joists, and looked disinterested. That was the calm before the storm. Once they got used to the attic. That is when the fun started.

Those of you who have dogs have seen this happen. The will go from quiet and intelligent to wild and running wild in "Oh, maybe ½ second." The pack behavior thing sets in, party time.

The deal now is that they started chasing each other. "Wow, what a cool place to play," is probably what was going through their minds. "This is great." But now, now they are not only running on the joists, their feet are slipping into the Celotex ceiling tiles. Like I said before, this stuff is not that strong. Now they start knocking tiles out of the ceiling. One here, one there, they probably took out 6 or so in a matter of thirty seconds. Of course, as soon as I realized what was going on I yelled "STAY, STAY" That at least cooled them off a bit.

Nils stopped right over a tile and stayed. He also went through the ceiling. His front legs and his head were in the attic, the back end of him is waving in the air over the living room. He was not too happy about this.

He did not know how big a drop is below him, but he can't get up in the attic again by himself. We did get lucky that I was not too far away from him. I was able to grab his furry butt and drag him into the attic. Now they both went back downstairs. I also gave myself a repair job on what used to be a perfect ceiling. Not that big a problem, I eventually sheet rocked over the tiles.

Chapter 18   SEEING IS BELIEVING

VISUAL POLLUTION

A problem in the burbs. You know the deal; some people must have no idea of what they look like, some of them must own a magic mirror that makes them better looking than they really are. These are the kind of people you see going out for the newspaper in their underwear, or a bath robe that always seems to be open to show off their naked body and they are not built like Mr. America.

I have a neighbor who recently went through Weight Watchers, now she looks really decent, but at one time she would be out there in the morning with her frumpy robe and fuzzy slippers getting the paper. At 230 pounds and 5'3" she was not what I wanted to see at 7A.M.

I also know someone who we see a few times a year. This woman is about 63 years old, and couple years ago we were going out with her and she commented that she has to watch the vertical blinds in her house cause she does not want the neighbors seeing her walking around naked in the house. To start with she has really short gray hair, clocks in at about 220 pounds and looks more like an old man than an old woman. I think if I walked past her windows and saw her naked I would make sure I left my glasses home the next time I went for a walk.

One guy I know has a habit of going out in front of the house in his underwear. This would not be bad either if he had a decent body, but again, he has dickey do disease, you know what that is? Where his stomach sticks out further than his dickey do. He has lost a lot of weight in the past six months as he has found out he is a borderline diabetic. Now he takes human bites.

The next thing I find to be a little ugly is the problems caused by people who seem to collect automobiles, and a ton of extra parts. I remember looking at a house several years ago. This was the exact situation. The guy next door had about 8 cars on the property. To look at them, I don't think any of them ran.

I could be wrong, but they all looked like clunkers. He also had enough parts on the property to make another 8 cars; transmissions here, wheels there, a pile of tires in the back and a dozen seats scattered across what could have been a front lawn.

I think I get the point across to you, though I will admit to going out in bikini underwear in hot weather to throw the dogs out. Then again, at least I work out in the gym 5 days a week. My mirror and my wife do not lie to me.

Since I originally wrote this chapter, the guy who thought he had diabetes turned out to be a wrong call, who knew? Put the weight back on and then some. He should be headed for the fat farm.

RELIGIOUS WARS IN THE HOOD

This goes to show you, that you do not have to go to a foreign country to get involved in a religious war. If this did not happen to me in person, I would not even bother with it. But I did get a kick out of this episode.

I have a guy named Adam who comes around to visit. He is a Jehovah Witness. He and his wife started coming around several years ago. Now at the time, I told him right up front. "I was raised as a Catholic, and only do church for weddings and funerals, and that all depends on who is getting buried or married. I don't practice my religion, so don't think I am going to do yours either."

My idea of praying is when for example; I am painting something in the house, and some paint drips off the brush and hits an area that is supposed to be painted the same color. "THANK YOU GOD." That is about the size of it.

So a few weeks ago it was one of those rainy, cold, cloudy days around here. You know the kind of weather, the kind that makes you think suicide is a good idea.

The doorbell rings on the front door. There are two reasons I know it is the front door. I have two different chimes for my doors (big deal) and also my dogs are going nuts running for that door. The bell does not get rung all that often, so when it does I almost fart with excitement.

WELL GOLLY. IF IT ISN'T TWO, YOUNG, IDEALISTIC GUYS TOTING SOME PROPAGANDA FOR THE MORMONS.

Now I have a friend of mine whose son got into this religion a number of years ago. Got to a point I was calling him "Rev." I do not know what gets these people all fired up, but they can go from a drinking womanizer to a holy worshiper in no time flat. Maybe they have had a close call. You know, like running a motorcycle through a tractor trailer and living. That kind of stuff. So now I go down to open the door, just because I am either curious or stupid. Maybe both.

These two young guys are out there in the rain in short sleeve shirts giving me the speech. Now I am a decent kind of guy and also do not want to be sued for negligence, so I tell them to get in the enclosed porch before they get sick. I am old enough to be their father, so I feel it is my duty to help them stay alive long enough to smarten up.

So for maybe 20 minutes or three days, I am not really sure. They go on and on about God, the Bible, Adam and Eve, whatever they can pull out of their briefcases. They insisted they had to leave me a book on their religion. So I took it just to get rid of them. I think it will work fine to keep my workbench from rocking if I put it under the correct leg. I also told them about the Jehovah Witness guy. Sort of like telling your wife about an old girlfriend who would do any disgusting thing you asked.

Well, just as they were leaving, who pulls up? You got it, the Witness guy. Shit, just like having your wife catch you in bed with another woman. So I tell them who this is and send them on their way. But now of course, the witness guy sees these guys and wants to know if this is company. By now he should know this is not *my* company at least not late in the afternoon wearing ties. Most of my company wouldn't know a tie if it was twisted around their necks. My tie thing is the same as the church thing; so I tell him, "Nope they are not company, they are your competition."

I almost had to bite my tongue to keep from laughing. Gave him the straight story on them. I have nothing to lose here. So to make a long story short. I talked to him for a while, and he asked me what they had to say and so on and so on, like an industrial spy. Except we were not talking about cars or washing machines. After a short time, he decides to leave. At least I was smart enough to put on a hat and jacket so I would not freeze my ass off.

Ten minutes later, I look out the front window of my house, and here are the WITNESS GUYS. They always seem to travel in pairs; maybe one is a security guy. Who knows? And the MORMON GUYS.

They are all in the street in the rain all *not* dressed right. Freezing their asses off, waving their hands, and quoting spiritual and bible stuff at each other. I could hear them now.

"He was MY convert, NO mine, NO MINE, I SAW HIM FIRST. I WANT A PIECE OF THIS SINNER." Think about it; many wars are done over religion, or some other faith based idea, whatever. I thought they were going to have a fist fight in the street. I was putting my money on Adam, the Witness guy. He is much bigger and heavier. Now if you can picture this.

Adam is about 6'2" and about 260. He is not taking this lying down. Nope. His eyes widen; his breath gets deep, his chest is heaving, he is gonna fight. He reaches in his pocket. He digs all the way in and whips out his Bible. Runs his finger down a page and with a BOOMING VOICE. A voice like Moses leading the people through the parted Red Sea. He starts quoting scriptures.

This guy is amazing. He knows shit that nobody knows. He can dig into a Bible and pull out stuff on any subject so fast; you would think that he wrote the book himself. Ask him about a plumbing problem in your house; and somewhere in that bible, he has some line which seems just the answer. He practically breaths this stuff. His nostrils are flaring; the veins in his neck stick out like a fire hose. His eyes are wide. He is going to kick ass.

Now the young guy goes for his Bible. He is not going down without a fight. This reminds me of the movies with the old time gunfight. They are squaring off and taking aim.

Adam starts with some stuff about creation, and the young guy is taking a shot back with the Heaven and the Earth. Their seconds are right behind them, with backup Bibles. They are shaking with excitement waiting for a chance to tear into the other side.

You know the deal. We all know.

Almost as if it is a God Given Right. WE ARE RIGHT NO MATTER WHO SAYS WHAT.

I had to get a cup of coffee. I can't take this much excitement in one day. Every religion claims that the people from all the other religions are going to hell.

That being the case; from a logical standpoint we will all go to Hell. Bring your bathing suits or go naked. I hear it is hot there. Can I arrange for cold beer to be delivered? I drink Rolling Rock in 7oz. glass bottles.

At some point these guys all got soaked to the skin and left without punching each other out. By time they left; they were so cold their chattering teeth were interfering with their speech.

Maybe they can pick this up again during the summer, when it is about 90 degrees. When it gets too messy, at least I can hose them down like dogs in heat. Maybe I will be a sport, and bring them some of those 7oz. beers.

CROOKED WALLS

When I was out doing carpentry work for a living on my own, I would occasionally run into someone who thought he knew more about the work than I did, or at least acted that way. My father used to get these guys every so often. They would give him a line such as "I would do the job myself, but I don't have the tools." He would give them just as stupid an answer. "Hell, I will rent you tools by the day." The whole thing was just silly.

I was doing a job for a guy in my area; he had a big contemporary home in the next town. To look at the place it was really impressive. It had all kinds of odd shaped windows, and high ceilings. Also a wide open layout, with a river behind it. Don't let the river thing look like a big deal. In the summer when the water got low, it stunk and there were 10 million mosquitoes. Not my problem. This guy was supposedly some kind of real estate professional, at least that is what he told me.

You would think if he were in this position, he would have a better clue of how to sell a house. The only reason I was aware of this, is that he was trying to sell this place at the time. For example, in the living room was a large kerosene heater which was vented to his chimney. Now if I were selling this house, I sure as hell would not have an item like this in the home. First impression that gives is that the heating system was not up to speed. Plus, the single pane windows that did not help.

Someone came over to see the place and asked him how big the hot water heater was. They were talking about gallons. That is usually how we judge these things. He is telling them it is six feet tall and two feet in diameter. I had to go outside and laugh so I did not crack up in his face.

I am not sure if he ever really sold the house. I was there opening up a wall for him. His kitchen was next to the dining room, just a doorway in between. I was moving some cabinets and a microwave oven so I could open up this wall and make a more spacious look here. His idea, good idea. The wall was a weight bearing wall.

So he took out the microwave, disconnected it. He hired an electrician to re-wire it in a different location. I guess he did not think I could do it. I didn't care. It was an annoying job and I am not a licensed electrician anyway. Then I took out some cabinets. This worked out fine, the lower base units were going to come to the top of the lower wall. This would leave a space of maybe 4 feet above the cabinets so he could see straight through to the dining room. Just had to finish off the top of the wall by the cabinets and the bottom of the wall above the opening. The piece by the cabinets was easy, just a small shelf.

The wall above it, had been cut, and I decided to put a good header in there to support the part that was no longer supported by the bottom half of the wall. Of course I had to set all this stuff up ahead of time in case something was going to sag. I opened the ends of the walls, and framed up some 2 X 4's to hold the header and built a header. Being a heavy duty freak, I made the header out of 2 x 10's. I didn't want it to come down at a later date. So far we are doing fine; except for the time I accidentally shut off the wrong circuit breaker and shut down his stupid computer for a few minutes.

I got this big header all built and installed it above this opening, did it all by myself. This was a double 2 x 10 with a plywood spacer about 10 feet long. Got it in place, all nailed. Now I covered it with sheetrock. This part has to be flush with the existing wall above the opening.

There was a track light set up near this wall for some reason, and it would shine directly on the joint where I was finishing the wall. Now with spackle, this is not always perfect looking from step one, the stuff has to get built up in a couple of layers.

The guys who do this for a full time job are usually much better at it than the average carpenter. I do it well enough to get the job done. So I had this wall pretty well finished and *"Mister I Have All the Answers"* comes along and starts giving me a song and dance about how he can see a small ripple in the face of the wall. Mind you, I am not done yet. That always annoys me how people like to interrupt someone before the job is finished. Idiots, wait till the job is done before you whine.

He starts to go on and on about the walls in this house being perfect. Now anyone can tell you, this is an illusion. There is not a house in the world where everything is perfect. It is the nature of the materials and people's abilities to work with them. So I let him rant for a few minutes. He is really full of himself and the stupid house.

When he has almost passed out from carrying on; I ask him to pick out one of the perfectly straight walls in the house. He goes right for a long living room wall. "Perfect, absolutely perfect." He was all excited. Here is where it really bit him in the ass.

I had just bought a brand new four foot aluminum level. This thing still had the UPC label on it. It was cleaner than most women I ever dated. This thing was about as close to perfectly straight as can be made with a machine. I handed this tool to him. "Here do me a favor, take a look down this level and see if it looks straight to you." I asked. So he holds it up, looks straight down the length of it. "Absolutely perfect." He tells me. This is what I expected him to say, he is just painting himself into a corner. "Now where is that perfectly straight wall you were going to show me?" I asked.

Right here, and makes his move. "Good," I am thinking. At this point I took the edge of this level, and laid it flat on the wall, and rocked it like a see saw. Of course the wall is not as straight as this level. That is almost impossible. I knew I was taking an outside shot at this, but it was worth it. All of a sudden he realized the perfect wall was not all that perfect and it was time to shut up.

Guys with big mouths always seem to get themselves into situations like this. I know this; so I do not try to tell anyone I live in a perfect house. I couldn't live here long enough to make it perfect. Besides, I have a life.

This brings me back to my cousin Steven. His name will pop up in my books here and there. All you ever get from him is how perfect his crap is. "This couch is imported from Italy" or some other nonsense. He wouldn't know an Italian couch if it came with salami stuffing in the seats.

A few years ago we were down there for coffee and cake. My Mom was also there. Now a bit about my mother. She was 90 last month and still sharp as a straight razor. Her arthritis slows her down a bit, but her mind is still real sharp. She basically grew up with my father, not from childhood, but married him when she was fairly young, and got to see him do a lot of carpentry work. My Dad did that work most of his adult life. Did a lot of good work, made mistakes, learned from his mistakes and other peoples mistakes. He was a smart man.

Now my mother was along for this ride. When he needed someone to hold something in the shop he would call her if there was nobody else there to help him. She helped him with sheetrock, wood, plaster, electricity, plumbing.....everything.

And she was paying attention. She is no dummy. So after 30 something years of this stuff... NOBODY FOOLS MOM WHEN IT COMES TO RENOVATION WORK.

So we are at Stevens' house having coffee and he starts going on and on about all the wonderful work he has done there. He does decent work, but likes to think he is Michelangelo. NOT. So my mother got a little fed up with his mouth and asked him to show her some of the work. She was ready for him. He walked her around the house flapping his mouth about all this work and she kept pointing out small mistakes. Nothing big, but not perfection. He came back to the table a lot quieter.

He loves to try this one one-upmanship crap on me all the time. I don't even get involved, or try not to get involved. He and my brother Bob do enough of it for all of us. I will on occasion mention something he has done wrong if it is a real screw up. I remember the time he built some kind of big tool box near his driveway for garden tools. Oh, he was proud as could be about how well he built it. It's got this, it's got that, and on and on. Let's be realistic. It is a stupid tool box.

I let him go on for a few minutes. This box was about the size of a small tool shed. Then I quietly pointed out to him that he had installed the siding upside down on the damn thing. He made sure he fixed that before Bob got a look at it. HA.

This was an experience I had several years ago. I would not do this, just out of common decency. But then again, some people do not have any decency. I was doing carpentry then, and working for clients. There are people who will complain that all the contractors are crooks. This guy was sort of a crook, but people should also meet some of the customers.

I had one guy where I put a floor in a bathroom for him. He had been doing the work himself but hurt his back and was sort of out of it for a few days. Meanwhile he wanted to keep the job going. He would buy old homes, fix them up and turn them over for a profit. Not a bad thing to do. He showed me a trick he used to use. Talk about crooked walls.

Some old homes have plaster and lath walls; these will sometimes hold up forever, and some of them will get dry and eventually start to sag and lean and look sort of like they will fall off the framing. He had a home with that problem. Chances are they were not going to fall apart, but he wanted to make sure prospective customers would not even think this.

He would take a wall like this; usually some tall, long wall and he would wallpaper this wall. He would do this with some large pattern, usually some kind of floral design. Wild flowers, leaves, twigs, branches, that type of thing. Nothing with a geometric pattern.

This wallpaper would now hide the bad wall, and distract the buyer from realizing they had a potential problem. Regular nice guy. So if you every buy any old homes in Long Branch, NJ, make sure you take a good long look at the walls.

Met another guy living in Colts Neck, NJ. Expensive area, period. Horse farms, celebrities, big shots. People have been spending over a million dollars for homes there for years. Another area I could not afford. I saw a home there few years ago. Someone had fixed it up some.

I saw the before and after, and the place was small. You could put this place inside mine and ride a bike around it. The priced it for somewhere like $650,000, and I am pretty sure they got it. This story is not about this home. It is about that home the other guy had.

This home was a big, beautiful colonial type house. There were walls in this house that ran thirty feet to forty feet long. Nicely done, lots of fancy trim, nice paint work. Aside from that, let's be realistic. It was built just like any other house in this country, stud walls, sheetrock, and so on.

This man called me out to take a look at this job. Here is what he wanted to do. Two jobs. One job he wanted to do was to put Formica on the walls behind the sink and counters in his kitchen. Formica is the name used for a laminate that is widely used for counter tops and cabinet facing work. There are a few companies who make stuff like this, but the brand name stuck so people treat it as a generic type thing, much like the oat cereal that we can buy. People still call the Shop Rite brand Cheerios, even though the box says Shop Rite.

The problem with using laminate here is simple. This stuff is thin, it bends and it will follow the shape of the wall. So if the wall has a small curve from one end to the other, so does the laminate. I explained this to him. I suggested ceramic tile. One job I talked myself out of. That is fine it would have come back and bit me in the butt. His other job was just as goofy.

One reason people come up with ideas like this might be just lack of proper information. Either that; or they think they will catch some contractor sleeping and get more job then they really wanted to pay for.

He had a long wall between his living room and his dining room, just taking a guess, 40 feet. There was beautiful wallpaper on one side of this. That was in one room. The other side had all kinds of fancy chair rails and trim. Nice work.

He wanted to put a seven foot opening between the two rooms. This was not a bad idea, easy access. Here is the problem. This wall was holding up the top half of the house. This meant that it was going to have to be re-supported with a big header. Either he did not know this, or he was trying to play me out.

When I told him it was going to take me a week to do this job because of the framing problems and doing the appearance work he thought I was kidding him. He said to me, and I quote..... "All you have to do is cut the wall, and put some trim on the edges." His second story floor would eventually end up being part of his first floor. That job also went in the trash. I am not sure if he ever did either of those jobs. All I know; is I am glad I did not do them. Experience helps.

Chapter 19   GOOD PLANS DO NOT ALWAYS WORK

SCOTTS STOCKADE FENCING

I have this neighbor I have mentioned, his name is Scott. I see him a couple times a year. When we first moved in I would see him more often, this was one of those times. Right after he moved in here, he needed some stockade fencing or some kind of fence.

Well, we had some stockade up so I said to him. "Why not get some of this stuff, the prices are not too bad, goes up halfway easy, and it will go along well with the fencing I have up already." Good thinking on my part I guess. Now we only had a small problem with this.

Today if we go to Home Depot, if I want to get something really big and do not have a truck, they will rent me one to bring the items home. Say for example, I was going to do roofing or siding where the materials are not going to fit in the car, this type situation.

If I remember right, this was before Home Depot was here. There was a store called Rickel's. This was a smaller version of Home Depot. They had a lot of things for homeowners. I think the first two years we lived here we kept one employee there working from all the stuff we got there. They eventually went out of business. But that is where we went to get Scott's fencing. He was still married to Barbara at this time.

So with me trying to be a good neighbor, I said to him. "We can take my van and pick up the fencing. What could it weigh? Twenty pounds a section." Duh. I have always been in pretty good shape so I have a tendency to guess weights wrong when it comes to building materials. For some stupid reason; I thought we could fit the pieces inside the van. That does not work with six foot high fencing.

So he and me and Janice and Barb all pile into the van and head to Rickel's. He and Barb were planning to go out for dinner that night. I guess he figured it was not going to take all that long to pick up the fencing.

Bedtime Horror Stories for Homeowners

We get to Rickel's, pick out whatever he needed and now load the van. The fence posts fit inside fine. They were 8 feet long, and the van could take that fine. Now we get to the fencing pieces. I guess there were about ten of these.

Not being a total jerk, I have rope and a big heavy strap clamp in the van. We decide to put the fencing on top of the van. There are no racks on it, but the van is old and who cares? By the way; these were not twenty pounds each, more like eighty. No problem. Idiots. This was like the Three Stooges at work.

Between the four of us, we did manage to get all this fencing on the roof of the van, about 800 pounds of it total. Talk about top heavy, this makes an SUV look good. We tied the pieces down, clamped some of it, whatever it took to make it stay put.

We were only going to drive for about 15 minutes, and if we drove slow and careful, this was not going to be a problem. I am surprised I didn't break the windshield with the weight on top of this van. We crawled home through the back streets. This is what drunk drivers do. Less chance of getting a ticket for overloading. I do not know if the weight was going to be a problem, but the weight distribution was scary.

We did get the van back to his yard in one piece. Now we had to unload the van. This went fairly well, I think. I stood on a ladder near the roof and I would push a section of fence to him and the women and they would stack it against the garage wall.

Took us maybe 15 minutes to get this done, about five minutes more and the posts were out. They never did get to go out that night. By time we got done unloading the van, Barb was soaking wet with sweat and dirty and mad as hell at Scott. Janice and I went home, got naked took a shower together and had some kind of supper. I don't think he saw Barb naked for quite a few days.

A/C FIASCO

First thing you want to know about me, I do not really like air conditioning. I will take a fan any day of the year over air. For some reason or other; I freeze in A/C. I especially dislike it when someone keeps the house at 66 degrees when it is 97 outside and expect me to sit around in this. I will take my drink and go outside.

When we moved in to Pughaven North we did not have central air, we had a window unit. It was in the front bedroom of the house. This thing weighed about 90 pounds, and could have been scary to install, except that I hooked a piece of wood across the top of the frame so it could not fall out the window and land in my neighbor's alleyway.

I lived with this for about 20 years. Janice would fire it up when it got hot, I would go sleep on the living room floor. "How can you sleep there, she would say?" "Watch" I would bring a blanket, and a pillow, throw them on the floor, open the front door and all the windows and I was in business. Out like a light. She has trouble sleeping in a bed; I could sleep in my crushed stone driveway.

So four or five years ago; we came across some extra money, maybe somebody left it to us. I am not sure. She does the check book. All of the sudden Janice is thinking CENTRAL AIR. Her aunt had hired some local company to install a unit in her old house in the next town, and was telling Janice how nice it was to come home to a cool home.

Before we even got the system installed, I told Janice. "You run this thing too cold and I am sleeping in the yard." Like she cares, she said to me. "Will you be safe there?" "Of course, I will take Lacey and a gun, nobody will bother me." Lacey is half pit, half boxer she is a sweet dog and would lick you to death, but not everyone knows that. Fortunately Janice keeps the A/C at a decent temperature so we have never had to resort to this situation.

Bedtime Horror Stories for Homeowners

So, we get the estimator over here to take a look at the place. We have a low attic with truss framing, great system. I even told the estimator. "Look in the attic, make sure you can get the air handler up there." He never looked, he was sure it would fit. Right there I should have sent him packing. This is what happens when I do not follow my gut reactions.

Janice sets up a contract with these guys, a certain size unit, price, taxes all that stuff. I was in on this also, so I can't drop the whole problem on her. Like I said, I should have sent them packing.

Day one the techs show up with a van, and drop this big compressor unit directly in front of my side door. This is the door we use to get in and out of the house 99.9 % of the time. I don't even have a key for my front door since I lost it last year.

I asked the guy, "Where are you going to install that thing?" "Right here." He says, and he is serious. I say to him. "You can install it right up your ass if you think it is staying there." Same problem, gut reaction. I told him to find some place in back of the house to put this stupid unit. They ended up putting it in back of the house behind the kitchen near the corner of the house.

That was the start of this mess. I was doing free-lance artwork at the time, and was working in the back yard. I told them that if they had any questions about the house, to come out and ask me, since I had done a lot of work here. Fine. I was there making some big signs for a playhouse in Elizabeth, NJ.

I come in a couple hours later to see what is going on. The crew is running pipes and vents at this point. My dining room ceiling has a mural on it; it looks like four big skylights with the sky showing through the skylights. One of the vents is sticking out of a part that looks like the sky. I mention to the tech. "Do you really think you would see a vent sticking out of the sky?"

I tell him, "Put the damn thing where it looks like part of the ceiling, I will fix the damage here." I figured he was so used to following orders, he could not see the problem. That for starters.

Then they ran a pipe down from the attic through the back part of the back bedroom ceiling, not near the wall. No, more like 16 or 18 inches from the back wall and 24 inches from the side wall. This ties up my entire back corner of the room. I am not amused. At this point I wanted to get rid of these clowns; Janice is just going along with the program. Then we get back into the dining room. They had run a 6 inch pipe through the corner of the mural and into the wall that goes into the kitchen. I still have a photograph of this I keep in the dining room to show people. When I questioned this, they suggested I box it in. When they sold us this job, we were getting a speech about their master carpenters, nail bangers. As an added bonus, the air handler was installed in my big closet that I had built in the back bedroom.

This closet was originally 13 feet long, and because of this, they ate up about 4 feet of the end of the closet. I even told them I would put in a pull down stairway so they could get to the attic without killing themselves. They insisted this had to be done this way for maintenance. They lied.

The only maintenance is the stupid filters. And they screwed up on that deal too. They put in the wrong vent, no filter. I had them drop off the right vent with a couple of filters. I installed it myself for the next summer.

One time they left was on a Friday, I was pissed. Janice had a heart attack a few years earlier and was giving me a story about chest pains. I was ready to send her to her mothers' until we got this worked out.

Ten o' clock at night, I took my cordless drill, made a hole in my kitchen ceiling, and drilled a hole through the upstairs wall that lined up almost perfectly with the pipe that was going through the back of the bedroom. Got an idea.

Saturday morning I rip out the upstairs pipe, and the one in the dining room. I built a wooden box, with insulation, that runs up the back wall. It is only three inches deep and a foot wide.

It hooks into the pipe in the attic; which by the way, was loose when I originally checked it. We would have been air conditioning the attic. Now I hooked this to a vent on a different part of the kitchen ceiling about a foot away and on a different angle. I also added a vent going to my hallway where they said there was no way to run a vent. I could have added another one to the bathroom, but I needed one room for me to go when the A/C is on. The one in the hall is close enough to do the job.

The tech says to me on Monday, "We are going to charge you extra to fix that." I answered "Like hell you are, that is staying that way, come here dummy, I will show you what I did." I showed him. He was impressed.

Eventually they finished the job; they were supposed to be out of here in a couple of days, took more like six days by time we got done fighting over stuff. I should have put the stupid thing in myself. I can tell you, the air handler would be in the attic.

As it is, there was supposed to be some kind of emergency shut off installed in the system in case of a leak. Good thing we had a permit, the building inspector picked up on that goof and got that worked out.

The tech that thought he was a genius tried to put it in the system, blew out some part, a relay or something. Fortunately they had a couple of guys who actually knew what they were doing. I think for the most part those couple guys were on some other job.

Even when they were ready to leave, there was a hole about a foot by four feet left in my ceiling. The idiot says to me "It can let the hot air out." "Yeah, and let my heat out all winter too you moron."

They had one guy who was smart enough to cut a piece in there. By the way if you do have a central air system in the winter, you may want to close the vents so the hot air from your regular heat does not sneak up into the vents. Save a few bucks on your heat bill. Just open the vents again when it is time to use the system again. This works in houses like mine where we have radiators. If you have hot air heat these usually use the same vents so you can't do this.

My cousin Steven gave me this tip. The system was installed in October, so we never used it that year. Next year comes around; we have company from out of state for the weekend. It is hot; we kick on the A/C and get nothing but hot air. Of course being a Saturday we can't get anyone out here to check it out.

Turns out there was a leak by the compressor, since it was under warranty, on Monday we got one of the techs out there who had a clue and he got it going. He was also the guy who hooked me up with the new vent with the filter. I don't expect to recommend these guys anytime soon.

STUPID SHOP ROOF

There are times we all make mistakes. Here is one I did that could have been a lot worse, bear with me. When I moved in here, the back yard was empty. I think at one time there had been a garage, but nothing when we got here.

My father died in 1983, and because of this, I was left some really good tools. I got a lot of hand tools, an old table saw, and a radial arm saw. I still use these tools. So for a couple of years I had the big saws down in the basement. This is not a place for them. It is low, and small. If I had any large pieces of wood; these were always a problem to cut.

So I said to myself; "What I can do to make some kind of outdoor shelter that will not cost me a fortune, but still be able to bring these tools outside." At the time, I came up with what I thought was a good idea, duh.

I built a floor in the yard near a fence I had out there. The floor was built on pressure treated 4 X 4's, with plywood. There were no walls, just the fencing which I used for two of the four walls. I added two more sections of fencing to make it look like a small fenced in area. Just that was not too smart; I have no idea what I was thinking.

So now, I came up with this idea of making a curved roof on top of these fences, sort of like a half barrel shape where the water and snow would run off. I ran 2 X 4's across the fence posts, and built this semi round frame out of PVC pipes, I then attached some cheap plastic corrugated material to the PVC, with the grooves running in a direction that would run water and snow off the top. As goofy as it looked, it actually worked for a couple of years. That was till we got a real industrial type snow storm one year.

This was one of those snows that come in at night when I am sleeping. I didn't think too much about it, I just figured I would clean it off in the morning. This is where the plan crapped out. The snow came down really fast and dropped about 10 inches of wet, heavy, snow on the roof. This is the kind of snow that weighs like concrete.

The other problem is that I could not get to the back of the roof without going around the block and getting at it from my neighbors' yard. I get along with the neighbors so this would not be a problem.

As it worked out, I did not have to go to the neighbor's yard, I was working like hell with a big broom and a step ladder to scrape the snow off this "roof" and hoping I would get it off before I had a problem.

This must have been God's way of paying me back for being a cheapskate. Halfway across the roof, the whole thing just caved in. It went down like a big piece of plastic, buried the tools in about a foot of snow and made me look like a fool.

There was snow in everything. I had snow in tool boxes, on the saws; and in my supplies. Fortunately it was not too cold out at that point, no wind either. I spent the rest of the day cleaning snow off everything and covering all the stuff with a big plastic drop cloth. Later, I got my act in gear, and built regular walls there, framed the roof with trusses and put a real roof on that. I actually tried corrugated fiberglass roofing material the first time over the trusses.

They even sell these special pieces of wood with curved surfaces made just for this type work. Now at one time, this fiberglass was made fairly strong. I know buildings where the roof has been made out of this, and it has lasted for 50 years. The new stuff is crap. It has no material strength, and cracks like a potato chip. After about two years of putting up with this stuff, I pulled it all off, rebuilt the roof using trusses, plywood and regular roofing shingles. Much better.

Chapter 20   SOMETIMES I GET LUCKY

CHEAP FANCY DOORS

Every so often, one of us gets lucky. Not like hit the lottery lucky, or have someone leave us a million dollars lucky. Just a little better than usual type lucky. This is a good luck story.

Our house has two entrance doors, one in front, and one in the back. Actually toward the back of the house, but on the side where the hallway sticks out. This is not too important, but both doors face the front of the house.

So for several years we have had old doors on the home. The one in the back actually came off a building in Red Bank, NJ. My father had replaced it with another door on the building, and he and I put that one on the house. The original door on the house had a bunch of small windows, and Dad felt this was a security risk. In some ways I would agree with him.

That door from his job had three small windows at the top. In the business, these windows are called lights. So that is the door that was on the side of the house. The one on the front of the place was here when we moved in. It was a similar door, and since you really cannot see both doors at the same time unless you are standing across the street, it was not a big deal.

But, Janice and I had looked at these fancy doors you see on homes these days. These are the doors with a big piece of glass and leaded glass in the door. They come in all different designs, and the door surfaces can run from real wood, like oak, to fiberglass which looks like oak. They also come with metal surfaces which are smooth. The price range of these doors usually starts at around three or four hundred bucks each up to several thousand depending on the door and trim. So for the most part, we were not going to get doors like this unless we got lucky or someone threw out a couple. We got lucky.

Bedtime Horror Stories for Homeowners

I was in the local Home Depot one day. I guess maybe 5 or 6 years ago. Hard to keep track of time when we are having so much fun. Anyway, I ran across a pair of doors which was originally set up to open in one opening. The two doors were set up to meet in the middle with a large wooden frame.

The idea is to use these as a main entrance door, and getting things like a big couch or a cow or some other large item into the house becomes a little easier. You see these every so often on homes.

Well, these doors had a damaged frame. It was not going to function the way it is supposed to work, so the price on the doors was marked down. The original price was somewhere around $900. I am sure someone screwed up here. I saw they were marked down, and had the clerk run a scanner on the tag. Get this, hold on to your ass; the price was $108 for the pair.

So before someone changed the price, I jumped on this like a wolf on a chicken. I figured they were probably supposed to take the $108 off the original price and sell the unit. I do not know this for a fact, just guessing.

Before I got this unit out the door, I had some guy want to buy one of the doors from me. "Nothing personal, but you are out of luck Bubba." If I went home and told Janice I did something like that, I would never hear the end of it. I would never live that long. But coming home with two doors for $108. I was a hero, a genius, a fart smellow.

Now these turned out to be fiberglass doors which are fine with me. That stuff does not rot. I have a 40 year old surfboard made of fiberglass which lives in my back yard and it is fine. Not pretty, but still functional. Sort of like me.

Since the frame was damaged anyway, this was not a problem as it was going to be useless in my situation. I needed two frames either way. Also the walls on this house are thicker than some homes, as the place has been renovated several times. Between building up the inside walls and the outside ones, our walls are closer to 10 inches thick.

There are some homes today with extra thick walls made this way for energy efficiency, but they are scarce. A regular wall is about five or six inches thick depending on the siding.

So in the interest of getting these doors installed, I got some of the special weather stripping that the Stanley Company used on these doors. I got some plywood, and trim, and built two new frames. I also put in good locks, the kind with a life time warranty. Total cost including the two expensive locks, the trim and everything ran me about $400 for the entire job.

Now I have two matching doors which not only work fine, but are pretty. These doors were originally painted dark brown. In the interest of doing something different and making people wonder. I painted them purple this year. A very light purple, I call it sky blue pink. Janice will not let me call them lingerie purple.

LOCKED OUT

I have been told that locks keep honest people of our homes. I sort of agree with that, I worked for an alarm company for a short time years ago. I didn't make much money, I was living in Beachwood at the time and people there did not even bother to lock the homes most of the time. Wrong job; wrong place, but I did learn a few things about security in buildings. One thing I picked up was that they told me burglars will come in a window and go out a door. That makes sense.

Almost anyone can get in a window unless they are too fat to get in the opening. In that case, maybe they should get an honest job where they can work off their fat ass.

I had locked myself out of the house; not paying attention, not stupid, just not paying attention. I got locked out once. I was sunbathing in the nude, in the yard, with nothing but a towel. I found a nail, opened a screen and climbed my naked ass in the back kitchen window. I have helped neighbors get into houses where they got stuck outside. They were usually amazed how easy it is to do this.

Now my in-laws are the other extreme. I just hope they never have a real emergency where someone has to get in the house. Not that it is impossible to do it; just that something is going to get broken.

They lock everything all the time; maybe it is a throwback to older times. I am going to visit them tomorrow, if I think of it I will have to ask my father in law about this. When we visit, the inside doors are locked. The storm doors are locked, all the windows are locked. It is like trying to get into Fort Knox.

I have gone down the basement to get a screwdriver and had to knock on the door when I came back because someone locked it on me. Good thing I usually have Janice with me, she at least understands me and I can always call her with my cell phone.

Bedtime Horror Stories for Homeowners

Chapter 21   PLAYING WITH FIRE

JACKIE'S NEW GAS STOVE

Here we have another fiasco. I have a friend named Jackie; she has a fairly large house with older appliances that need to be changed. For several months she had been cooking on two burners of an electric stove, the other two were shot. The big microwave on top had stopped working months ago. Here is another kicker; this gas stove was supposed to be installed 6 months ago. The old workman left her with the stove sitting on the kitchen floor in a box, and half the plumbing work installed.

At this point, she asked me if I had any idea how to put one of these in; of course, I have to do the macho thing and say. "Sure I can put it in for you" At least I would get paid to do this.

So I took a ride over there to check this out. There are a bunch of pipes installed in the basement. These are because the old stove is an electric one and the new one is gas. The home had been converted to gas about 15 years ago, and gradually as appliances crapped out, the electric ones were replaced with gas ones.

The plumber also left some plumbing tools there. This was good. There is one of those things with three legs and a gadget on top with a chain grip that holds pipe in place. You use this to cut and thread pipe. I looked at this thing and have no idea what to do with it. Then again I am not all that dumb, so I soon figured out how to do this.

She has a son who lives here with her. His name is Jimmy. He was about 35 years old and has some idea of technical stuff. This comes mainly from his hobby of HO trains.

Bigger stuff, this is just a bigger version of the trains. So he has to stick his nose in here to see what is going on. Fortunately he just was there when I was looking at the job, and not there when I was doing it. He seems to be nice enough to me, but he and Jackie have a tendency to get on each other's nerves.

So I show up in the morning to get this thing installed. Pretty straightforward deal, first rip out the old 220 electric line that is behind the stove, install a 110 line for the new stove and the hood, and then hook up the gas lines. This does not look too bad.

To start with I had to find the 220 breaker in the circuit box. I dragged in an electrician friend of mine to do this electrical stuff. Not my house. Got lucky, they were marked. We shut it off, checked it with a meter, and checked it with the old stove. I am sure it is off. Now he took the old outlet apart. Don't pay too much attention to how it was wired, looked really simple, sure. It took us 15 minutes to put the stupid wires back in this outlet after I pulled them through the kitchen floor. There is a strange way they are attached to the box, and I was not familiar with this system. Okay, so we play around with it and get the damn thing rewired. Now I go to the main circuit box and mark the circuit as dead, and make sure it is off. We left the old wiring all attached in case someone ever wants to use a 220 line in the basement for something like a table saw or a really, really big flat screen TV.

The wiring went really easy. I ran the wires up through a hole in the kitchen floor where there were other wires going into the kitchen. I found a place to splice these in, and in about an hour or so, we have the two boxes upstairs running for the new stove and the hood. This is an hour or so after we got the 220 line worked out.

Oh yeah, something else I forgot to tell you. I am doing this while having a small medical problem. I had an enlarged prostate; this has not been a big deal for a couple of years.

Of course it has to flare up a few days before I started doing this job. At this point I was wearing a leg bag which I have to empty every so many hours.

That is not too bad considering that the prostate shut me down previous to this and put me in the ER for a couple of hours so I could drain a gallon of piss. I almost felt like a human again.

So we get the electric going, and now it is time to finish the plumbing work with the gas pipes. Now I could not figure out why this guy dropped this job, I did figure it out a few hours later. I have now installed a bunch of pipes, and a shut off valve. I have one connection to make. This is the connection to an inch and a half gas pipe in between the floor joists.

No big deal shut off the gas. No problem, this is a week before Christmas, and it is maybe 25 degrees outside. I figure it will take me a half hour to pull out the plug, and connect the pipe and get it running again. Sure. Now I know why this guy dropped this job. That plug must have been installed by Superman. I tried every big and small wrench I had on that fitting. Cursed at it, heated it with a torch, tapped it with a hammer. Put WD 40 on it. That fitting was not coming out.

By now I am calling this guy names plus the guy who installed the pipe in the first place. Why didn't you put in the stupid stove 15 years ago Bozo? The only thing I have in my favor is that I do not get trapped in a box when something like this happens.

I ended up tapping into a pipe near the heating system, using tees, reducers and some back yard engineering to make it work. I even put the shut off valve in a good spot. Now this seems to be the end of the story, almost, but not quite.

We try the stove and nothing happens. All the pipes are connected, the electric is working, but we can't get a flame out of the burners. I would turn on the burner and where there is supposed to be gas there is nothing.

The clicker things are going clik clik clik clik, but no flames. About this time, Jimmy comes home. He is a fairly big guy, maybe 5'11" and 240 pounds. So one of the first things I think is "Good, he can help me hump the old stove out to the curb, get rid of that thing."

He works in an office, so he has to change his clothes or he was going to look like a mess in about 5 minutes. Good clothes off, work clothes on. Let's get this show on the road. Now he decides it makes sense to take the big microwave off the top of the stove. Mind you this thing has been on here for several years and not hurting anyone.

I suggest we just throw them out together sort of like being married, till death do them part. NO, NO, NO, he insists he has to take this thing off here. Fine, give him something to do while I figure out why the stove will not make fire. By time he pulls about 20 screws out of it he thinks maybe I have the right idea. So we ever so gently, slide the stove across the floor on a rug and gently move it to the double doors at the front of the house.

Maybe he is under the impression that someone will want this relic. I have a different approach. I give it a good push and it goes down the steps like a big drunk, hits the sidewalk and starts to roll. I thought he was going to cry.

 Give me a break, it is an old stove. It is full of grease. It is sticky. It is late in the day and it is dark. Do you really think anyone cares how we move this thing to the curb? We dragged it to the curb and then another 40 feet or so to put it at the edge of the property. The garbage men really do not care; they are just here to take it away.

So now we go back to the new stove. We check all the gas fittings for leaks with soapy water; not with a match like a buddy of mine does. That guy is gonna get killed someday doing that. No leaks. Still no flames.

I send Jimmy downstairs to shut off the valve, and then put it on again after I pull the flexible pipe off the back of the stove. "OK…turn it on." I yell to him. Gas comes out of the flex pipe. It is making noise. It stinks. I am sure if I put a match in front of it, I could scorch the ceiling. OK, so I am convinced the gas is fine to this point. We check the valve on the gas regulator of the stove. This thing is a joke. It has a tiny little itty bitty, small piece of junk steel that has to be put either on or off. The book shows where it is located.

It is so small you damn near need a magnifying glass to find it. Well, we put that on. Still no gas. At this point, I am tired, I have a full tank of water on my leg and I decide to call the Sears service guys for a suggestion.

You know the deal. You call up and get one of these make believe voices on the other end. Press one for this, two for that, and so on for about half hour.

When I finally get through to a real person, they offer to connect me to the service guy. Then the line goes dead and I get that other stupid message. "I am sorry your call did not go through." This pisses me off. We never had this when I was a kid. We had a phone that had the dial that you had to turn for each number. You dialed a number and it always worked unless you dialed it wrong and then someone who was a real person would tell you it was a wrong number.

After getting connected to the same woman for about the 4th time, she gives me a direct number to call. This call goes through some of that crap till I get hooked up to Roberto or whatever his name is. Probably some guy in India. We make an appointment for someone to come out the next afternoon. I tell Jackie "I will come back in the morning for my tools" It is about 8:30 P.M.

Next morning I come over her house. Pile all the tools in the car and tell her "Let me show you where the cut off valve is for this stove so when the Sears guy gets here, you will know." Son of a bitch..........the valve is off. I turn it on, we go upstairs turn on the stove and like magic, it works. "Call Sears, and cancel the service call Jackie." Jackie came to my house for dinner that Christmas, and brought over some cooked veggies and a casserole that she did on that stove. Happy, Happy, Joy, Joy. Now as soon as the urology guy got me worked out, I had sex with my wife to celebrate getting the stove going for Jackie.

FIRE IN THE TOOL SHED

We had neighbors a number of years ago who lived two houses away from us. They eventually moved and now live about three houses away in a different direction. I have no clue.

They were nice people. Italian family, grown kids, quiet. What I did not know then, and it is not any of my business; the husband used to process sausage in a shed he had in the back yard. I guessed this was an old tool shed at one time.

One night, about 3A.M. middle of the winter we hear knocking on our front door. A lot of yelling, my dog is going nuts. I have no idea. By the way these people only spoke Italian. About all they knew in English was Hello and Goodbye.

 So of course when they are trying to tell us about this problem there is a lot of body language going on. We didn't need too much explanation. When I ran down the steps to the kitchen to see what was happening, I looked out the kitchen window. This window faced the shed. There were flames 20 feet high coming out of it.

Well I did the smart thing. I called the fire department, and then I took a photo. Turns out, what caused the fire was him cooking sausage in a low pan in the shed. It bubbled over and took out the shed.

That was a hot fire though, we stood in the snow on the sidewalk at least 50 feet away and we were plenty warm even just wearing bathrobes and flip flops.

Another fast fire story. This happened in my house in Beachwood. The house had a crawl space that opened to the yard. This was where I lived with my first wife.

One year we went out somewhere for New Years Eve. I forget where, must have had a real good time. I don't know what time we got home, but when we did and tried to use the sink in the kitchen, the pipes were frozen. This house was not too good in the insulation department.

So thinking I have a good idea; I went out in the crawl space with a coffee can full of pine needles. The whole yard is full of them. They are dry, they burn like the Hindenburg.

I now commenced to light up these needles and hold them under the frozen pipe in the crawl space. There was a small area about 5 feet square where it was like a tiny basement connected to the crawl space. I was standing in this area. Only problem here, is that the flames did not do much for the frozen pipes. But, they did light up the floor joist under the kitchen floor. This was not working according to my plan.

But not being a panic type guy, I step out to the side of the house, and bang on the side of the house to get Lorraine's attention. "HEY LORRAINE, CALL THE FIRE DEPARTMENT." I yell. She says "Why?" "SO I CAN WISH THEM HAPPY NEW YEARS." Well, she got the picture and called them. Within five minutes; probably less, we had a police car there and the cop blew the flames out with a fire extinguisher.

Now the fire department shows up. I know these guys want to track down any loose flames in the house, so before they destroy the place with axes. I went up to the kitchen, and took out a piece of the wall right over the site of the flames. Meanwhile I had put my dogs on the back porch and locked the door. The firemen are all over the house, climbing on the roof, looking under the place. They were sniffing and peering to see if there was a problem; fortunately there was none. The dogs were going absolutely nuts. I felt like I was living in the SPCA.

I have an old friend who I knew even before this marriage, her name is Rose. She brings this story up every so often; she will never let me forget it.

This is a current story for the end of this chapter. If it were not so goofy I wouldn't even bother. A controlled fire no less. This happened to me today. I was headed for my favorite adult toy store....A.K.A...... Home Depot.

THE EMBARRESSING FIRE ALARM

I needed some stain, and a drill bit. I feel it is patriotic to keep the economy going. I was about two minutes from the store when my cell phone rang. Now this is New Jersey. One of only four states where it is illegal to talk on a cell phone while driving. It is also one of only ten states where you are not allowed to pack heat, these things fit together here. Anyway it was Janice on the phone. I don't usually pack a gun, but the phone is usually with me.

I was stopped at a light so technically I guess I was not driving since I was stopped. Long red light, short conversation. Tells me, Rachel called her. I am thinking? "Who the hell is Rachel?" I know one woman by this name who works at a county park where I teach classes, but she never calls me. Probably afraid I will tell her one of my crummy jokes, so I ask Janice "Rachel Who?" "This is Rachel who lives near Jackie." "Gotcha." This is a friend of ours. This lady hangs out with Janice more than with the two of us, so they are more buddy / buddy.

"Wassssup?" Turns out the house across the street from Rachel had a lot of smoke coming out of the chimney, and she was getting concerned. Wanted to know if she should call the Fire Department or talk to me, as I am a technical type guy. Fooled her, I was five minutes away so I told Janice to call her back and if it looked too bad she should call the Fire Department.

This woman is sort of very proper. She works in a college library and would feel embarrassed to call the police or the firefighters. Some people are like that.

In about 4 minutes I pull up in front of her house, she comes flying out the front door. Okay, not exactly flying, but doing some serious walking.

She points to the home across the street. It is a nice ranch house, looks fine and there is some smoke coming out of a chimney, nothing too unusual. I asked her if there was anyone home at the time.

She was not sure, the neighbor's truck was parked in the street in front of the house, but when she rang the bell she got no answer, and expected to find him dead. I smell wood burning, so I tell her not to get too excited. I tried the bell. I have two of these stupid bells; they run on batteries and if the batteries die, no bells.

So instead of getting nervous I used a ring I wear on my right hand. This is a huge steel ring I made out of a big steel nut. It replaces a college ring I had gotten. Turns out the college ring was made of stainless steel instead of the white gold that was on the ad. It is just like most other stuff I got from the school. Useless, don't let me go there.

I did get some of the money back. I sold it to some wise guy who had a jewelry buying service in a mall. He would give you a lower price than the other places, but since I knew someone else in the business and found out I got screwed, I figured something, is better than nothing. I remember, I paid a phone bill with the money I got from the original ring. This new ring I made is almost custom made for knocking on doors. Sort of like knocking with a hammer, a big hammer. Two or three shots and the man comes to the door. He is fine, Rachel is relieved.

We tell him about the smoke coming out of the chimney. He comes out to take a look and makes some comment about burning wood. "Oh Yeah, there was some composite type wood in there, and it started melting. I guess that is what is causing the smoke." No big deal. I figure he is going to just let it burn off. Not like he is toasting marshmallows over the toxic fire.

We go back to Rachel's house. She asks if I would like a cup of coffee. Is the Pope Catholic? "Sure, if it's not a lot of trouble." Turns out she had just made a pot. See, I can also smell coffee in friends' homes. What a guy.

At this point, I am sitting in her living room with her dog Sadie sitting on my lap, some kind of little poodle type dog. Cute mutt.

This dog is slick, sees the coffee cup and figures out there will be food and I look like an easy touch. Dog is not only cute, but a mind reader.

Someone had called the fire department. We sat and watched exactly what Rachel did not want to have happen if she made the call. It started out with one fire truck; this went to two and then three trucks. Also, a couple of cars. Big Ugly SUV types, a couple of Police cars were soon there, I am sure half the payroll of West Long Branch Emergency Department was headed here. It is a quiet town. Aside from busting drunken students at the local college, there is not much going on.

Some of these guys were going in and out of the neighbors' house, some were walking around the property, and some were just standing in the street in uniform trying to look important. It always amazes me how you can take a cop who is out of shape, put a well-tailored uniform on his fat butt and make him look almost impressive. Does not work all the time, but on occasion.

These official type guys tied up the street for at least 20 minutes, my new car was parked right in front of the house and all I was worried about was getting it hit by some guy having a testosterone rush on the way to the fire.

After they all realized that this is all that was going on, they all got back in the vehicles and hit the road. Rachel was embarrassed for the neighbor. I would rather be embarrassed than roasted. I finished the coffee, gave Sadie a few pieces of oatmeal cookie and headed back to the store.

Chapter 22 WATER STORIES

STEVENS' HOT TUB

My cousin Steven lived in this house with his wife Marilyn. She is the one who was married to my brother Bob at one time. That is another tale. Okay, so now Steven has done a ton of work on this home. As best I can tell, he wanted to erase every trace of anything Bob ever did there. The only thing Bob ever did there that was not erased, was Bob doing Marilyn.

So Steve put in central air, new siding, a deck, a screen house, a new roof. Some new landscaping, took out the load of rocks and stuff that Bob used to store in the front of the property. I've got to say he did a nice job on the place. Bob lost interest in the marriage and the home, so he just let it go. (This is how it could become a handyman special).

At some point Steve decided it was time to put a hot tub on the deck. Now, because he is not sure the deck will really support the hot tub; he rebuilds the deck. Ca Ching. Then has to get some high end electrical wiring put in to run a hot tub, and some plumbing to make the water work in this hot tub. Then he had to go get a hot tub. I am not sure what he paid for it, and I don't really care. But at some point he installed this thing on the deck.

Steven will not drive five minutes to visit someone; his favorite line. "We'll be here." He expects everyone to come and visit him. When he got the hot tub I guess he thought people would flock there to get wet. I don't have to do that, I live five minutes from the ocean. But one night we took a ride down to visit anyway and were going to do the hot tub thing with him.

When we went to the hot tub, I showed up wearing a Red Speedo. I am in pretty good shape so I can get away with a suit like this. What Steven did not know is that I had a Blue Speedo on under the red one. So he and I get in the hot tub and he is showing me all the whistles and bells on the thing. This makes a waterfall, this makes the lights go on.

This gives you a massage, this is a temperature control. Only the best. He seems to think everything he ever buys is always the best, this is debatable. So after about twenty minutes of this silliness I pull this deal on him.

I call Janice over by the tub; she is not going in at this point. I say to Janice "Hey Babe, can you hold this for me?" and give her the red Speedo. I have been going to a nude beach for years so I have this reputation for nudity.

Steven starts getting crazy. "The neighbors, they are going to see you naked." I answer. "Get lost I am under water, what the hell are they going to see? Think about it." There are a million bubbles in this tub. He can't see what is going on, the neighbors can't see either

Now that I have handed Janice the suit; I start moving over toward Steven, like I am going to get real friendly with him. He starts scurrying away from me like I am going to sexually assault him. He is yelling like a little girl. I keep moving and he keeps moving. We are sort of playing tag in the tub. Finally I said to him. "I guess I'm going to get out, you're no fun."

He is about to go nuts at this point figuring the neighbors are going to get a show. I am not hung like a horse so who cares. He still thinks I am naked.

At this point I climbed out of the hot tub and laughed my ass off at him. I think he kept this hot tub for maybe another six months before he decided he was tired of it and sold it. I actually helped him and bunch of other guys move it to its' new home. We used a rented truck from Home Depot and got it from Steve's deck to someone else's place in under an hour.

THE SUMP PUMP FIASCO

This is how you screw up big time.

Years ago, I put a sump pump in my basement, the pump went in fine. The pipes going to the pump were in wrong. I did not know this. Somehow, when I installed the pipes, I put them in upside down. The pipes I used had three holes every few inches on one side.

The pipes that go in the ground have to be laid with the lowest end of the pipe being set near a big plastic barrel which has holes in it. One end of this pipe goes in one of these holes. This brings water to the sump pump which then pumps it outside. Some people will hook the outlet pipe from the pump to a drain pipe, but this is actually illegal in some locations.

These holes in the pipes are supposed to face down toward the earth, not toward the sky. Somehow I learned how to put them in the wrong way. I do not know if I was taught wrong, or if I was not paying attention when my father put them in his house, or maybe he did them wrong and did not know it either. My brother Bob told me he put pipes in one of his houses the same way, so maybe this was a family problem.

The kicker here is that the pipes will work like this for several years. The water from the ground will fill them up, flow to the pump and go out the pipe. The problem is that this water carries dirt or sand with it and at some point, the pipes fill up with that dirt. Now we have something similar to a constipated snake.

The water will hit the pipes, but because they are full of sand, the water has nowhere to go but up to the floor. This is the floor I am trying to keep dry. So for about 17 years the pipes worked. This is a long time to think things are working fine to find out there is a screw up, sort of like finding out you are adopted at age 17.

Bedtime Horror Stories for Homeowners

My first reaction is that there is water coming in the outside walls. Remember, I did not know that the pipes were in wrong. So a few years ago I dug up the dirt by the foundation, put tar and plastic on the outside walls, added foam insulation outside of that and backfilled the dirt. I figured this would solve the problem. It did not. This job also involved moving my neighbors' fence so I had room to dig, and doing it when they were on vacation so one of the kids would not fall in the trench. Fortunately, I had the time and the physical strength to do this job.

It seemed to help somewhat, so for a couple of years I thought I had it solved. What probably happened is that there was water sneaking in the walls that I did not know about, and that was part of the water in the basement. Now I was not getting a lot of water, but if it rained for about 3 days, I would get maybe 2 quarts of water on the whole floor. Not much, but who needs it. Water creates mold and other ugly stuff so I was determined to get rid of it.

So at the age of 59, I now decided to go after the pipes again. Now I am still in pretty good shape, mostly because my wife told me if I got fat or bald I am out the door. So a couple weeks before Christmas, I rented an electric jack hammer and tore up about 60 feet of trench on the outside edges of the floor. The basement has a low ceiling about 6 foot so using a sledge hammer was out of the question. I would have been tearing my heat pipes off the beams.

Maybe if I was about 18 inches tall this would work, but at that size what would I be using? A one pound rock hammer? So off we go to the rental place to get the electric jack hammer. Now this thing weighs about 70 pounds and has an awkward shape, plus it moves when you fire it up. Think of an electric pogo stick.

It comes with two different bits to destroy the concrete, either one will do a pretty good job. I used to have a van, got rid of that last year when I decided I did not have too much use for the monster, so now I threw the tool in the back of the old Honda Civic hatchback and headed home.

Bedtime Horror Stories for Homeowners

In my case, I at least knew where the pipes had been placed so I had to dig them up with the help of the electric jackhammer. (Hint: If you use one of these, make sure you have a good dust mask, not one of those cheap paper ones. Also a pair of ear plugs or those earmuffs you see construction guys use).

Part of the problem here, is also that in 20 or so years we have collected a lot of stuff. You know STUFF. The crap that everyone picks up here and there. Things like shovels, camping stuff, coolers, and the kind of clutter that we use for everything in our lives. This *"stuff"* now lives in our basement. It is going to be a cold day in hell when I go for a storage unit somewhere.

This is why people in foreign counties hate us; we have too much *"stuff"*! So I have no place to put all this stuff except in other parts of the basement or piled up on itself. We also do Halloween parties every year so the basement has been decorated with all kinds of strange things, including a full size ghost made of clear plastic that has been sprayed with some chemical that makes it glow under a black light.

So I piled things on top of things, instead of having a throw away party first. I could have dumped about a truck load of things before the fact, but that makes too much sense. Besides I wanted to get the pipes in before the winter got ugly. I got lucky; the weather was pretty warm that year for Christmas and New Years'. I remember taking the dogs out in the middle of the night, 2A.M. Fifty five degrees; it was almost as warm as Florida. We are in New Jersey.

So; trying to be organized I piled things on top of each other in the center of the floor, figuring that I am working on the outside edges of the floor. This makes sense. Then after I tore up most of the trenches, I decided to move my washer and dryer and all the stuff on that wall to make a trench on that wall. After all, that area was looking a little damp these days, and as long as I was paying for the stupid tool I might as well use it.

Now I moved all those things to the center of the floor. The washer and dryer are sitting on a platform I made out of a bed frame and some ply board years ago. This kept them off the floor and makes it easier to load and unload them. I moved the whole platform with a big steel bar, hoping like hell that I would not kink any water hoses.

This is after the rest of the basement has a huge mess in it. Then again, it's not like anyone who is coming for Christmas is going to come down the basement. Who cares?

The make believe storage table on this side is piled high and comes away from the wall like moving a bag full of bricks. There was a big tool box I had built at one time in this corner that was made of particle board. This is basically wood chips glued together. That was falling apart. That got torn apart.

When I get going, I am like a pit bull, I do not let go. Now I get the busted up concrete worked out, and return the jack hammer. The guy at the rental place knows me for several years so when I tell him what is going on, he just nods his head. I am sure inside his head is the thought "Idiot, you should have rented some Mexicans to do the job. Stupid old man!" Anyway we got the tool back in time to not have to pay for two days rentals. I have a reputation as the cheapest guy in New Jersey, and don't want to ruin it.

I got back to the house; it is maybe lunch time, and survey the mess. I am not the kind of guy who panics, and will also make sure I eat my meals. You can't do real damage on an empty stomach. At this point in my life I have a problem with cholesterol, so I have started eating oatmeal every day for one of my meals. This was lunch. There was a time it would have been a sub sandwich. By the way, this has worked for me, my numbers are much better in only 6 weeks. Get back on track you fool.

So now we start; and by we, I mean ME I often think of myself in the plural. Maybe I have a split personality or think of myself as more than one person. Or maybe, I am just nuts. Anyway, now comes the job of digging up the floor where the trenches are.

Bedtime Horror Stories for Homeowners

I ended up with three or four big piles of dirt, and about 20 of those milk boxes full of broken concrete. You know the boxes, the plastic ones that have printed on them something about misusers' will go to jail. If you don't say anything I won't. I am not doing this as a full time job here; I have other things which get in the way, such as work, dance classes and sex. Besides like I said before, who is coming down here anyway?

I am working here about three hours a day, but at least do not have to go to the gym. I actually lost a few pounds over the holidays instead of putting it on like most people. Got a good workout doing this job.

To make a long story short, I managed to dig up the old pipes which for the most part were full of sand, added a second sump pump on the washer/dryer wall and got the pipes buried before our next big rainstorm. This by the way, keeps the basement dry as dust. Makes me a happy camper.

I also found out there is now a stocking that goes around the pipes to help keep out dirt. I made sure I used that stuff all the way around, cleaned out the old sump pump well and replaced it with a new one that is engineered better.

The pump still works fine after over 20 years, amazing. I wonder what the new one will do. I also got rid of a lot of the old concrete floor by busting it up and using it for fill with the new pipes along with some small stone. With some luck, this will last a few years like 50 or so.

In between, the washer developed a problem, seems there was some kind of gunk in the drain. Had to spend a few hours in there to make that work again. There are 4 clean outs on that drain pipe. I flushed them all out and now it works fine. This stuff never ends.

Also broke the stupid switch on the washer trying to watch the machine work. You know the switch, the one that will shut off the machine if you open the door when it is spinning like a top. This is to keep someone from putting a hand in there and losing an arm when it is on spin cycle.

I had jury rigged a temporary switch on it, and since there are only two adults living here who are both smart enough to keep our hands out of the machine, I am fairly safe till I get the proper switch on it again. Besides, Janice sends me down there to do the wash half the time anyway. I have since replaced this machine.

And, one more thought. We had new rugs installed here about 3 months ago, light green. They go right to the basement door. On the basement side of the door we have small pieces of carpet to collect dirt that I drag up from the basement. After I got the mess under control I used a novel approach to cleaning these rugs. These rugs are made from recycled soda bottles. Really. No kidding.

Keeping this in mind, I took these small rugs outside, used squeeze clamps to hold them to a fence, sprayed them with a hose and dish washing detergent and then vacuumed them with my shop vac. They look at least as good as new. If you don't believe me, call my wife.

Chapter 23 DEALING WITH ANIMALS AND FOOLS

MEESE AND OTHER CRITTERS

You get the idea. Goose, Geese. Mouse, Meese. Everyone gets a mouse in a house once in a while. It is going to happen. I do not care how tight you have the place closed up. If they decide to move in, you have a border. Simple as that. A full grown mouse can get through a hole the size of a dime. A dime is not worth much these days, so you may want to glue one up somewhere to remind you of this story.

I am one of those wacky animal lover types. I am a vegetarian because of this. I have always liked animals, I still do. Any kind of animal will do. I still go to zoos, and petting zoos. I have to pet any dog that comes near me. This makes Janice crazy sometimes. When I try to pet the police dogs at an airport, she will grab me and yell, "Get away from that dog." So you know where I am coming from.

So when it comes time to get rid of a mouse, I hate to try to catch them in a spring loaded trap. I know they carry germs and all that stuff. Kids also carry germs, ask any school teacher. I feel bad for the poor stupid things (mice) when I realize that most people have no use for them and would just as soon go after them with a shotgun.

I catch them with humane traps. I tried a few commercial ones with some success, and even built one from an old pepper can and some junk I had lying around the house. That was a sort of Rube Goldberg, goofy looking thing, clumsy looking but it worked. It eventually got beat up so I trashed it. I have a commercial one now.

One year for some reason, I started having a lot of mice in the house. I can go for three years and not see one. That year; I am not kidding in one month, a mouse a day for a month. I was starting to wonder if it was the same guy coming back for more food. The only reason I think not, is that I dropped them off in a park 2 miles from my house. That is a lot of walking on those short legs to come back for scraps.

I had one mouse who showed up on a counter top in my kitchen. I set up the humane trap, ran a line of cheese pieces to the trap. He would sit up like a squirrel and eat one, and go to the next one until I got him in the trap. He then figured out how to open the door and got out on me.

But I am smarter than he was. I did the same thing, caught him the same way and this time I taped the door shut. Hell, I am no fool, I am a college graduate. I took him to the park that night and on the way I explained to him that a bunch of his friends were out there and he should look them up.

We came downstairs one morning and there was a little, tiny, baby mouse sitting next to the wall. He was so small I almost did not see him. He was so young; he did not know enough to make a run for it. I caught him with a coffee can and a magazine; he also went to the park. I even leave some food with these animals to give them a head start on the rest of their lives. At least Janice and I are on the same page with this issue.

Had another mouse one time; not dumb animals at all. He was grabbing dog food on me; I had a wet suit hanging in the hallway for when I go surfing in cold weather. I went to use the wet suit one day, took it off the hanger, and as I moved it, I would say about 3 or 4 cups of dry dog food fell out of the legs. I know I did not put it there.

I did feel terrible about one poor mouse here. The guy fell in the water bowl for the dogs and drowned, that was sad. Amazing thing about mice, they can climb trees like a squirrel, think about that.

SQUIRRELS

I have no idea what it is with some people who hate these animals. I get them here. I feed the birds and the squirrels also get in on the food. I do not care, I happen to think they are cute animals. I also do not try to pet them. My old neighbor Ray tried that once, the critter bit his thumb. He said it was like hitting it with a hammer. "Think about it Ray. They break nuts with those teeth."

My sister in law hates these animals for some reason. I do not even know why. She had a few on the property once, still does. One day she came out and smelled gas in the yard. "Sniff....Sniff....where does that come from?" One of these guys had chewed through the rubber hose on the grill and gassed himself. She did feel a little silly calling the fire department.

My cousin Steven; he is the neat freak. He did not like the idea of having to rake leaves in the yard. It also annoyed him that squirrels would dig small holes in his stupid lawn. Big deal.

So thinking he is being clever, he took all the trees out of the yard. Actually at this point there was one real big oak tree and a couple of scrawny little ones out there. The birds and squirrels had nests in the big tree. Lesson: don't mess with Mother Nature.

The trees came down. A couple days later, his wife took their Lexus to work. That is as far as the car ever goes. At the time he had this car over a year, has maybe 4000 miles on it. I had a Honda Civic two months; I had 7000 miles on it.

So Marilyn took the car to work, it is fine. When she comes out and tries to start it, the lights on the dashboard looked like a Christmas tree. Having no idea what was going on; the car did start. She somehow got the car home. I think they actually got it towed.

Turns out the squirrels that were displaced decided to move into his car, made a nest and ate some of the wiring under the car. He got lucky the bill was under $200. They might have chewed about ½ inch of wire. Knowing the Lexus dealership, that is about all they would do for that kind of money.

When my brother Bob was still married to Marilyn, they had a squirrel trying to make a nest in the attic. Bob likes to think of himself as the Great White Hunter. He came up with this idea of trying to get the critter out of the attic by shooting at him up there with a 12 gauge shotgun. I am glad he mentioned this to me before he did it. He would have done a lot more damage than the animal.

Then again, when Bob had his landscaping business, he was building a deck for someone. His helper saw a raccoon under the deck. Another rocket scientist. This guy takes a nail gun and shoots the poor thing. Bob called Marilyn to bring a shotgun out so he could kill the coon. "We were putting it out of its misery." He said. If they left it alone in the first place, there would have been no misery.

This happened in our yard about 10 years ago. My dog Sammy would go behind my shop and start barking like crazy. He was loud anyway so this did not seem like a big deal. Turns out, there was a mother possum and 3 babies living in some wood I had back of the shop. Not wanting to try killing them off, I asked my vet what I should do about them. He suggested cat food and Animal Control.

I blocked off that area to keep Sammy out of there, fed them for a couple of days and they left of their own. Most animals are like your teeth, if you ignore them, they will go away.

We did have a possum in our yard when we had Noah. He was funny; he didn't really know that to do with it. I saw him following the animal, butting the possums' tail end with his nose so it would leave the yard.

We feed the birds every morning. Bob had made me a nice bird feeder a couple years ago. We fill it every day. Even when we go away we get someone to do this. I think the birds appreciate this. I also have a fountain and a bird bath. The birds like to drink water out of both of them. Some of the small birds, like sparrows will sit on the pipes and drink out of them, this makes us all happy.

Got to watch out for birds though. They are beautiful, but sometimes do not realize where they are going. One day I was in the yard doing some kind of work. I kept hearing some kind of strange noise in one of my downspouts. Got closer to it, a scratchy noise and really animated. This got my attention.

Took the downspout off. In the top of it was a small bird that had gotten in there with no idea how to get out. He had managed to get past one of the elbows before he got stuck.

I took off the elbow and away he went. My friend Jackie, similar situation. Now Jackie is a nervous type person and does most everything in a hurry. The old saying "If you do not have the time to do it right, how are you going to find the time to do it over?" She should have this tattooed on her body somewhere.

She was running out of the house one day like the house was on fire. No fire, just the way she was headed out. As she was going through the yard; same thing, heard some kind of strange noise in a pipe.

She had no idea of what it was. For all she knew it could be a squirrel, or a snake or a gorilla. She taps on the pipe, more noise. Gets panic stricken. Calm down Jackie, easy does it. She calls me to help. I live about 5 minutes away.

I tell her to cool off. Go sit down before she has a heart attack and I will have two problems to deal with. I get over there about five or six minutes later. Having this previous experience with my downspouts I took a guess that there was not a gorilla in there. I got some of the tools in her garage and within a minute or so...this little bird was out and gone. Probably took longer to calm Jackie down than it took for the bird to come back to normal.

I had a raccoon in my garden one time. At least I saw him before the dogs did. I had to keep the dogs in the car till I chased him away. I guess he did not read my sign. The sign is for people who will get out of their car; step over the short fence and trample my vegetable garden. The sign says. "Please keep your big ugly feet out of my garden. This means you, thank you."

MOVING DAY

This usually is a really fun day. It actually can be a good time with the right people and some decent planning. I don't care if you are moving out of a one bedroom apartment or you mothers' house, the rules are the same.

To start with, make sure you have everything packed the way you would if you were going to send it west on a wagon train. No matter who moves you, it's not their stuff so if something does get broken, it is still *your* something. The person will grovel and apologize and maybe even get you some insurance money. That will not replace your teddy bear which got mangled in the spring mechanism of a recliner.

Also make sure the stuff is packed and ready to go. I helped a buddy of mine move a house full of junk for one of his girlfriends. "Everything is ready to go!" "Yeah right." There was about a foot of everything all over the girls house with everything from dog food to designer panties all mixed together. These people were removing drapes and washing them as the move was going on. Want to hear the best part? The drapes were coming out dirty, mainly because they ran out of detergent three days earlier.

Make sure the people helping you are dependable. This is very important. Even if they are alleged "professionals" they may be a problem. If you hire someone to move you, they may not be better than your brother with the big truck and the strong back. I met a moving man who must have picked up his help in the dark by feeling the tops of their heads for splinters.

These guys actually moved an antique table 75 miles by standing it on its legs with boxes piled on top. Needless to say, when the truck arrived, the base of the table was in a few more pieces then when it started. That stunt cost the mover a trip to a furniture repair shop.

If you decide to move yourself, there are a few things to remember: mini vans don't replace trucks, and friends work cheap or free, but be prepared to keep the beer and the food in the action. Also, if your friends help you move they might like the favor back sometime. This is great if you own a Victorian and they buy a ranch.

Don't pack boxes too heavy either, you don't want all your male friends to sound like a girls' choir at the end of the day. If possible, move the furniture in a logical order, this way you are not trying to hump a 300 pound convertible sofa over a dining room set.

Move delicate items either before or after the big move, this increases their life span. Make sure you have a set of keys for the new house. Also keep pets out of the way. A dog will stay put till you try to carry something big and heavy down the steps. Your first step will probably be on the dog's head.

Allow time for coffee breaks and the bathroom breaks that follow. Make sure everyone knows where the bathroom is and that there is toilet paper. Nobody should have to share the back yard with Fido. After the move is over, make sure everyone is fed, hook up the strays with blind dates and throw everyone out. And to steal an idea I saw on a rental truck. "On moving day, wear deodorant."

There is one short tale I have to put in here even though this was only a move from one apartment to another. This was someone I helped move three or four years ago on Christmas Day. Normally people do not work on this day in my neighborhood but my wife Janice was still working as a nurse and doing a 12 hour shift.

A woman we both knew was being moved out of an apartment that was part of a home where the landlord decided to renovate the house and throw all the tenants to the wolves. They would be "allowed" to come back when the work was done.

Please, give me a break. Our friend was only moving about a mile, but that was still a move. I will call her Patty; I could see her getting crazy if she thought I was putting her life on paper.

I had picked up the rental truck the day before. This truck should do the job. My brother Bob was up here in Jersey for a week or so and had volunteered to help me move her. I told him to just help me get a few heavy items out and then get lost, or he would lose the entire day.

Janice was at work at 6:45 A.M. I had breakfast with the dogs. Bob was not here yet so I decided to take a look and see how Patty was doing with her packing. I had dropped a load of cardboard boxes there during the week with some tape. I was hoping that she would be all packed and ready to go. This was like hoping I would hit the lottery this week.

I drove over there at about 8 A.M. She had not touched a thing, there was a huge mess all through the apartment, there was almost nothing packed. I suggested she have some breakfast and get with the program. Told her I would be back later with Bob and the truck. I figured about 10 o'clock. I called Bob at my mother's house and told him to take his time. Bob got to my house about 9:30. We had some coffee.

I told him about the situation, so he would not get too worked up. Not like he had any reason to get upset, Patty was nothing to him anyway. We got to her apartment about 10 A.M. Had a truck, straps, rope, a hand truck and a thermos of coffee.

First thing we had to do was to get Patty let us in, that was easy. The door was open. We found her in the apartment with one hand on the doorknob of the bathroom and her other hand on the corner of a wall so she could keep the bathroom door closed. I asked her what she was doing.

"One of the cats is in here, and I do not want him to take off." I did not want to look uncaring, but I did point out to her that we were going to have to put the cats in carriers or cages or something so she could let go of the door and do something useful. One cat was easy to catch; the other one took us about 20 minutes to round up and put in a crate. They were not too happy about this, but I was not there to make the cats happy.

I asked Patty "Did you get any breakfast?" "I had a beer" was her answer. I was not impressed. I guess there are carbs in beer. I did not know at the time that she had a serious drinking problem. Fortunately she has kicked that habit. I think the doctor telling her that her liver was shot may have made an impression.

So after we got the cats under control; Bob and I backed the truck up to the back door and took out whatever big items we could get out without a big fight or repacking. Meanwhile, Patty finally got moving ever so slowly and started to pack stuff from the kitchen. It took Bob and me about an hour to get a big TV, a couple of dressers, a bed and some other big things in the truck. We then drove across town to put the stuff in her new apartment. We left Patty to putz around with whatever she could pack. I told Bob to follow me with his car so he could leave.

By time I got back to Patty, she had packed a few boxes, not too many, but at least she was doing something. Since this was not my stuff, and she was about as helpful as a glass eye in a keyhole, I did my best to pack as much as I could with the least amount of energy. I could tell I was going to be the one doing most of the work here. Meanwhile I am not getting paid. This is a favor for a friend.

I was doing things such as putting a big box on the floor, pulling the entire bar out of a closet and dumping everything off the bar right into the box. Not doing any damage, just not folding everything neatly.

I did the best I could to help her put any breakable stuff in boxes with care. In the middle of this business, one of her silly neighbors came down and started to tell me I was making prisoners out of the cats by keeping them in cages. I asked him if he wanted me to shove his skinny ass in a cage next to the cats. He got the point and left. If he was that worried, he could have stuck around and helped.

This mess went on all day till about 7 P.M. when we finally got all her stuff to the other apartment. Her big concern was where we could get some beer. And big as life she knew where to find beer on a Christmas night at 7 P.M.

All I wanted to do was go pick up Janice and eat supper. I did not want to bring Patty along, I had already seen too much of her for the day.

When you do help someone move, try to get people to help you who at least understand the overall picture of what is to happen. I mentioned this guy Joe with the girlfriend. When we did that move for his friend, we ended up throwing things out the windows because the doorways were all blocked up.

At one point we were taking stuff out of the closets with the original tags still on these items. Not wanting to sound like a troublemaker, I think it would have been nice to have this stuff already packed.

Even when we were loading a van there were problems. Some people have no concept of space or distance. When we did get a number of boxes ready to go, I set up what was like a fire brigade type line. This was like where they used to pass a bucket of water from the truck to the fire one person at a time, and the end person got to throw the water.

I set up a line like this with a number of people to move all these boxes from the house to the van. Had to line everyone up like a bunch of Kindergarten kids and explain the concept of moving boxes from one person to the next.

You would think this was rocket science to look at the blank stares on their faces. Most of these people were college graduates. So much for higher education.

I just thought of my first wife when we moved into the house in Beachwood. As soon as her car got packed, she hit the road as if it would kill her to stick around and help the rest of us get out of there. At this point we were almost done, so it was no big deal, I think it was her attitude that annoyed me. My van was packed so tight that my dogs rode to the new place lying on top of the engine cover. Before you get involved with a moving situation, give it some serious thought.

NO HOME

What the hell is this about? I know we all have to work to make some kind of place to live, but what is it with homeless guys? I can almost understand when you see some woman with a couple of rug rats on the street; I figure her old man dumped her and the kids and left them hanging, but what is with these guys you see on the streets.

Perfect example, I was in NYC last weekend; the weather was fine. I see some guy who is maybe 35 years old standing on the sidewalk with a sign says "Homeless Vet." There seemed to be no physical problem that was stopping this guy from working in K-Mart or Home Depot; in fact a lot of these companies make a big deal about hiring people with disabilities.

Also, if I were going to be homeless, which I choose not to be; why would I do that in a northeast city where the best heat comes from the subway heat vents? These vents were not installed to keep people warm on the streets. As best I can tell, these were put in to get heat away from the trains in the subways so those people who do work at K-Mart, do not have to get there all sweaty from riding in a train that is 110 degrees.

If I were going to do the homeless thing, I would do like a guy I met years ago. His mother lived in New Jersey and he lived with her. Now even though I live in this state, that does not mean I am in love with it. I guess he got sick of living at the bottom of the food chain with low paying jobs. This is what he did.

He cashed in the mothers house after she died, took the money and the last I heard, was living in Hawaii in the jungle. Think about it. Like myself, I have tourist friendly skills. I play guitar very well, professional level. (Find me on YouTube, Paul Pugliese guitar solos)

I could move to the jungle like this guy, get a job at a hotel, or sit outside one with the case open and make a few bucks. If I am living in the jungle with maybe a guitar, a bike and a handful of clothes. How much money do I really need? Oh yeah, my surfboard, I need that.

Bedtime Horror Stories for Homeowners

I hear that Hawaii has health care for everyone who lives there. Maybe in another 200 years the rest of the states will smarten up to this deal; or would they rather wait till someone gets sick and costs 1000 times more money to get back to health. Check out the PBS film "Sick around the World" on the internet, get educated. Or the Michael Moore "Sicko" movie.

I also do caricatures, I draw these at parties. Places like Hawaii, again I could do the jungle thing, pedal into the tourist area and make some $$.

In the year or so before I met my wife I had taken a van to Florida with a sketch pad. Big as life, I made a living doing caricatures of people. I worked at restaurants, bars, art shows, and flea markets. Anywhere I could get set up. My biggest expenses were food for me and my dogs, and gas in the van. I had a great time. Like they say, "Home is where you park it."

I do not know if it is still like this, but back then you could park in a shopping center parking lot and sleep there during tourist season because the campsites were filled and the state would rather have tourists parking by the Piggly Wiggly than drive back to Minnesota or whatever other cold state they live. I saw campers the size of Greyhound buses in these lots and they were fine.

Plus get this. The state had free campsites where you could live for 2 weeks in season or a month off season. Can't beat that with a stick. I met a couple from Australia who had gotten out of the rat race, packed a small tent and some other stuff in a Pinto station wagon and had been on the road for 8 years. They even had a four year old kid with them. Now that is one way to educate a kid. By the way, he was an engineer and she was a teacher so these are not uneducated people.

Don't show him where the states are on a map, take him there. I am also a big believer in home schooling. My neighbor home schools her three kids who are high school age. Her husband teaches in the local high school. Hummmm.

THE DEAD PHONE ISSUE

Now; we all have telephones in this country, even people who live in trailers and cardboard boxes have some kind of phone. Maybe a cell phone, or a hard wire type, whatever. Well, this is fine till the phone does not work. Sometimes that happens when there is a big storm. Fine, our phone is out but so is everyone else's so who cares? We can all hang out in someone's living room and wait till the service comes back. We can have a no phone party, or something like that.

Our situation did not work like this. What did happen is that we had two phone lines in the house. One for talking and the other for a dial up service with AOL. This is a simple system. The reason we had the two lines is because if one of us was on the computer looking at porn or some other important site, and the other person wanted to call home, the line would be busy. So that is why we had the two lines. This worked for several years. So eventually, my nephew Tony became a computer geek and gave me a computer that he rebuilt. There was something wrong with the modem on it, so when I tried to go online, it did not always work properly. I got the computer for nothing so I didn't want to complain.

About that time, Verizon kept sending me an e-mail about a DSL line which is basically a fat phone line. I also was getting ads in the regular mail on this subject. When I would put in my phone number on the website, I kept getting a response that the number was not available for that service. There was a phone number there on the site, so for laughs I dialed it. I guess I am a glutton for punishment.

I got some young guy on the other end who checked things out and determined that I could in fact get the DSL line; and with the free installment kit, and the fact that I could get AOL on the cheap or for nothing the deal kept getting better.

I could also get rid of the extra phone line which would save me almost as much as the DSL line was going to cost me; plus from what people told me it was faster and I could enjoy the internet even more than before. Sure.

About a month ago I got the kit, and installed it with the filters and wires and all that good stuff. Took me about an hour. I didn't go online till that night but it did seem to work fine once I got it all fired up. So now we had to call AT&T to take out the second phone line. That seems simple enough; you call up, and go through a phone tree till a live person gets on the line. Now Janice called them and told them "I want to disconnect _one_ phone line here. This is the number."

The other number she had when she was young and single, way before she met me. That number has been hers almost as long as her name has been hers. So for four days this worked fine. One morning I tried to call my mother's house. No dial tone on the kitchen phone. That phone has worked a little funny since the time I got pissed off at someone and threw it across the dining room, but it does usually work.

So now I go upstairs and try the phone in the bedroom, same deal. Now I go to the computer and try to go online and get some message about not being able to connect. Fine, as a last resort I call the house number on our cell phone. I get a message about this number has been disconnected, I am not amused.

Of course when I tell this to Janice, she is not too happy. So now I go around checking connections on my phone lines and realize we have been cut off. As best I can tell, the phone company got annoyed that we dropped the one line and figured they would annoy us for a while by knocking out all the service. I might be wrong, but I might be right. One more thing; you will notice lately that if you call for any type of technical support, you are talking to someone in India or China. The people all have names like John, or Maria, but with the Indian accent you feel like saying: "Come clean Habib, my name is not John either." Well anyway that was the situation. So now what do we do?

First Janice gets on the cell phone and dials this 800 number that she has on her bank statement. You say, "Who has an 800 phone number on a bank statement?" Anyone who pays bills online. She has her own way of running a checkbook. It is so confusing, that I told her if she dies before me; I will have to put her funeral on a credit card because I have no idea what the balance is in the bank.

I told her if I die before her, maybe she will get lucky and have it happen on a Tuesday. That way she can throw me out with the big garbage on Wednesday. I can see it now; she is telling the guys with the garbage truck. "Watch that one bag there, it is sort of heavy."

Now she gets on the phone and hits a phone tree. You know the deal: Dial 1 for English, and so on through any number of stupid options most of which do you no good anyway. At first she has it going pretty well, that lasts for about a minute.

She says to me "You better do this!" Then, I think she remembered what I did with the kitchen phone and decides to give it another shot. Well she starts out full of sweetness telling the guy (John) about the problem. This is after she gives him her name, address, her mother's maiden name; the dogs shoe size and the date she lost her virginity.

I am not entirely sure what he is saying since I can only hear part of the conversation as I am cooking pancakes. She is explaining to him about the single phone line which was supposed to be taken out, and so far being pretty polite about this. He tells her it is going to take 3 to 5 working days to get the phone line back up. "Wait a minute kids, this is bogus. The line was working as of 10P.M. last night. It didn't take 3 days to shut it off. Let me talk to a supervisor."

Now there is a wait with some jazz type music on the line. I think these are the same people who do music for porn flicks, sounds a lot like the same music. Like none of you guys ever rented a porn flick.

"Come clean like Habib, you lying sack of shit." Well she gets a "Supervisor." I can picture them all in some basement in India with a bunch of phones and computers. They are all bunched together doing this work, drawing straws to see who the supervisor will be today. They are probably making about $3 an hour. Which over there, is probably big money and they are thinking they are cleaning up.

Now she gets Tonya. I wonder if this is the girl with the ice skates from the Olympics several years ago. So now Janice goes through the whole verification business again; and the entire story. This is getting more stupid by the minute.

The pancakes are done now and I have them on dishes with pot covers on them to keep them warm. This does not work too well. If I leave them too long, they will be like eating cardboard.

Now sometimes, even something really serious seems funny to us; like watching some guy fall off a ladder and hitting the concrete. It is not funny for him, but for some reason it cracks us up. This is what has started to happen here.

Poor Janice is talking to idiots on the other end, and lying through her teeth telling them she has kids here and the place will fall apart without a phone. She tells them she is using a borrowed cell phone to do this call. She didn't tell them she borrowed it from her husband, and the only kids we have are two dogs. Well, for some reason I start thinking this is funny.

I don't know why, but now I start cracking up. I had to leave the kitchen with the cardboard pancakes and go laugh in the living room 40 feet away so they could not hear me. This happened twice.

Now guys, you know what happens when you laugh at something your wife does not think is funny. You get the sour look and even if she does not say a word, you know she does not see the humor in this. I would usually get the "You think this is funny?" question. If I say yes and continue to laugh, you know my love life is shot for a few days, or weeks. This depends on what I found to be funny.

Bedtime Horror Stories for Homeowners

She ended up talking to John, then Tonya, and then some other guy named Mark. Then some woman named Jill. And son of a bitch, she switched Janice back to John when Janice asked for her supervisor. By now Janice looks like she is going to cry, and she has stopped being polite. It is more like "Your idiot technician shut off two lines instead of one here. How hard is it to count to one, Dummy?"

"I can't believe you hire people who are that stupid. No wonder it takes 3 to 5 days to get the phone reconnected. I bet there is a switch somewhere that goes on and off and that would do it." By now she is really mad, and I am telling her "Look at it this way, we have the cell phone with some time on it and if they get it going in 3 days it is no big deal since we get free weekends anyway and today is Thursday." When someone is as whipped up as Janice is there is no logic to be had.

To get to the point; as of Thursday we were told it is three days, take it or leave it. When we do get back online we are looking for another phone company. The guys at Verizon only sent me some stuff in the mail today which would cover all my service for $55 a month; or so they say, we will see.

Now we are using the cell phone, this is another joke. At one time I had the original really, really, really cheap plan. A big $20 a month. WOW! The only problem is that during weekdays I got a big 60 minutes a month for weekday calls. The weekends were unlimited.

So, I got into the habit of doing most of my cell phone calls on weekends. And you may have had this happen. Go over by 2 minutes and the bill almost doubles. Hell, I am not calling South America. I was calling thirty miles south of here in the same state. So I got a better plan that for $29 a month. We got 300 minutes and unlimited weekends. That seems to work better. We usually are way under the 300 minutes. There are certain people to whom I have not told we have a better plan. There is a reason for this.

Bedtime Horror Stories for Homeowners

I have a few people who will call me for the stupidest reasons in the world. Perfect example; my friend Rod, he is a nice enough guy. A little strange but he is OK. He will call me up with something like "The FDA just approved a drug for overweight dogs." Now this tells me maybe he thinks my dogs are fat, which they are not. Or more like, he heard this earth shattering news on some PBS radio station and thinks the entire world should know it. He should be built as well as my dogs.

So as of today which is Friday, I am working on this book, this also gives me another story. By the way, I left the cell phone home with Janice last night in case she really needed it. When I left there were about 180 minutes on my time which has to last me till next Sunday. Actually, I guess Friday since I get the free weekends.

After I got home, she told me her sister Gloria had called AT&T and got connected to someone who told her the phone would be up and running today. I just checked it. Nope, dead as dirt. Of course even though Janice will scream about me going over the time on the cell phone; I notice it took her and her sister 25 minutes to discuss this issue.

Two thoughts about the phones....I had a hard time getting a DSL line here. I live 20 miles from New York City, as a crow flies. My brother in law who lives in the middle of North Carolina has had a DSL line for the past year. Also on cell phones; I have a friend Steve who got a cell phone several years ago.

When he was using it at home it would not work indoors, he had to go in the driveway to talk. I can only imagine what the neighbors were thinking. "Five degrees outside and this nut with the PHD is talking on the phone in the driveway. Maybe he loves cold weather." I talked him into getting a better phone and a better plan.

Ok, I am back to reality. I thought I may have gotten this mess under control. Maybe I thought I saw a pig fly by here today. This is probably how a deer feels when it jumps over a road. "I'm flying, this is great." Then he gets hit by a semi. I thought AT&T was bad.

Amateur stuff. At least they had an excuse, their support staff is in India. Now I am dealing with Verizon.

So Mr. Smith said to me. "Your DSL line will be up by Tuesday." This was on a Friday. Now remember, my regular phone line is also not working. Fine I can live with this for a few days. I have my cell phone with unlimited time on weekends. Just not get wild during the weekdays and blow the minutes.

Well, on Monday I get a dial tone. "This is great; they got me going a day early." Here is the kicker; it was AT&T who hooked me up, not Verizon. How do I know this? Call 411 for information and see who answers. Whatever company has your phone service will come on with "AT&T Information" or "Verizon Information" or "Jack's Phone Company in the Garage Information." Someone at one of the phone companies tipped me off to this. Occasionally they do tell you something useful.

This was almost 3 weeks ago. I still do not have my DSL line. I have talked to at least 10 people from Verizon about this. Got everything from "Your Modem is not connected" (Wrong, it is) to "There is a repair issue in the lines." "So fix it. This is not rocket science."

One woman even said to me: Get this.... "You can't have our hardware and software for the DSL line." "NO, I am reading the Verizon stuff off a tattoo on my wife's ass, you moron."

Tell you the truth if I didn't have a website that makes me a few bucks every so often; I would probably drop all this internet stuff completely. My wife buys stuff online which I have done once in 10 years. She also pays some of our bills online, which I think is bogus too. I hear the biggest business online is porn, and even that? How much of that can you look at?

By now, I feel like I am working at Verizon. There are people there who know me by my voice. By the way, I have taken to audio taping these phone calls now. First, so I can keep my information straight; and also if I have to sue Verizon, I have some real proof.

In the public library there used to be a set of books called the Standard and Poors Directory where anyone could look up information on companies. Things such as CEO's home addresses. Those books are not there anymore. There is now some fake version of this, which is almost useless. It gives names and the company address. I got to the Vice President of Allstate once with his home address to fix a mess we had with that company. I guess they do not want us poor people to have access to the rich ones.

Since my DSL line is off and I do not want to tie up our regular phone line, I went to the library to look up some big shots name. I did that about 5 days ago. I did dig up a corporate address and the name of the CEO from Verizon. NO, I am not going to give this info to you. He will probably be in another company by time this book gets in print. I also got phone numbers of the executive offices in New York for Verizon. Time to hit from the top down.

First, I tried the civilized approach. I called up nicely to that number. Got a different person each time. At least they would recognize the name of the last person to whom I spoke. That is the line they told me.

So for the best part of a week I farted around talking to these "executives" to try to work this out, basically got nowhere. By now I am losing patience. So I sent a letter to Mr. CEO. Not like I really expected it to ever get to his office. I figured it would hit the circular file in about 10 seconds.

Well, as of yesterday, I almost had to clean my shorts. I got a call from some woman who claimed to be from his office. I explained this mess to her in a way that was really simple. Now see if you can picture this analogy. For those of you, who do not know what analogy means, go find your dictionary and look it up.

I told her. "Suppose I went into a Subway sandwich shop and decided I wanted a bag of their potato chips; and one second later I realized I was hungry and ordered the Value Meal which includes the chips, a sandwich and a drink?"

If the price of the chips have not been put in the computer, all they do is work out the new deal. Simple enough. Now, compare that to having a DSL line and wanting to add a regular phone line.

(DSL line = the potato chips)... (The complete package with the DSL line and phone service would be the Value Meal). This is how I expected to explain it to Verizon. We all have to eat, so there is some common ground here.

To make sure this made sense; I did stop at a Subway in town. The guy who owns it is Indian, so the scene is perfect. I ran the chips and sandwich idea past him and he got it the first time. Then I told him how I was going to approach a phone company with this analogy.

This is what I got. "You must have Verizon, that company very bad." He continues. "My friends have many problems, it is bad company. They make you crazy!" Now this is with his Indian accent and the way he uses grammar. I was laughing so hard, I almost wet my pants. By the way, I did not even tell him who the phone company is that is giving me the problem.

The executive lady from Verizon talked to me yesterday, claims she can get it all worked out. I will have to see where this goes. By the way, I can't even order the DSL again for 3 to 5 working days. Will keep you posted on this deal.

FIVE DAYS LATER:

OK, so 5 working days went past and I got a call on my answering machine from one of the women in one of the "executive" offices. She tells to give her a call. The first thing I did before I called her was to call AOL and see if I can order the DSL line from Verizon as the $55 deal, and still keep my AOL screen names. According to "Steve" with an Indian accent there, this would work out fine. So now I call her office.

She is not available, but someone else finds my file. She tells me that I can order this DSL line and it will be on about the 22nd of Feb. I will believe it when I see it. It will be interesting to see what happens with the billing. She also wanted to send me all the hardware and software to do this. I told her, do not bother, I still have the stuff from the last time I ordered this.

Now as an aside; I love practical jokes, I have played a lot of them. Good sophisticated ones. The kind that take a lot of thinking. One of my favorite involved having my cousin thinking he had won a Corvette. I had about 20 people involved in that one including someone I have never met in person but was kind enough to get the phone number off a pay phone by Wal-Mart in Hilton Head SC. So I could not get too pissed off about this joke.

Remember I told you about the woman from the top offices of Verizon? Let's say her name is Mary. She is the one who suggested I call AOL in the 5 working days; she also gave me two phone numbers to use to call. I thought she was really being nice to me.

Good thing I am not dating this broad. When I tried to use these numbers to call AOL this is what I got. The first number is out of service. Okay, maybe her phone list is outdated. Who knows? When I called the second one, I got a machine which said "Want to talk to fun people?" which sounded sort of bizarre; but I dialed the number they gave me. It was an 800 number. Got hooked up to a sex line. It started out with some crap about "Hey big boy, want me to talk dirty to you?" Or some stupid thing like that. If I want that, I can either bother my wife or find some lonely women in cyberspace to do this for nothing. She must save these two numbers for people who actually make her work. At this point, I am still waiting for the DSL line to be connected in the next week, will keep you up on that deal. Okay, so this has been an ongoing story but I *think* things have finally gotten worked out. Verizon called me a couple weeks ago and told me the line was going to be connected. They had also told me I needed hardware and a CD to make this work. I screamed at them.

"NO NO NO. I already have the stupid hardware; it is sitting all over my house waiting to be reconnected. I have had this junk since you put in the DSL line in 6 weeks ago. Now just send some guy out with the big white truck with your logo and hook me up, thank you." Now I have two computers. I am typing this book on my old computer and the DSL line in on my not so old one. Watch me go online later and it will shit the bed. Seriously, so far the DSL line is working ok. Let's hope it continues. End of story.

BUSTED BY THE FUZZ

DEN DE DEN DEN.... DEN DE DEN DEN, DENNNN. Think Sergeant Friday, Joe Friday, Dragnet, 1950's cop show. He was a detective. I am glad they gave him a first name and didn't just call him Friday. Names are strange enough. I knew a girl who called herself Sunday. I had to ask her if that was spelled like the day or the dessert. Her given name was Gertrude, no wonder she changed it. What the hell was her parents thinking? This chapter is not about names though, it is about cops.

Most times when detectives are depicted in a movie, TV or a book, they are sort of sharp, and suave, except for Colombo. He is more like the real thing. I am only writing this chapter because it happened today and I did not want to lose my grip on the situation.

I took my dogs to the park for their play date with their buddies. I do this on weekdays and they have a bunch of other dogs who meet us there. I don't spend as much time as some people there. I do have other activities to keep me busy.

As I was pulling out of the driveway, I noticed a four door sedan in the driveway next to mine. I do not recognize the car or the two guys sitting in it. They are middle age type guys, sort of non-descript. There is also a car in the driveway across the street, and the homeowner has moved his truck out of that space. Plus there was another car parked around the corner.

My first thought is that this is a bunch of religious people who come around and give us literature about the Jehovah Witnesses, except these people were not dressed as sharp and they were not getting out of the cars, plus the Witness people usually park on the street not in driveways.

Bedtime Horror Stories for Homeowners

My next thought is that maybe my neighbor who does carpentry work is meeting someone to discuss a job. Too many people. Then I think maybe these guys are out to re-assess the taxes in the area, I hear that is going on recently. All the cars have the municipal type license plates. The thought of a home invasion came into mind, but these guys did not look the type, too old and fat. I thought of staying home and getting my meat cleaver and machete ready. I was tempted to call the cops on them. Turns out these *are* the cops.

I took off for the park, and called to tell Janice to lock the door and call me if anything stupid started happening here. She was going out anyway and was not too concerned. Told her I would see her when we got home. I forgot about these guys. Took the dogs out to play. We saw some of their friends and had a good time even though I was running late today. I had gotten up last night around 1 A.M. I could not sleep and worked on my computer till 5:30A.M. Got a couple hours sleep and off we go.

By time I came home, Janice was still out wherever she was going, so I got home first. The cars were still there. I see my neighbor Pete walking down the street. I motion him over to my driveway.

Nice and quiet I ask if he has a clue what is going on. He has always been really street smart and spots stuff like this quickly. He tells me these are cops and they are setting up a bust on someone. I say, "It is not me; I am not doing anything illegal." He replies… "Me neither, I got to go, getting some work done on my heating system." So we leave it at that. A minute later Janice comes home. I tell me what Pete said.

Now she is trying to figure out who is getting busted. We know our neighbor's pretty well so we figured it was nobody we knew. Most of these people have been here for years'.

I had some running around to do, the bank, the car wash, and a couple other stops so off I go again. I am at one of the other neighbors' homes and get a call on my cell phone from Janice.

She commences to tell me there are about eight police cars on the street and some young guy in a tank top was being cuffed by the fuzz. At this point there were the regular police cars out there. I said, "Fine, when I get home we can discuss this." She had no idea who the guy was in the cuffs and did not recognize his Honda. We also have no idea of why he got busted, and since it is none of our business, we don't really care.

The regular cops were there till at least 2 P.M. They were milling around the area. I have no idea what they were up to, and like I said, it's none of my business anyway. The thing that cracked me up about this whole incident was the detectives. These are supposed to be undercover guys and women, but anyone who lives around here could pick them out in a heartbeat. I don't think they could sneak up on Helen Keller.

CONCRETE AND THE BLIND OLD LADY

This is about a job I helped my father do years ago. We would do concrete work once in a while, Dad was not wild about concrete work; he was also not wild about starving. So you do what you have to do.

There was an old lady who got in touch with us to do some concrete work. The good part is that we were doing this in the summer. The bad part is that we were doing this in the summer. Concrete waits for nobody. When it starts getting hard it is worse than an over anxious bridegroom.

So we went and set up forms for the job. There was a fairly big driveway and a sidewalk. It was Dad, me and this guy Nicky. Nick worked with Dad for quite a few years, a good worker, a nice guy, great helper. I don't think he had the temperament to actually do contracting himself. That is a whole other ball game.

So the forms are up and ready from the day before. We are there about 7:30 A.M. and it was going to be a hot day. You can spot days like this; it is 70 at six in the morning. I happen to like hot weather, but if you don't like hot weather, it is not much fun.

The lady who owned the property was maybe 75 years old. Just taking a guess. She was mad at the world, half blind with an eye patch over one eye, and she would sort of put her hand over the other eye to keep the sun out. If you think about it, this is not too bad. If the job did not come out perfect she couldn't see it anyway.

There was a trucking company across the street. We watched her scream at a guy for violating her air space when the back of his truck hung over her sidewalk. We knew we had a winner on our hands. At least she pretty much stayed out of the way when the concrete truck showed up.

Dad used to always get fired up when one of these trucks would arrive. You would think he had stock in cement or sand. I would be glad to have them come and go. But Dad; WOW, he used to get wild.

I guess the up side of this is that his adrenalin would be pumping so he would get a lot of work done. The concrete truck got there about 8:30. It was already getting hot. I guess it was kicking in about 80 degrees; it was going to be a fun day. This was also a fairly big job. We had a driveway that was about 10 or 12 feet wide, by maybe 30 feet long, plus a sidewalk that was about 3 feet by 16 feet. It had a potential to turn out fine or to be a real mess.

We had a lot of experience with stuff like this, so at least we had our forms all set. The truck was barely able to turn far enough to pull out his chutes. This guy was good though, and got them going fine. He was probably out of there in a half hour. Dropped the load, took the check and split. Now it was up to us.

Nicky was a good worker, as were Dad and I. Pop had the most experience so he was running the show. We shoveled the slop, pushed it, pulled it, we used a long 2 X 4 to level it. We were in good shape, even considering the heat. We were moving along fine. The weather kept getting hotter.

We sprayed the concrete with a hose a few times to keep it wet, had little choice, and you do not want to get it too wet. That can cause problems. Nick was working one section and Dad and I would work another. Then one of us would move around. This went on till 2 P.M. Forget lunch; we did that with a tool in one hand and food in the other. Sandwiches are always more fun this way. The old lady would stick her face out there every so often like she had a clue what was going on. She was probably bored being stuck in the house. At least she did not give us any crap.

Got to be about 3 P.M. By now the weather had peaked to about 100 degrees, and is going down to maybe 97. This is not the best weather to put a job like this on the map. But we finally got the mess all worked out. The edges were done, it was flat. Looked pretty good. It was going to dry like stone.

Now Dad says "There's a bar across the street. Let's go get a couple of beers over there." Nicky did not drink beer but he was game for some soda. We hit this place; they had these small glasses about 7 or 8 ounces of draft beer.

I don't think any of us even tasted the first two that went down. We sat there for probably a half hour drinking and cooling off and went back to see how the mess across the street was doing. It was fine, the old lady was fine, and we were fine. Everyone was happy as pigs in dirt. We picked up the tools, made sure the concrete was blocked off so nobody could walk through it. We told the old lady we would see her tomorrow and hit the road. Next day, we came back, ripped out the forms, got paid and got lost. Another day on the job.

BOB AND THE BASEMENT APARTMENT

My brother Bob had a house in Manchester, New Jersey at one time. A ranch house similar to the one he built in Tennessee, but with less land in Jersey. He had one great item in the Jersey home. He had a full basement and it had high ceilings. That was one nice basement. For most of the time he lived there, he used it for parties and storage. Had the storage area walled off. Then his daughter Dana got married to Matt. Next thing we know, these two have twin boys.

I forget where they were living at the time, but for some reason it was not working out. I know for a while, before they had the kids they lived with Marilyn and Steven. But after they had the boys I am not sure. So now Bob works out some deal where they were going to move into his basement. He was going to make an apartment there for them.

Bob walled off the basement into separate rooms, put in a bathroom with a toilet that would flush up instead of down, put in a big exit window as a way out if there was a fire. He built it, I helped him paint it. Steven called me on a Saturday to help Bob paint it. "The guy is going to kill himself painting this place. He needs some help." So not wanting to have to put on a suit and tie for a funeral, I took a ride down there to help.

When I got there, Bob was already started. Steven was standing around like he thought he was some kind of supervisor. Matt was standing there as if Bob was hired help. I remember telling Matt there was a roller downstairs with his name on it. He did squat; Steven painted maybe 4 square feet. Bob and I did 99% of it. Big joke.

I remember stopping there before the "kids" moved in. I am not sure what the fight was about, but Bob and Dana were screaming at each other. I felt like I was on the Jerry Springer show.

At some point Matt and Dana moved in there. Bob thought he was going to collect rent. This deal lasted about two months and fell apart, I am glad I was not involved.

Chapter 24   BACK ON THE BLOCK
                THE HOUSE AS AN ART PROJECT

One good part of a house is the way it looks; the tricky part is making it happen. Go see the home, Falling Water by Frank Lloyd Wright. It is somewhere in western Pennsylvania. That, is a distinctive structure. It has made magazines and art books; there are all kinds of interesting things going on here. I visited the home last year, very impressive. Now most of us have no chance of ever moving into a place like this. Simple reason, we could never afford it. I forget what the tour guide told me the cost of the Falling Water when it was built, In today's market, it would be several million. That takes most of us out of the loop.

So as an alternative, there are guys like me who are frustrated architects. I went to college to be an art teacher, this was after two years at night studying mechanical engineering, and several years of doing renovation work with my father. So my background is sort of strange. I have been doing sculpture work for about 40 years, along with painting and drawing and photography.

This brings me to a few ideas I have done in my own home. One is a curved wall in a hallway. Now this was not done just to see if it could be done. It is part of a closet. The hallway was originally just an entrance to three bedrooms. Two of the bedrooms were small so we decided to make them into one bedroom and make a big closet. Old homes never seem to have much closet space. So if we were going to make a mess anyway, why not do something with some visual appeal? This is that story.

The bedrooms were at the top of the steps in our home. There was a landing which was sort of an "L" shape. The long part of the "L" had a doorway that led into one bedroom; the short part of the "L" had a doorway that went into the other bedroom. There was a wall between these two bedrooms. There was a small closet in one of the bedrooms.

One thing I wanted was a decent closet with this room. Since we did not have kids, and were not planning to have any, this made a lot of sense. So, the first thing we had to do with this job was to take out the wall between the two rooms. These old homes were built with plaster walls and lath.

The mess from destroying plaster walls or ceilings is unbelievable. You can take a piece of old plaster the size of a dinner dish, and bust it up with a hammer and make enough dust to cover the floor of a small room. And this dust flies. When you take out plaster; I don't care how many drop cloths you have, or how the room has been sealed with plastic, this dust will somehow find its way into the rest of the home, and the neighbors' home too if the windows are open. (Try hanging a damp sheet in the doorway).

We did the best we could to seal off the bedroom doorways with plastic before we started the mess. The best part is that we were living here full time and sleeping in the front bedroom. So, at some point I had to stop talking about the mess, and actually make it. Now the wall between the bedrooms was not a support wall which was good, I didn't want to get involved in a deal like that. The trick now was to take this wall out with the least mess possible.

The first thing I did was find a mask to keep the dust out of my face and my internal organs. This is easier said than done. There are these small paper masks which are sold for this purpose, these are basically a joke. I have used them.

Better to use one of those heavy duty masks with the filters on the front. You know the type; they look like a gas mask. Another problem I have with masks is that I wear glasses, so when I breathe, my breath works its way up onto the glasses and fogs them up.

Nothing like a guy with an electric saw; a pry bar, a hammer, and impaired vision. If I were also deaf, maybe that would help. With all the windows open in these rooms, I commenced to take off trim, plaster on the wall and the part of the ceiling where that wall crossed that part of the house. It made a sizable mess.

The dust was flying out of the windows with the help of a box fan. It looked like the house was on fire most of the time. I also removed a hardwood floor from one of the rooms to keep the floor on both sides of the new room level. I used this floor somewhere else in the house.

The job did not take all that long to rip out the wall, but it made a dust storm that covered everything that got in the way. I did the job in the summer so I could have the windows open, so this dust managed to sneak into the first floor through any open windows. We did not have central air in the house and would keep the windows open for air. It was quite a mess. So at some point, this wall was gone. I now added another wall that ran the opposite direction along what now became the long side of the room. This was for my long closet.

This wall ran from one side of the house to almost the other side of the home, about 13 feet. I made the closet about 3 feet deep. Now I still had the doorway on the one room intact, so I left that alone. I could have just squared off that wall in the hall and had my closet, but that was too simple. I now built a curved wall at the end of the closet in the hallway. Since 2 X 4's do not curve, I did the top and bottom plates of the wall with pieces of plywood. I used ¾ inch plywood cut in a curve, made several layers to build up the thickness and ended up with a radius of about three feet.

We also decided to take out the plaster in the hallway when we did this job. I tore that plaster out one night when Janice was at school. She came home and it looked as if we had had an earthquake. The four or five layers of drop cloths were like a joke. I told her if she wanted, she could go visit someone for a couple hours while I cleaned up the mess. She was a good sport, put on some old clothes and helped me get the mess out of here. This was already about 10 P.M.

Took us till midnight to make the hallway clean enough to use. So now that the plaster is off the walls in this hallway, we took out the ceiling in that hallway. It was taking a hit anyway, so why not be big shots? The original ceiling was just a horizontal ceiling.

What we did, was starting at the outside end of that ceiling, I framed it toward the center of the house, and made a short cathedral type ceiling in the hallway. This ceiling starts before the curved wall, intersects with that wall and goes the length of the hallway. At the high end, it sits 18½ feet above the floor. Very impressive. The entire hallway is painted white to help keep this open look. The only art work is a hooker rug with a picture of a leopard. This is on the wall that faces the steps. Janice did that work. This hallway is like living inside an abstract sculpture piece.

At one point later on, I added a small strip light just below the top edge of the steps. This light is activated with a sensor and gives us light for going up and down the stairs without using the track lights. This uses less electricity, and does not flood the entire hallway when one of us decides to go downstairs at night.

Bad enough you want to go to the bathroom half asleep or the dogs want to go out. I don't want to light the hallway like a construction site on the highway. The strip light works fine.

WHAT HAPPENED TO THE HARDWOOD FLOOR?

At the time we did this job; I was working at a vocational school teaching high school kids to be carpenters, or at least trying to teach them. A lot of these guys are there just to skip out of regular high school or stay out of jail. That is another story in itself.

One of the better things about working at this school is that there were tools there that I do not own. One of these was a planer. This is basically a machine which is like a big electric plane.

A plane is used to shape wood, and take off a thin layer of wood a bit at a time. In the old days these were all manual, but several years ago they were also made as a portable tool which could be used to clean up wood, or take wood out easily. Well, the planer machine is a big version of this tool. The one in the school could handle a piece of wood up to a foot wide and 4 inches thick. It has a lot of guts.

th one of these tools is that there is a bed on the bottom d on top there are blades that rotate toward the operator. The wood is fed into this machine, and the blades cut the thin layer of the wood from the wood. Now this is supposed to be used with clean wood, with no nails or finish. The wood I pulled off the floor had no nails left in when I got done cleaning it. There was a finish which was probably shellacked. This was a wood finish that was popular before polyurethane was developed. The finish on this wood was old and fragile, so I decided to take it off.

I took the wood into the shop one day, and ran it through the planer to take off the shellac. It took that finish off faster than a football player taking the uniform off a cheerleader.

I took the wood home, cut it to short lengths, and installed it in my dining room. I put foam insulation on the walls, with some 1 X 2 strips, added some electrical outlets, and put the recycled wooden floor vertically on the walls on two sides of the room.

I added some trim to make chair rails at the top end of this wood. This is probably the best looking trim work I have ever done in my life. I put a light oak finish on the woodwork to go along with the dining room set.

THE DINING ROOM CEILING

As I told you, I went to school to be an art teacher. I never got a full time gig as a teacher in that field, a lot of politics in New Jersey. So I did free-lance artwork, I still do it. I have a piece in a show locally as I type. I have a lot of talent in the field, and with the proper marketing, I may have made a decent living. If you want to see some of my artwork, go on line to www.ppugartist.com.

Anyway, we have this dining room which is probably the best dining room in the family. It can seat 10 easily, and when I move furniture around, I have had sit down dinners for up to 20. I don't serve them, they have to serve themselves.

Bedtime Horror Stories for Homeowners

So a few years ago, I guess I ran out of big physical projects in the house. I decided I wanted to do a mural on the dining room ceiling. Now I had this idea for quite a while, but had never done it. This job fell into the faux painting department of art work. There are people who think this is a new development in the art field. Don't kid yourself, it has been around forever.

Think about it, Michelangelo was using this when he did the Sistine chapel. Well I am no Michelangelo. I could not clean his brushes. It is scary the talent that man had. I can only imagine what he could do with the technology today. Like they say; it took him four years to do the ceiling in the chapel, he could have done it faster with a roller.

Anyway; using his type ideas, I have no problem stealing ideas, I painted my ceiling in the dining room. There is a crystal chandelier in there that is about in the center of the room.

It works well visually and throws a lot of light, so of course that is going to stay for the long run. What I did, was to paint the ceiling so it appears to have four openings in it. The openings look as if they are angled from the ceiling to the outside of the house. Sort of like you took a picture frame and held it flat on the ceiling. I did this with various shades of gray paint to create this illusion.

Where the openings intersect is on the light fixture. I then painted the areas inside these "openings" to look as if we are looking at a blue sky with some clouds. It is very cool. This is the kind of stuff you see in mansions in a place like Newport, RI, they also used a lot of faux painting there. It took me about 14 hours to do this job. It took me three years to convince Janice that I could do it. She said to me "What if I don't like it? Or it looks stupid?" This is why paint companies make stain killer; we would just repaint it white, duh.

My biggest problem is that even though the ceiling is 9 feet high, I have never been able to get a photo of the entire ceiling even with a wide angle lens. No big deal.

Stop by for a visit sometime, see it live, have a cup of coffee.

THE BASEMENT DOOR

At one corner of this room is a door that leads to my basement. It was here when we moved in, and is basically one of those cheap hollow core doors that people put in just to close a hole in the wall. It was stained a dark walnut when we moved here. That was no big deal except that it was sort of dark with the rest of the room. What I did with this door was neat.

I painted it with acrylic paints and made it look like a panel door, put in fake angles, and shadows. From across the room it looks as if it is an actual panel door. I have had people walk up to it and run a hand over it to see if it is real or fake.

Again stop by sometime. If I ever get the guts to rework my website, I will show these jobs on it. Right now the website works, so I don't want to screw it up.

Of course being an artist, I have work all over the house; everything from a five foot square abstract painting in the living room to a fake six foot sub sandwich which graces the top of my sofa. There are paintings, sculpture, and photos inside and outside the home. I have also taken out some of the wood panels from the bedroom doors and replaced these with stained glass, have also added stained glass to a kitchen cabinet door. When I get around to it, there is a stained glass piece I am going to finish for the transom over the front door. I am presently working on this piece. It is a sunrise over the ocean with a surfer and his board.

One of my recent projects was to install a short fence between my property and the tool shed my neighbor installed. We painted flowers all over this fence to create the illusion that they actually grow there. In good weather, we have flower pots that blend in with the fence. In the winter it is too cold to bother looking at it.

CHRISTMAS AT HOME

The year 2008 was the first year since I know Janice that we were able to do Christmas dinner without a song and dance. She retired from nursing that year, so for once, she was not working on that holiday. When she did 8 hour shifts, she could at least come home and have dinner. When the shifts went to 12 or 13 hours, that deal killed the holiday.

This is probably Janice's favorite holiday. She starts with the Christmas music the day after Thanksgiving. My house is wired for sound; I feel like I am living at the mall, and she plays this music till the middle of January. By time she stops playing this music, heavy metal starts sounding good.

I go along with her with the decorations. We have the fake tree; pine needles make a big mess so we avoid that. Besides we can leave this one up till June if we want. That includes the ancient Lionel train set that goes around the base of the tree, the tracks are attached to an old piece of plywood that fell off a sign job I did years ago.

The dogs bark at the trains, Lacey tries to eat them. It is fun watching her get zapped when she puts her wet nose on the track. She has a high tolerance for pain; I would have to boost the voltage by a couple hundred volts to get her attention. Then again, that would burn out the locomotive. I added an electric eye with an alarm this year to keep the dogs away, it works.

We put garlands up on the windows, hang cards off beaded strings; a small ceramic tree is on the server. All kinds of small decorations are all over the place. One year my friend Rod came up here. He cannot keep his hands off anything.

I rigged up a fake decoration with a red bulb sticking out of a reindeers' face. It was set up so if the bulb got screwed in, it would set off this thing that sounded like a car alarm.

he would mess with it within one minute of
 room. Took less time than that. When it went
ng like a little girl for me to shut it off. I just
..... to loosen the bulb and keep his grubby fingers off it from now on. We have a crowd for Christmas. Usually our parents, actually her parents and my mother. My dad has been dead for years.

Sometimes we get some family here. Most times we end up with a lot of friends. I can turn our dining room table sideways, add another table and actually feed 20 people sitting down. Not bad for a home that people told me was a good starter home.

People bring food and deserts and sometimes, something to drink. We force them to sing Christmas songs. I actually have song books I put together for this. That way, I don't get this lame excuse that they do not know the words. Not that it makes much difference; we still sound like a bunch of dogs in heat, either way we have a fun time. Look me up on youtube.com sometime. (Twelve days of Christmas, puppy version. We both sing on this one).

If it is up to Janice, she will use paper dishes or those Styrofoam ones. This helps the clean-up part. For several years we had to chase both our mothers out of the kitchen. They were either trying to help us cook or wanting to do dishes. My Mom would even bring her own rubber gloves and apron. Too funny. I told them we had domestic help for this stuff.

Two years ago our oven crapped out the week before the holiday. We borrowed a large toaster oven from my mother, used our smaller toaster oven and made a great dinner. We do not let small problems stand in our way. Merry Christmas; Happy New Years' and all that crap.

PAY ATTENTION, I WILL BE BACK WITH MORE STORIES

This is the end of this book and the stories contained, keep an eye out for more books with similar type stories. The books will have similar titles, which is not just due to laziness, it is due to the thought that people may get the idea the books are connected, and if you liked this book, you may enjoy the others. I plan to put on similar covers with other outrageous houses.

At this point I have another complete manuscript and enough notes to do a third book. People are always telling me new house stores, so this could go on for quite awhile. It has been a pleasure writing these stories for you.

Look for the complete story of RAT-A-FOOIE in book number 2.

RAT-A-FOOIE

This is not to be confused with the dish ratatouille. But if you want to pronounce this title in a way that is compatible with this story, just think of Peter Sellers, Inspector Clouseau, Pink Panther movies. By the way there is no rat in that dish, even though I understand some people actually cook and eat these rodents...YCCCCHH.

SĚNOR-SIR, THE RAT

Now guys, you have a chance to make this an interactive chapter.
That means if you have a sense of humor and some coordination we can have some fun. If you decide to just read the chapter that is fine. Here is the interactive part: First, sit up straight and put your hands on your thighs, right on right, left on left. Sounds like something they would have us do in the U.S. Army.

Bedtime Horror Stories for Homeowners

Now what I want you to do is quickly slap your thighs in a right, left pattern, so they are like small drums. After about five or six slaps each, clap your hand together. This is the interactive part; there will be a part of the story that tells you when to do this. Back to the story. Pay attention, this tale is also educational.

Anyone who has read any of my books knows I am an animal lover. This is why I am a vegetarian. I do not expect anyone to agree or disagree with me; what you do is your business. I am one of those people who catch bugs and mice and turn them loose somewhere else. The bugs usually go out the door, the mice I relocate a few miles away.

So a couple months ago, it was the middle of the night and I had let the dogs out to water the grass about 3 A.M. We do this sometimes. I was standing in the kitchen and this mouse comes charging across the floor like a runaway train. I was sleepy; he looked like a big mouse, so big deal, set a trap for him. I have done this before. The next night I set a trap. This routine went on for several nights with no results. I did not see anything that looked as if he had moved in, so I guessed he took a hike.

Summer of 2009, I went into a hospital to have a kidney stone removed; this was supposed to take three days. Go in Monday, get out on Wednesday. "We do this all the time." Says the surgeon. "Fine, so get it done." To make a long story short, there were problems. I was in there for, get this....28 days. I should have been getting a salary by time I got out of there. While in there; about 4 days before I left, Janice announces that the mouse I have been trying to catch may be a rat. This was either the biggest freakin' mouse she had ever seen or a small rat. I tell her, "Leave him alone, try to stay out of his way and when I get out we will catch him."

ABOUT THE AUTHOR

Paul Pugliese spent a good part of his life employed as a carpenter and also taught carpentry for a short time. He was considered as a replacement for Bob Vela' when Vela' left This Old House.

He has owned two homes in his life and is quoted as saying "If I couldn't fix things, I could never afford to own a home." He still has a shop in his back yard which he uses for home repairs and as an art studio. He lives in New Jersey with his wife Janice, and his dogs Lacey and Luther. He lives in what he considers a good location. He is five minutes from the ocean, a hospital, a train that will bring him to NYC, and fifteen minutes from just about everything else he needs.

Paul plays guitar, works out in a gym and surfs. He is having a fun time with his life.

CONTACT ME

If you have any comments, or any stories you would like to put in one of my books, please contact me at paulwriterguy@aol.com. I take a while to get to my e mails, but I do get to them. The best way to let me know is to put the words "house stories" in the subject line. You can leave me either an e mail address or a phone number and a name so you don't think I am a crank call. Thank you.